CAMBRIDGE

Official Cambridge Exam Preparation

COMPACT

B2 FIRST

THIRD EDITION

B2

STUDENT'S BOOK

WITHOUT ANSWERS

Peter May

Cambridge University Press
www.cambridge.org/elt

Cambridge Assessment English
www.cambridgeenglish.org

Information on this title: www.cambridge.org/9781108921879

First published 2012
Second edition 2014
Third edition 2021

20 19 18 17 16 15 14 13

Printed in Great Britain by Ashford Colour Limited

A catalogue record for this publication is available from the British Library

ISBN 978-1-108-92187-9 Student's Book without answers

Contents

MAP OF THE UNITS

UNIT	TOPICS	GRAMMAR	VOCABULARY	READING
1 Living day to day	Daily life People	Present tenses Present simple in time clauses	Adjectives ending in *-ed* and *-ing* Character adjectives Adjective prefixes and suffixes: *-able*, *-al*, *dis-*, *-ful*, *-ic*, *im-*, *-ish*, *-itive*, *-ive*, *-ous*, *un-*, *-y*	Part 7: multiple matching
2 Differing tastes	Food and drink Restaurants Relationships	Past tenses	Fixed phrases	Part 6: gapped text
3 Changing places	Travel and tourism Transport Festivals and customs	Modal verbs Adverbs of degree	Dependent prepositions	Part 5: multiple-choice questions + long text
4 Getting creative	Entertainment (film, music, arts) Leisure	Verbs followed by *to* + infinitive or *-ing* *Too* and *enough* Present perfect	Phrasal verbs with *on*	Part 6: gapped text
5 Making your way	Education, study and learning Careers and jobs	Future forms Countable and uncountable nouns	Phrasal verbs with *take* Noun suffixes: *-ant*, *-er*, *-ian*, *-ist*, *-or*	Part 7: multiple matching
6 Setting the pace	Health and fitness Sport	Relative clauses (defining and non-defining) Purpose links	Medical vocabulary Phrasal verbs with *up* Sports vocabulary	Part 5: multiple-choice questions + long text
7 Feeling the heat	The environment The weather	Conditionals 1–3 Mixed conditionals Comparative forms Contrast links	Phrases with *in*	Part 6: gapped text
8 Moving ahead	Science Technology	Passive forms Articles	Communications vocabulary Science and technology vocabulary Collocations	Part 5: multiple-choice questions + long text
9 Breaking news	The media Celebrities	Reported speech	Media vocabulary Noun suffixes	Part 7: multiple matching
10 Shopping around	Shopping and consumer goods Fashion	Adverbs of manner and opinion *Wish* and *if only* Causative *have* and *get*	Clothing and shopping vocabulary Phrasal verbs with *out* Extreme adjectives	Part 6: gapped text

USE OF ENGLISH	WRITING	LISTENING	SPEAKING
Part 3: word formation	Part 2 informal email: getting ideas, informal language	Part 1: multiple-choice questions + short texts	Part 1: talking about yourself
Part 2: open cloze	Part 2 article: narrative linking expressions	Part 2: sentence completion	Part 2: giving opinions, comparing
Part 1: multiple-choice cloze	Part 1 essay: linking expressions, for and against	Part 3: multiple matching	Part 3: turn taking, suggesting, speculating
Part 4: key word transformation	Part 2 review: descriptive adjectives, recommendations	Part 4: multiple-choice questions + long text	Part 4: asking for and justifying opinions
Part 3: word formation	Part 2 formal letter of application: formal expressions, achieving aims	Part 2: sentence completion	Part 1: talking about future plans
Part 2: open cloze	Part 2 letter: informal language, purpose links	Part 1: multiple-choice questions + short texts	Part 3: agreeing and politely disagreeing
Part 4: key word transformation	Part 1 essay: contrast links, for and against	Part 3: multiple matching	Part 2: comparing: *-er, more, (not) as … as*, etc.
Part 1: multiple-choice cloze	Part 2 article: reason and result links, involving the reader	Part 2: sentence completion	Part 4: adding more points
Part 3: word formation	Part 2 report: recommending and suggesting	Part 4: multiple-choice questions + long text	Part 2: keeping going
Part 4: key word transformation	Part 1 essay: extreme adjectives, for and against	Part 3: multiple matching	Parts 3 and 4: decision-making

1 Living day to day

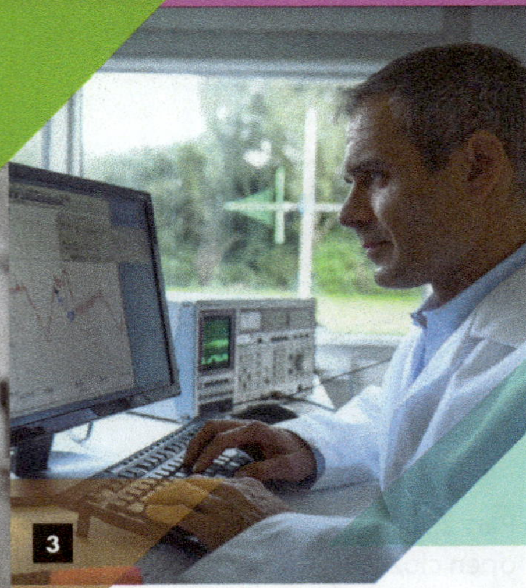

1 **Look at photos 1–3. What do you think a typical day is like for each person? Think about:**

- when they do things like having meals
- where they go and how they travel
- who they see
- what they do to relax
- how they feel at various times of the day

Part 7

2 **Look at the exam task. Answer these questions.**

1. How many people are there?
2. Is it one text in sections, or is it several short texts?
3. What's the topic?
4. What kind of information do you need to find? (e.g. *Which place … ?*)
5. How many questions are there?
6. Can you use letters A, B, C and D several times each?

3 **Look quickly at the text. What are Becky's main activities in each section A–E?**

4 **Look at this Part 7 example question and the underlined words in the text. There are references to this in parts A, B and E. Why is A right? Why are B and E wrong?**

Example:
In which section does she mention doing intensive physical exercise? A

5 **Do the exam task. Underline the words or sentences that tell you the right answers.**

Quick steps to Part 7

- Look at the instructions, title and layout, then read quickly through the questions.
- Remember that the information you need may not be in the same order as the questions.
- Be careful with words that only ***seem*** to say the same as a particular question, but in fact mean something quite different.

Exam task

You are going to read an article about a student's daily life. For questions **1–10**, choose from the sections (**A–E**). The sections may be chosen more than once.

In which section does the writer

talk about something she does only once a week? **1** ____

refer to a time when her life was less complicated? **2** ____

explain why she sometimes has to pay for her meals? **3** ____

state she is sure of her ability to combine study and work? **4** ____

suggest that some may be surprised at something she chose to study? **5** ____

remark on something about her culture that makes her proud? **6** ____

describe a habit she feels is good for her health but unusual for a student? **7** ____

indicate that she sometimes misses a meal? **8** ____

express her admiration for the scenery at the university? **9** ____

suggest that she had difficulty adapting to university life? **10** ____

Exam tip

When you have finished, make sure you have answered all ten questions.

A day in the life of a Canadian student

by Becky Bradley

A I greet the bus driver with a cheery 'good morning!', as is the norm here rather than the head-down mutterings common in other countries at this early hour. Before becoming a geography and psychology student at the University of British Columbia, I had a set daily routine – which seemed to make everything simpler. My morning routine has changed drastically over the years at university but now, in my third year, I like to think that I have finally mastered it. After the 10-minute ride on the 99 bus, I thank the driver – another wonderfully Canadian practice – and head to UBC's gym for a fairly demanding workout before class. Breakfast varies, in terms of when, if and what I eat.

B My first lecture is at 9.30 am, on globalisation. I have this course twice a week and love it. This class finishes at 10.50 am, allowing plenty of time to stroll or jog to the next lecture. UBC's Vancouver campus is located on the Point Grey peninsula, a stunning site sticking out into the ocean, so this is an enjoyable commute. After my class on environment and sustainability, I have my Spanish literature course at 1 pm. You might be wondering why I am taking a Spanish literature course as a geography and psychology major. This is because, as an arts student at UBC, I have a literature requirement to fulfil, and I've always been really interested in Spanish so decided to combine the two.

C Now it's 1.50 pm and I am done with classes for the day … except on Wednesdays, when I have a three-hour sports psychology lecture in the evenings. At lunchtime I try to save money by bringing leftovers from dinner the night before. However, I still like to be sociable at lunch so I normally meet a friend in our student union building called the Nest. If it's a nice enough day (not raining), my friend and I will probably eat on the grassy mound just outside the Nest. If I have left my lunch at home or was too busy (lazy?) to prepare food, I will grab a bite to eat at one of the many eateries in the Nest.

D Where I study in the afternoon depends on whether I am studying in a group or not; if studying solo, I enjoy the Hogwarts-like atmosphere of our main library. However, my afternoons are not always dedicated to studying since I do have two campus jobs. As a UBC student ambassador, I give campus tours to young people interested in studying here. My other job is working at UBC's Alumni Centre as a secretary. Because UBC is my employer, it is flexible with my academic schedule and limits my number of hours per week. Many students don't have jobs, but I choose to work because I feel confident I can balance the time commitment with my course.

E My evening schedule varies. Sometimes I go for a long gentle run in the beautiful park near my home, but most evenings involve lots of studying for my courses. And, of course, dinner, when my five housemates and I eat and talk together. It's a chance for us to share the highs and lows of the day and feel relaxed spending time with each other. My schedule is consistent with an approximate bedtime of 11 pm. I am unlike most of my peers in going to bed this early, but sleep is crucial to my overall well-being and something I must prioritise because it impacts my day significantly.

Adjectives ending in *-ed* and *-ing*

6 **Read these words in the text and complete the sentences with *-ed* and *-ing*.**

demanding (A)	stunning (B)
interested (B)	relaxed (E)

1 We use adjectives with .... to describe how somebody feels about something.
2 We use adjectives with .... to describe the thing or person which causes the feeling.

7 **Complete the sentences with *-ing* and *-ed* adjectives formed from the verbs in brackets. Then answer these questions about yourself.**

1 Which day of the week do you feel most .... (relax)?
2 What's the most .... (amuse) film you've ever seen?
3 Do you ever feel a little .... (stress)?
4 What's the most .... (depress) news item you've heard recently?
5 When do you feel most .... (motivate) to study?
6 Are you .... (worry) about the environment?
7 What do people find .... (surprise) about you?
8 What's the most .... (puzzle) thing about the English language?

8 **Compare a typical day in your life with that of Becky. What are the different times in your day like, and how do you feel? Use words from Exercises 6 and 7.**

Listening

Part 1

1 **Look at the photos. What are the people doing? How much time each day do you spend: a) studying or working, b) travelling, and c) relaxing with friends?**

2 **Look at question 1 in the exam task. Answer these questions.**

1 How many speakers will you hear? What is the situation?
2 Part 1 questions may focus, for instance, on gist, detail, function, purpose, attitude, opinion, genre or agreement. What is the focus of *What does she say?*

3 **Read the recording script for question 1. Which is the correct answer (A, B or C)? Why? Why are the other two wrong?**

> Back in my student days I often stayed up until well after midnight. I needed the recommended eight hours' sleep so I had trouble getting up the next day and I'd sometimes be late for lessons. *Nowadays I can manage on far less than that* ← B but *I need an alarm clock in case I'm still asleep at six.* ← C I also need to stick to a regular bedtime, switching off my laptop and phone well before then or else *I end up lying awake for ages.* ← A

4 01 **Work in pairs. For each of questions 2–8, ask and answer the questions in Exercise 2. Then listen and do the exam task.**

> **Quick steps to** Part 1
> - Don't choose an answer until you've heard the whole extract.
> - You can always change your mind about an answer while you're listening or when you listen again.

Exam task

You will hear people talking in eight different situations. For questions **1–8**, choose the best answer (**A**, **B** or **C**).

1 You hear a woman talking about her sleeping habits.
What does she say?
A She finds it easy to fall asleep at night these days.
B She doesn't need to sleep as long as she used to.
C She always wakes up before six o'clock in the morning.

2 You hear two people talking about weather conditions.
What are they doing?
A sitting in a railway station café
B walking past a sports centre
C waiting at a bus stop

3 You hear a teenager talking about her new home.
What does she think about it?
A It's too far from where she studies.
B It's in a very quiet part of the city.
C It's very similar to her previous home.

4 You hear part of a radio programme about a coastal area.
What is the speaker doing?
A suggesting a beautiful place for people to live
B studying the wildlife next to the sea
C describing the local effects of climate change

5 You hear a man talking about his work.
What is his job?
A salesman
B language teacher
C office worker

6 You hear a man telling a friend about a mistake he made.
How does he feel now?
A amused
B relieved
C worried

7 You hear a woman making a phone call.
Why is she calling?
A to cancel an order
B to make a complaint
C to reschedule a delivery

8 You hear two people talking about travelling into the city centre.
What do they agree about?
A the time to set off
B the type of transport to use
C the road to take

Exam tip

Have you chosen an answer for every question? Even if you're not sure, you could be right.

Grammar

Present tenses

Page 99

1 **Match extracts a–g from the recording in Listening with rules 1–7.**

a That north wind brings snow.
b They're always talking about building more.
c They sell hot food, too.
d The remaining human inhabitants are starting to follow.
e I mainly work from home.
f I'm calling about my order.
g He's working night shifts all this week.

We use the present simple to talk about:

1 a routine or habit
2 a permanent situation
3 something which is always true

We use the present continuous to talk about:

4 something happening right now
5 a temporary situation
6 a situation that is changing or developing
7 something irritating or surprising, using *always*

Note: verbs which describe states, e.g. *think, own, have, understand*, are normally used in simple tenses, but some can be continuous when they describe something we do, e.g. *I'm thinking of buying a bike.*

Stative verbs

Page 99

2 **Correct the mistakes in these sentences written by exam candidates.**

1 I suppose that you are knowing the area well.
2 This afternoon, people are playing games and have fun.
3 I know that you are hating your job. In my opinion you should look for another one.
4 I wait for you to call me back.
5 Nowadays, I'm preferring to walk to school.
6 In summer it's nice to go for a walk and having a picnic in the park.
7 Sara, can you see me? I stand in front of the coffee shop on your left.

3 **Complete the sentences with the correct form of the verbs in brackets.**

1 Jack's in, but he .... (talk) to someone on the phone at the moment.
2 Scientists believe that sea levels .... (rise) because of global warming.
3 My dad .... (quite often / go) swimming on Sunday mornings.
4 My neighbours .... (always / listen) to loud music late at night. It's really annoying.
5 That notebook on the table .... (belong) to me.
6 I .... (live) with my parents while my house is being decorated.
7 In the UK the sun .... (set) quite early in winter.
8 Look! Ellie .... (wave) at us.

Present simple in time clauses

Page 99

4 **Look at these extracts from the recording in Listening. Do all the verbs refer to the future? What tense do we use after time expressions like *when*?**

When I start there next year I'll be fine.
Parking will be a nightmare once we actually get there.

5 **Choose the correct option.**

1 I *buy / 'll buy* some new shoes when I *go / 'll go* shopping at the weekend.
2 I *wait / 'll wait* here until you *come / 'll come* back later on.
3 As soon as the meeting *finishes / will finish* this afternoon, I *call / 'll call* you.
4 I *don't / won't* move house before I *start / 'll start* my new job next month.
5 By the time you *arrive / 'll arrive* at 8.30, I *am / 'll be* ready to go out.
6 I *take / 'll take* the dog for a walk once I *get / 'll get* home.

6 **Complete the sentences about yourself. Then tell your partner.**

1 I'll have a meal as soon as …
2 I'll take the bus next time …
3 I'm going to buy a house when …
4 I don't think I'll have a holiday until …
5 I won't have a coffee before …
6 I think I'll watch TV after …

Part 1

» Page 128

1 **In Part 1, the examiner may ask you questions like these. What are they about? Which verb tense would you mainly use to reply?**

1 Where are you from?
2 What do you like about living there?
3 Tell me a little about your family.
4 Which time of the year is your favourite? Why?
5 What do you enjoy doing when you are on holiday?
6 What do you use social media for?

2 **In pairs, read this example conversation from Part 1. What is wrong with Sam's and Elena's replies (1–6)? Correct two mistakes. Then study the Quick steps for ways of improving the other four replies.**

Examiner: Sam, is your routine at weekends different from your daily routine in the week?
Sam: **(1)** Yes.
Examiner: Why?
Sam: **(2)** I am staying in bed later, of course. I go out with friends after lunch.
Examiner: And what about your routine at weekends, Elena? Is it different from your daily routine?
Elena: **(3)** Not really. I have to get up at about the same time.
Examiner: Why?
Elena: **(4)** Well, I have a job in a coffee shop and I'm going to work early. It's a long way from my house. And I arrive home late every day.
Examiner: Sam, how often do you read online newspapers or use social media?
Sam: **(5)** Repeat.
Examiner: How often do you read online newspapers or use social media?
Sam: **(6)** Not often. I don't like them much.

Quick steps to Part 1

- Be friendly to the examiners and to the other candidate.
- You can politely ask the examiner to repeat a question. Ask: ***Sorry? Could you say that again, please?***
- Don't just reply ***yes***, ***no*** or ***I don't know***. Give reasons (***because …*** , ***so …***) or examples (***such as …*** , ***like …***).
- Use as wide a range of grammar and vocabulary as you can.

3 **Elena says *I arrive home late every day*. Look at these expressions and answer the questions.**

every hour or so | from time to time | most weekends | five times a week | hardly ever | now and then

1 Where do frequency expressions like *every day* go in the sentence?
2 Which one means 'almost never'?
3 Which two mean 'occasionally'?

Exam tip

Think about how, why and when you do things, so you can give a full answer.

4 **Work with a different partner. Ask and answer the examiner's questions in Exercises 1 and 2. How well did you answer the Part 1 questions? How good were your partner's answers? Tell each other what you think.**

Character adjectives

5 **Find out what kind of person your partner is by asking them questions 1–10. Give examples, using expressions like *now and then* and *nearly always* in your replies.**

What are you like?

1 Do you think about what other people need or want?
2 Do you usually expect good things to happen?
3 Do you behave in a way that is silly and not adult?
4 Do you like telling other people what to do?
5 Are you good at dealing with problems?
6 Do you get annoyed if things happen too slowly?
7 Do you want to be very successful in life?
8 Are you easily upset and do you know when others are upset?
9 Do you find it easy to make up your mind quickly?
10 Do you do things that nobody expects?

6 **Match the adjectives with questions 1–10. Do you think they describe your character correctly?**

ambitious | bossy | childish | decisive | impatient | optimistic | practical | sensitive | thoughtful | unpredictable

Reading and Use of English

Forming adjectives

1 **Underline these prefixes and suffixes in the words in Speaking Exercise 6. One word has both a prefix and a suffix.**

-able -al -ful -ic im- -ish
-itive -ive -ous un- -y

2 **Form character adjectives from these words with the prefixes and suffixes in Exercise 1. Be careful with spelling changes.**

adventure aggression anxiety
artist caution cheek compete
emotion energy enthusiasm
fool generosity greed help
pessimist polite popular
rely respect sympathy

3 **Correct the mistakes in these sentences written by exam candidates.**

1 My job can be quite stressing.
2 He is a very charmful host; everyone likes him.
3 I eat a lot of fruit and vegetables, so I think I'm very healthful.
4 We really enjoyed our stay in the hotel in spite of the disorganising staff.
5 I'm helpful and socialful, so I'd like a job working with new people.
6 I won't invite her to visit again because she was rude and unpolite.

4 **Complete the sentences with the correct form of the words in brackets. In each case add a prefix and/or a suffix.**

1 Our neighbour has lost her cat, so she's feeling quite .... (depress).
2 Not many people have signed up for the new football club, so the coach is feeling quite .... (pessimism).
3 Question 9 in the quiz was quite .... (challenge), but I got it right.
4 Dan felt .... (refresh) after his three-week holiday.
5 People seem .... (enthusiasm) about the TV show. Few are watching it.
6 The staff disliked the boss and they were .... (sympathy) when he lost his job.

Part 3

5 **Look at the exam task. Answer these questions.**

1 How many gaps are there in the text?
2 What do you have to put in each of them?
3 Does this task mainly test grammar or vocabulary?

Quick steps to Part 3

- Read the text quickly to find out its purpose and main points.
- Look at each word in capitals, then the words next to the gap. Do you need a noun, an adjective, or another part of speech?
- Does the word in capitals need more than one change?

6 **Quickly read the text, ignoring the gaps for now. What is the purpose of the text? What is each paragraph about?**

7 **Look at the example (0). Answer these questions. Then do the exam task.**

1 What kind of word probably goes between *the* and *results*?
2 Does it describe how someone feels, or what causes a feeling?
3 What suffix do we use for this?
4 If this suffix begins with a vowel, how does *surprise* change?

Exam task

For questions **1–8**, read the text below. Use the word given in capitals at the end of some of the lines to form a word that fits in the gap in the same line. There is an example at the beginning (**0**).

Example: 0 SURPRISING

Very different but best friends

We often assume that people have similar personalities to their best friends, but the **(0)** .... results of recent research **SURPRISE** indicate this may not always be true. It seems that in friendship, unlike in many **(1)** .... **ROMANCE** relationships, opposites often attract.

For example, an optimistic person can provide a balance if the other is not. In the same way, someone who is shy can benefit from the **(2)** .... **POPULAR** of their sociable best friend by being introduced to people they would never have the **(3)** .... **CONFIDENT** to begin a conversation with on their own.

In **(4)** ...., as a close friendship develops, **ADD** two people may gradually become much more **(5)** .... For instance, a highly **LIKE** **(6)** .... individual might listen to what a **ADVENTURE** rather more **(7)** .... best friend says and **CAUTION** take fewer risks, while in turn encouraging their friend to worry less and try new things. So taking each other's advice and helping one another can build a relationship that is cooperative, not **(8)** .... **COMPETE**

Part 2 informal email

Page 120

1 Look at the exam task and answer these questions.

1 Who has written to you?
2 What does this person want you to do?
3 What style is the extract from the email written in? Find examples of the following:

a contracted forms, e.g. *I'm*
b short, common words, e.g. *got*
c simple linking words, e.g. *because*
d informal punctuation, e.g. dash (–)
e friendly expressions, e.g. *tell me*

Exam task

This is part of an email from an English friend, Alex.

To:
Subject:

I'm lucky because I've got really good friends – especially those I've known since I was a kid. I don't know what I'd do without them! So tell me, how important are friends to you? Who's your best friend and what do you like about him or her?

Looking forward to hearing from you soon.

Write your **email** to Alex in **140–190** words. Do not write any addresses.

Quick steps to Part 2 informal email

- Look at the task, including any text, and decide who you are writing to, why, and which points to include.
- Note down ideas and decide how many main paragraphs you will need. Then put your ideas under paragraph headings.
- Begin ***Dear*** (***friend's first name***) and thank them for their last message.
- Keep to your plan and use informal language throughout.
- Close in a friendly way, asking them to write back. End ***Lots of love***, ***Best wishes***, etc.

2 Read the model email and answer these questions.

1 Is Lydia's email the right length?
2 Has she made any language mistakes?
3 How does she open and close her message?
4 What does she talk about in her introduction and conclusion?
5 Does she answer all of Alex's questions? In which main paragraphs?
6 What examples of informal language can you find?
7 What character adjectives does she use?
8 Which phrases of hers might be particularly useful when you write other emails?

Dear Alex,

Many thanks for your message. It was great to hear from you!

The first thing I want to say is that I completely agree with you about friends. I see some of mine almost every day and I really miss them when they're away.

My closest friend Nicole, who's also a student, is the same age as me and lives just down the road. We've been best mates for many years and we tell each other everything, but I think we've got quite different personalities.

For instance, I can be a bit indecisive at times, but she's very practical and gets everything done quickly. She's not bossy, though. In fact, she's really thoughtful. Whenever I get upset she's always sympathetic and then she finds a way to cheer me up – she's got a wonderful sense of humour!

I hope one day you can get to know her, and that I have the chance to meet your friends, too. Please tell me more about them in your next email. Write soon!

Best wishes,

Lydia

3 Think about these questions and note down some ideas for your own email to Alex.

1 What does friendship mean to you?
2 How often do you see your friends?
3 Who are you going to write about?
4 How long have you known each other?
5 Which character adjectives best describe your friend?

4 Make a plan for your email. Put your best ideas from Exercise 3 under these headings: 1 *Friends in general*, 2 *Best friend: who*, 3 *Best friend: why*. Then add some details, such as the person's age or job. You could put the points under each heading into main paragraphs 1, 2 and 3.

5 Write your email. When you have finished, check it for the following:

- correct length
- all the content asked for in the instructions
- good organisation into paragraphs
- correct grammar, spelling and punctuation
- suitable style of language

Exam tip

In the exam, make sure you leave enough time at the end to check your email for mistakes.

2 Differing tastes

1 **Look at the photos and answer these questions.**

1. What do you think makes a restaurant popular or unpopular?
2. Why do people enjoy eating food from other parts of the world?
3. What do you enjoy cooking?
4. What are the advantages of using online videos to help you cook?

Part 6

2 **Look at the exam task instructions. Answer these questions.**

1. What kind of text do you have to read?
2. What do you have to put in gaps 1–6?
3. Do you have to use all of sentences A–G?

Quick steps to Part 6

- Study the instructions, read the main text for gist, then look quickly at sentences A–G.
- Study the words next to each gap, then look for similar or contrasting ideas in sentences A–G.
- Look for: vocabulary links; grammatical links, such as verb tenses; reference words, e.g. ***these***; and linking expressions, e.g. ***but***, ***after***, ***too***, ***ones***, ***so***.

3 **Quickly read the text, ignoring sentences A–G for now. Answer these questions.**

1. Why did May have to learn to become a chef?
2. What does May's mother think of her cooking?

4 **Question 1 has been done as an example. Look at sentence E and the first two paragraphs of the main text. How do the underlined words link sentence E to gap 1? Why can't sentence E fit gap 2?**

5 **Do the exam task, underlining the words and phrases in sentences A–G and in the main text which are linked to each other in some way.**

6 **Find words and phrases in the text that mean the following:**

1. lists of foods and instructions explaining how to cook something (paragraph 1)
2. style of cooking (paragraph 2)
3. food cooked and bought at a shop but taken home to be heated and eaten (paragraph 3)
4. people who write articles giving their opinion about books, films, music, restaurants, etc. (paragraph 4)
5. be in danger of failing (paragraph 5)
6. property owned by a company or organisation (paragraph 5)
7. long flat surface where customers are served (paragraph 6)
8. advice (paragraph 6)
9. as 4 (sentence G)
10. real or true (sentence G)

Exam task

You are going to read an article about a woman who became a chef by watching online videos. Six sentences have been removed from the article. Choose from the sentences **A–G** the one which fits each gap (**1–6**). There is one extra sentence which you do not need to use.

Star chef learnt to cook by watching YouTube

The kitchen has no oven. The restaurant is almost impossible to find, and the head chef learnt to cook by watching YouTube videos. But Siam Smiles, a Thai restaurant located in a former railway building that is now a shopping centre in Manchester, is run by a woman who has become one of the city's most critically acclaimed chefs.

Lallalin Mahasrabphaisal, 37, whose friends call her May for short, has no formal training but simply learnt to cook by obsessively watching online videos. After returning from a busy day at the Thai supermarket she owns in Manchester – and after putting her three young children to bed – she would watch YouTube, memorising complex recipes without making a single note. 'I didn't sleep,' she said. 'I watched YouTube videos.' **1** Her menus continue to reflect what she learnt from him.

May said her main courses, which typically cost less than £10, do not always go down well with locals who are not used to very hot food. 'Once I saw a grown man burst out crying,' she said. **2** Of course, such strong flavours are an integral part of Thai cuisine and will hardly come as a surprise to most customers.

She was forced to learn to cook after a chef, who ran a small but successful café in the basement of May's supermarket, suddenly resigned. He gave her just two days' warning. 'We were very popular,' she said, 'and we had so many customers. **3** It's not about the money, it's about my love of Thai cooking.' She had no previous cooking experience. 'I would make my children ready meals and basic Italian dishes like spaghetti bolognese. Nothing special. Just normal home cooking.'

Critics began to take notice, with the restaurant critic Marina O'Loughlin, who now works for *The Sunday Times*, describing it as 'the most exciting thing to happen to me in Manchester for many years.' **4** These include noodle soups, curries, stir fries and salads.

When rents and rates in Manchester's Chinatown increased, however, May's modest supermarket-café began to struggle, and the building was repossessed by its owners in March. **5** At the time of the closure, the company was making a film about how she taught herself to cook using its tutorials, so it also helped May decorate the replacement premises.

It is simple. The kitchen consists of a fridge and two hot plates behind a counter. The room has ordinary wooden chairs and tables, and on the wall hangs a photo of the former King of Thailand. May's mother, Mamat Buatick, 58, said: 'I am very proud of her. Her grandfather owned a restaurant in Thailand so perhaps it runs in the family. **6** I am amazed at how good she has become since then. But it wasn't all from YouTube,' she insisted. 'I gave her some tips, too.'

A I didn't want to let them all down.
B She didn't take very much interest in cooking growing up.
C It was simply too spicy for him.
D She thanked him for being so helpful at such a difficult time for her.
E Her favourites include those of green curry and Thai basil dishes being prepared by the popular Thai chef, Ying Sak.
F Much to her relief, YouTube stepped in to set her up at a new location in the Great Northern Warehouse in the city centre.
G Other reviewers praised the 'tastes to lose yourself in' and 'flawless' authentic dishes.

Exam tip

Make sure you have chosen an answer to every question. There will be one letter you haven't used. Check that the extra sentence doesn't fit any of the gaps.

1 **Look at the photo. Do you ever buy from a food truck, buy street food or order a takeaway meal? Tell your partner why or why not and give examples. Use some of these expressions.**

convenience food | delicious | (to) heat up | junk food | packaging | portion | sit-down meals | tasty | (un)healthy | (un)hygienic | vegan | vegetarian

Part 2

Quick steps to Part 2

- Quickly read the instructions and all the sentences, including any words after the gaps.
- Decide what type of information, e.g. a person, an object, a place, you need for each gap.
- Wait to hear all the information about each point before you decide on your answer.

2 02 **Look at the exam task and answer these questions. Then listen and do the exam task.**

1 In question 1, what kind of word probably goes after *the*? What does the word *near* indicate?
2 What kind of information do you need for each of questions 2–10?

Exam task

You will hear a young man called Dave Simpson talking about selling meals from a food truck. For questions **1–10**, complete the sentences with a word or short phrase.

When Dave realised food trucks near the **(1)** .... were successful, he decided to buy one.
Dave managed to get money from a **(2)** .... to start his business.
Dave changed his mind about asking a **(3)** .... to help run the business.
Dave says he had difficulty creating a **(4)** .... to advertise his business.
Dave sometimes has to **(5)** .... in his truck overnight to get a good place to do business.
Dave says he sells more **(6)** .... than any other type of food.
At lunchtime, the majority of Dave's customers are **(7)** .... and students.
Dave particularly likes driving to **(8)** .... to sell meals.
To help make his business more environmentally friendly, Dave uses **(9)** .... that can be recycled.
According to Dave, the **(10)** .... in the food-truck trade tend to be low.

Exam tips

- Write your answers exactly as you hear them – don't try to use other words that mean the same.
- Read all your completed sentences. Do they make sense? Are your grammar and spelling correct?

Giving your opinion

3 **Now that you have heard Dave talking about running a food truck, do you think it is a good job to have? Use some of these expressions and give reasons.**

Actually, I'm convinced that ... | I'd say that ... | In my opinion, ... | It seems to me ... | Personally, I think ... | Well, my own feeling is that ...

Past tenses

Page 100

a b c

1 **Look at these extracts from the recording in Listening and answer the questions about the underlined verb forms.**

a Once I'd made that decision, the next step was to raise the money.

b … my friend George, who used to run a market stall …

c I would try to work out whether they were selling enough.

d I noticed all those by the shopping mall had queues.

e When I was drawing up my plans I felt it was essential to find a business partner.

f I'd been taking an interest in the food trucks.

Which verb form do we use:

1 for actions or events in the past?
2 to talk about something that was going on when something else happened?
3 when we are already talking about the past and we want to talk about an earlier event?
4 to talk about how long something went on up to a point in the past?
5 to talk, without using time expressions, about things we did regularly in the past but don't do any more?
6 like 5, but only for actions, not states?

2 **Correct the mistakes in these sentences written by exam candidates. In some cases more than one answer is possible.**

1 I saw that Amy carried a heavy bag, so I offered to help her.
2 She started walking back to the garage where she left her car the day before.
3 I used to be a shop assistant for about three years.
4 The party was something that we organised for weeks before his birthday.
5 We were very pleased when they bought the house as it was for sale for nearly three years.
6 It was dark, but it was clear that someone walked across the bridge.
7 People didn't used to worry about the environment.
8 I wanted to go to Rome because I used to wanted to be an archaeologist.

3 **Choose the correct form of the verb (A, B or C) to complete each sentence.**

1 My aunt and uncle didn't have a car, so they .... one last year.
A bought **B** used to buy **C** 'd bought
2 When I got home yesterday, I felt quite tired because I .... an exam all afternoon.
A used to sit **B** 'd been sitting **C** sat
3 I don't think I .... Holly before last week's party.
A was meeting **B** met **C** 'd met
4 Sean .... with somebody else all last summer, but now he's my sister's boyfriend.
A used to go out **B** had gone out **C** was going out
5 By the time he was 30, he .... one of the leading experts in his field.
A became **B** had become **C** was becoming
6 When I arrived at Micky's house, everyone .... a film on TV.
A watched **B** used to watch **C** was watching

4 **Use the given verb form to complete the sentences.**

1 This afternoon I saw my sister Eileen while I .... (past continuous)
2 I could see he was upset – his eyes were red because he .... (past perfect continuous)
3 Nowadays I follow quite a healthy diet, but when I was younger I .... (*used to*)
4 I made friends with lots of people when I .... (past continuous)
5 I had a lunch date with my new manager, but I was late and by the time I arrived she .... (past perfect)
6 When we were kids, our parents took us on family holidays where we .... (*would*)

Speaking

A

B

1 Look at photos A and B. We can use sentences a–f to compare two photos. Fill in gaps 1–8 with these words. You can use some of them more than once.

both	difference	different	other	same	similar	similarity

a In **(1)** ....both......... of these photos there are some people eating out, but in this one they're in a street café.
b In this photo there are two people, but in the **(2)** .... one there's a family of three.
c These two are **(3)** .... in age, about 30, unlike the family inside the restaurant.
d One **(4)** .... between the photos is that **(5)** .... show people eating a quick lunch.
e But in some ways the situation in the two photos is quite **(6)** ....
f The biggest **(7)** .... between them is that this one shows people laughing and enjoying a meal together, but in the **(8)** .... one they're looking at their food, not at each other.

2 Look at photos 1 and 2. Which of points a–f are the same or similar in the two photos, and which are different?

a the place
b the food
c the number of people
d the people's age
e the people's appearance
f what the people are doing

3 Look at photos 3 and 4 on page 96 and note down as many points of similarity and difference as you can.

Quick steps to Part 2

- Think about what you are going to say before you start speaking.
- Don't try to describe everything in the photos. Just mention as many similarities and differences as you can.
- When your partner is speaking, listen to what they say but don't interrupt. At the end, the examiner will ask you a question on the topic, so think about your own ideas.

1

2

Part 2

Page 130

4 **Look at the exam instructions in Exercise 5. What does Candidate A have to do? What does Candidate B have to do?**

5 **Work in pairs and do the exam task.**

Exam task

Each of you will be given two photographs. You have to talk about your photographs on your own for about a minute, and also answer a short question about your partner's photographs.

Candidate A: It's your turn first. Look at photographs 1 and 2. They show people buying food. Compare the photographs, and say why you think people choose to buy food there. Talk about your photographs on your own for about a minute.
Candidate B: Do you like to go food shopping? Why? / Why not?

Candidate B: Look at photographs 3 and 4 on page 96. They show people eating out. Compare the photographs, and say what you think would be enjoyable about having a meal there. Talk about your photographs on your own for about a minute.
Candidate A: Which of these two kinds of place do you prefer to go to? Why?

Exam tip

Don't panic if you don't know much about the topic or you are unsure what is in the photograph. Keep talking and use phrases like ***It may be …*** , ***It could be …*** , ***It looks like …*** , etc.

6 **Change roles and repeat the exam task.**

7 **How well did you and your partner speak in Part 2? Tell each other what you think.**

Fixed phrases

1 Replace the underlined words with these fixed phrases.

at ease | at first sight | break my heart | get on my nerves | is attracted to | keep you company | leave me alone | lose touch | propose to someone | takes me for granted

1. When I take my dog for a walk, I feel completely relaxed.
2. He keeps calling me early in the morning, and it's starting to annoy me.
3. It's sad when you move away and you stop communicating with your friends.
4. The book doesn't look very interesting the first time you see it, but it is.
5. It'll make me very, very sad if you marry somebody else.
6. Sometimes I think Jeff forgets how lucky he is to have me as a friend.
7. From the way Marta looks at Ken, I think she really likes him.
8. You become engaged when you ask someone to marry you and they say 'yes'.
9. I have a lot of work to do but my colleague won't stop talking to me.
10. I'm waiting for the 55 bus too so I'll wait here with you.

Part 2

2 Look at the exam task. Answer these questions.

1. How many gaps are there?
2. How many words must you put in each gap?
3. Are you given a choice of words to use?

3 Without filling in any gaps, quickly read the text and answer these questions. Then do the exam task.

1. What does the title mean? Is the writer still happy in this relationship?
2. What kind of text, e.g. a news item, is it?

Exam task

For questions **1–8**, read the text below and think of the word which best fits each gap. Use only one word in each gap. There is an example at the beginning (**0**).

Example: 0 AT

How we met

I've known Mateo since our school days, so it definitely wasn't love **(0)** .... first sight. In fact, back then he and his rather childish friends used to get on **(1)** .... nerves and I felt we had nothing in common.
So I was surprised to discover how much he **(2)** .... changed when we met up years later. I'd just split up from someone I'd **(3)** .... seeing for ages and was in no hurry to start dating again, but Mateo seemed to understand that immediately and I felt completely **(4)** .... ease with him.
Our friendship grew. When I needed someone to keep **(5)** .... company he was there for me. Whenever I was upset he **(6)** .... listen patiently and if I needed help I knew I could always count **(7)** .... him.
One day I woke up and realised I wanted to see Mateo every day. That evening I proposed **(8)** .... him; he said 'yes' and three years later I don't regret a thing.

Quick steps to Part 2

- Read the title and the example, then quickly read the text.
- For each gap, decide what kind of word you need, e.g. auxiliary verb, preposition.
- Don't use abbreviations such as ***etc.***, or contracted forms like ***won't*** – these count as two words.
- Use the correct verb form with the subject given, e.g. ***people were going*** (not ***was***).

Exam tips

- Make sure you have given one word for every question and that your spelling is correct.
- Revise verbs and adjectives + prepositions as these are often tested in Part 2.

4 Which answers complete fixed phrases from Exercise 1 and which complete past tenses?

Linking expressions

1 Match the underlined linking words with their meanings.

as soon as | at first | at the same time | between those two times | immediately | very surprisingly

1. Initially, he thought the course was easy. But then he realised it was more difficult than he thought.
2. The flight was at 9.15, but I arrived at the airport at 7.30. In the meantime, I had some breakfast.
3. Once Dan had woken up, he put the light on.
4. The thief broke the car window. Instantly, a loud alarm went off.
5. You are trying to do too many things simultaneously.
6. The door opened, but to my amazement there was nobody there.

Part 2 article

Page 124

2 Look at the exam task and answer these questions.

1. Who are you writing the article for?
2. Should you write mainly about the past, the present or the future?
3. How many words must you write?

Exam task

You have seen the following announcement on an international website for young people:

Had a great night out? If so, tell us about it!

Write an article about the best evening or night out you've ever had. We will put the best articles on our site next week. Send us your article, and you could have readers all over the world!

Write your **article** in **140–190** words.

3 Quickly read the model article and answer these questions.

1. Is the article about the right length?
2. Is the style very formal or very informal – or somewhere in between? Give examples.
3. Why will readers want to continue reading after the first paragraph?
4. Which part of the article does the ending refer back to?
5. Find and correct one mistake in each paragraph.

Out at night

Have you ever felt that birthdays were more fun when you were a kid? I certainly did on my 18th as I sat at home watch TV. Sure, people had given me some nice presents, but somehow the old excitement was missing. Then, to my surprise, the doorbell rang.

The moment I opened the door and saw my friends standing there my mood changed. 'We're taking you down town!' they said, laughing. You can imagine how delighting I was!

I quickly got ready and before long we were in a taxi. First they took me shopping, buying me any clothes I wanted, and after that we went bowling. For once I actually won! Then we had a delicious pizza before going to a fashionable nightclub, where we spent hours dancing and meeting with people, some of them quite famous.

Eventually I arrived home, but just as I was going to bed I received a text message. It was from one of the celebrities I had been talking to earlier, inviting me out for a dinner the next day. I think you will agree it had been quite an evening!

4 Read the article more carefully and find the following:

1. expressions the writer uses to speak directly to the reader
2. examples of the past continuous, the past perfect and the past perfect continuous
3. linking expressions that mean the following:
   a immediately **b** after a while **c** in the end

Quick steps to Part 2 article

- Plan your article, noting down points for all parts of the task.
- Think of a title that will attract the readers' attention, and also an interesting first paragraph to keep them reading.
- Involve your readers by using expressions like ***Do you ever … ?, You might think … but …*** or ***How would you feel if … ?***

5 Read the exam task again and write your own article. When you have finished, check your work as in Unit 1 Writing Exercise 5 on page 13.

Exam tip

In an article, you can give your own opinions using expressions from Exercise 3 on page 16.

3 Changing places

1 **How important are the following when choosing a holiday?**

- the harm to the environment caused by the journey itself
- the effect of tourism on the local environment
- the benefit to the local people and the local economy that tourism can bring

Part 5

2 **Look at the exam task. Answer these questions.**

1 What kind of text do you have to read?
2 What different kinds of question are there?
3 For each question, how many options are wrong?

Quick steps to Part 5

- Quickly read the text, ignoring questions 1–6 for now, to see what it's about.
- For each question, look only at the first part of the question or unfinished statement and read what the text says about it.
- Think about the answer in your own words, then decide which option (A–D) is closest to your own answer.

3 **Quickly read the text. What is the writer's main purpose?**

A to criticise the islands' tourism authorities
B to suggest an alternative way of managing tourism
C to describe an enjoyable holiday he had recently
D to discourage tourists from visiting the islands

4 **Read the first two paragraphs of the text on page 23 and answer question 1. Why are the other options wrong? Then do the rest of the exam task.**

1 The writer says the construction of the tunnel
A made the island of Vágar far more attractive to tourists.
B forced local people to climb a hill to reach their village.
C meant that Gásadular didn't lose all its inhabitants.
D enabled travel between the coast and Gásadular for the first time.

Exam task

You are going to read an article about tourists doing conservation work. For questions **2–6**, choose the answer (**A**, **B**, **C** or **D**) which you think fits best according to the text.

2 What does 'It' in line 20 refer to?
A the path
B the mountain
C the village
D the road

3 What does Jóhan say about closing the islands for the weekend?
A It was part of a long-term plan to reduce tourism on the Faroe Islands.
B It aimed to improve understanding between local people and tourists.
C It had nothing to do with making money for the Faroe Islands.
D It was intended to benefit the islanders, not tourists from abroad.

4 What is meant by 'logistics' in line 34?
A the most important reasons for doing something
B the main disadvantages of doing something
C the dangers to people involved in doing something
D the practical arrangements for doing something

5 How does Ditte feel about tourism?
A She doesn't want the number of tourists to increase.
B She feels the Faroe Islanders should visit other countries more.
C She wants local people's attitudes to tourists to remain unchanged.
D She thinks tourists aren't sufficiently interested in the local culture.

6 In the final paragraph, the writer implies that
A villagers fear they will have to spend more time rescuing tourists.
B he would advise against running similar projects elsewhere.
C he had been wrong to doubt the successful outcome of the project.
D locals are aware that only the volunteers got anything from the project.

Exam tips

- If a question asks about a particular word or phrase, work out the meaning by looking for examples, explanations, and similar or contrasting expressions in the text around the chosen word.
- Make sure you have chosen one answer for every question.

Sustainable tourism: why the Faroe Islands closed for maintenance

by Tim Ecott

When the north Atlantic islands shut for a weekend to all but 'voluntourists' doing conservation projects, it was a win-win for locals and visitors.

The road tunnel to Gásadalur was built 15 years ago. Until then, residents of this tiny village on Vágar, one of the Faroe Islands, relied on irregular boat access below the cliffs or, more commonly, braved the 45-degree slope of a narrow track that climbs 500 metres over the mountain south of the village. Only 11 people live in Gásadalur today, and without the tunnel it would probably have become one of the Faroes' abandoned villages. Today, I'm doing the climb with several local men, plus three mathematicians from Washington DC, a pharmacist from Glasgow, a civil servant from London, two Finnish students and two biochemists from Bratislava. They're all volunteers who have come to the islands as a part of a tourism initiative that declared the country 'closed for maintenance' for one weekend last month.

We 'voluntourists' (as Visit Faroe Islands calls us) have the task of clearing loose stones from the path, and hammering wooden stakes into the grass to mark a safe, easily visible route over the mountain. Historically, clearing loose stones was done by people from the village, but thanks to the road they rarely walk over the mountain these days. It is being renovated mainly for the growing numbers of tourists who explore this archipelago of rugged mountains, prolific seabirds and wild-looking sheep. Gásadalur also has one of the Faroes' most photographed sights: a waterfall that gushes straight from the cliff face into the Atlantic below.

One of the masterminds behind this weekend is Jóhan Pauli Helgason, development manager for Visit Faroe Islands. He says the project had several aspects: 'Yes, it was a marketing campaign but it was also about making genuine improvements to the tourist experience, and providing visitors and islanders with a proper cultural exchange. We see that as a more sustainable version of tourism for a country with just 50,000 people.'

Helgason managed the logistics, getting 105 volunteers from 25 countries safely in and out of the country and distributed across ten projects selected in collaboration with district councils. The sites included the puffin colony on Mykines Island, the natural rock harbour at Gjógv and – the Instagram favourite – the high cliffs at Trælanípa, where the archipelago's largest lake seems to float hundreds of metres above the Atlantic. One group of volunteers also went to the southernmost island of Suðuroy, with everyone staying in guesthouses and local homes. Crucially, no one fell off a mountain or twisted an ankle in the mud.

It is clear to anyone from the wider world that the Faroes are not suffering anything like overtourism. Most Faroese people see tourists as an asset, and are still flattered that people want to know more about their culture. Ditte Mathilda Joensen runs small-scale photography tours through her company Veingir. 'I want visitors to meet locals, and become friends. For me, tourism has to be a two-way process, and I hope we don't lose sight of that as we grow.'

Knowing the Faroes well, I admit I'd wondered if voluntourism would achieve much in practical terms. On the island of Nólsoy, local resident Tjóðhild Patursson was adamant that the visitors had helped this small community in a tangible way. 'Many visitors take the wrong track across the mountains. If they get lost or injured, we have to take care of them. Our local municipality hasn't had the time, the money or the manpower to waymark the route, even though we have been talking about it for a couple of years. What the visitors have achieved in just two days is remarkable.' The 'Closed for Maintenance' weekend may well be a vision of what tourism should be like for many small communities.

5 Find words and phrases in the text that mean the following:

1 something that is done to improve a situation
2 repaired because it is old and in bad condition
3 causing little or no damage to the environment
4 working together (with)
5 someone or something that helps you succeed
6 pleased by what someone said about them
7 forget about something important
8 absolutely sure
9 real, not imagined

6 Would you like to work as a 'voluntourist'? Why? / Why not? Where could they do useful work in your country?

1

4

1 **The photos show places the speakers in the exam task went to. Answer these questions.**

1 Which photo shows each of the following?
The Uxmal Pyramid, Mexico
Victoria Falls, Zimbabwe/Zambia
Manarola village, Cinque Terre, Italy
The Wave rock formation, USA
The Harbin Ice and Snow World, China

2 What do you think the speakers might say about each place?

3 Which three places do you think are the most impressive? Why?

4 Which other places would you add to a list of the world's top sights? Why?

Part 3

2 03 **Look at option A in the exam task. The key words are *light* and *good enough*. These words have similar or opposite meanings: *sunshine*, *visibility*, *darkness* and *poor*, *excellent*, *clear*. For each of options B–H, underline the key words and note down some expressions with similar or opposite meanings. Then listen and do the exam task.**

2

3

5

Quick steps to Part 3

- Quickly read the instructions and options A–H, and think about what you're going to hear.
- Underline the key words in each option. Before you listen, think of words or phrases that the speakers might use.
- The first time you hear the extracts, get a general idea of what each speaker says. Then, the second time you listen, check that options A–H match exactly what they say.

Exam tips

- Be careful if words in one option are mentioned by more than one speaker. Only one of them can be the correct answer. Don't just listen for key words, listen for the meaning.
- Make sure you have chosen one letter for each answer.

Exam task

You will hear five short extracts in which people are talking about their visits to famous locations to take photos. For questions **1–5**, choose from the list (**A–H**) the difficulty each speaker had getting the photos they wanted. Use the letters only once. There are three extra letters which you do not need to use.

A The light wasn't good enough.
B A technical problem prevented me taking more photos.
C Travelling to the location took longer than I'd expected.
D It was difficult to get permission to visit the location.
E It was too dangerous to take certain photos.
F The location was too crowded to get good photos.
G It was the wrong time of year to get the photos I wanted.
H The outdoor temperature was unexpectedly extreme.

Speaker 1		1
Speaker 2		2
Speaker 3		3
Speaker 4		4
Speaker 5		5

Grammar

Modal verbs

Page 101

a b c d

1 **Study Modal verbs on page 101. Then choose the correct option in these sentences. Say why it is right and why the other one is wrong.**

1 We *could walk / could have walked*, but it was raining so we decided to go by car.
2 You *mustn't / don't have to* use your phone in class. It's against the rules.
3 I can't find my key. I *had to drop / might have dropped* it outside.
4 You *have to / must* make less noise, children, while I'm on the phone.
5 You *shouldn't / don't have to* wear a tie to work.
6 She *may have been / must have been* late because her alarm didn't go off, but it's more likely that she got stuck in a traffic jam as the new junction is very busy.
7 I was at the restaurant just before 12.00 but I *didn't need to get / needn't have got* there so early because Tom was 45 minutes late!
8 She immediately started to cry and Mark realised he *can't have / shouldn't have* said anything.

2 **Say what the mistakes are in these sentences written by exam candidates. Correct the mistakes.**

1 I could find my key in the end and I unlocked the door.
2 Now I cycle to work I mustn't spend any money on petrol.
3 That job must have been a great opportunity, but it was not.
4 Before I could drive, I must take lessons.
5 We don't have to drive above the speed limit.
6 We needn't to reserve a table because the restaurant was empty.
7 A lot of people take the early train to London, so you can have to stand all the way.
8 You might already heard that we got married.

3 **Complete this phone conversation between two friends with the correct form of the verbs in brackets.**

Sally: Hi, I'm at the station but I can't see Paula. She **(1)** .... (must / miss) the 8.30 train.
Lisa: Are you sure? She **(2)** .... (could / get) the earlier train, and she **(3)** .... (might / leave) the station before you got there.
Sally: No, she **(4)** .... (can't / do). I got here really early, and saw both the 8.15 and 8.30 trains come in. All the passengers getting off **(5)** .... (have to / walk) past where I was standing, so I would've seen her.
Lisa: Have you tried phoning her?
Sally: Yes, but there's no reply. She **(6)** .... (must / switch off) her phone, or she **(7)** .... (might / even / forget) to take it with her.
Lisa: Hang on, I've just had a text from her, saying she's sorry but she slept through her alarm.
Sally: She **(8)** .... (must / have) a very late night last night!

4 **Use the correct form of the modal in brackets to reply to these comments. More than one answer is possible, and in some cases negative forms are needed.**

1 Lucy looks just like that woman she's with. (must)
2 I overslept this morning. (should)
3 In my last job, it wasn't compulsory to wear a uniform. (have to)
4 I left my phone on the table in the café and now it's gone. (must)
5 I didn't know the train company offered student discounts when I bought my ticket. (could)
6 I sometimes ride my bike without wearing a helmet. (should)
7 I've just seen a famous actor waiting at the bus stop. (can)
8 I'm sure I had some spare change in my pocket, but I can't find it. (might)

5 **Look at the photos and talk about what *might*, *may*, *could*, *must* or *can't* have happened.**

Adverbs of degree

Page 103

1 **Look at the rules for adverbs of degree on page 103. Then choose the correct options to complete the dialogue.**

Sam: So how was your journey to the mountains?

Jess: It was **(1)** *totally / pretty* good, overall. The train was **(2)** *slightly / really* late, though only ten minutes, and I was **(3)** *rather / completely* tired after **(4)** *quite / fairly* a long day, but once we got out into the countryside I **(5)** *slightly / really* started to relax.

Sam: Yes, sometimes I'm **(6)** *absolutely / a bit* surprised to find that I **(7)** *rather / very* enjoy train journeys, though the bus is much cheaper.

Jess: Yes, you're **(8)** *a bit / quite* right, but it was **(9)** *totally / extremely* impossible to get a bus ticket, because we booked the trip so late.

Sam: I know what you mean. I was **(10)** *absolutely / slightly* astonished to see how quickly tickets for the mountain bus sell out on a Friday evening. But, anyway, it sounds like the train was **(11)** *fairly / a bit* comfortable.

Jess: Actually, it was **(12)** *completely / extremely* comfortable! I slept most of the way.

2 04 **Listen to the dialogue to check your answers. Which other adverbs of degree are possible in each case except item 5?**

Part 3

Page 134

3 **Look at the exam task. Answer these questions. Then check your answers in the Speaking bank on page 134.**

1 Who do you talk to in Part 3?
2 For how long?
3 What kind of thing do you look at?

4 **Read the exam instructions in detail. What is the situation? What do you have to do?**

Exam task

Now, I'd like you to talk about something together for about two minutes. **I'd like you to imagine that a town wants to attract more tourists.** Here are some things that may help make a town more attractive to visitors. You now have some time to look at the task. Now talk to each other about **how each of these things can make a town more attractive to visitors.**

How could these things bring in more tourists?

- outdoor sports
- museum of local culture
- music festival
- theme park
- local cooking

Now you have a minute to decide **which two things would attract most visitors to the town.**

5 05 **You will hear Elisa and Carlos, two strong students, doing this task. The first time you listen, answer these questions.**

1 Do they discuss all the prompts?
2 Do they take turns speaking?
3 Which two things do they choose?

6 05 **Complete the expressions used to make suggestions and speculate. Then listen again to check your answers.**

Right, **(1)** .... start?
I think **(2)** .... quite a good one.
So **(3)** .... the next one – the music festival?
Talking about summer, the theme park's **(4)** .... for the town.
OK, that's four of them done. **(5)** .... the last one.
Which two shall we choose? **(6)** .... the museum.

Quick steps to Part 3

- Take turns with your partner as you talk about each of the prompts.
- Make suggestions, using expressions like ***Let's …*** and ***Why don't we … ?***
- Use modals to speculate, e.g. ***It may be …*** , ***It couldn't be …*** , and adverbs of degree.

7 **Work in pairs. Do the exam task, using expressions from Exercise 6.**

Exam tip

Start speaking as soon as you can and don't spend too much time talking about one item. You only have two minutes for this part.

Reading and Use of English

Dependent prepositions

1 **Look at the underlined words in the extracts from the recording in Speaking Part 3. Then decide which preposition (*to*, *with*, *of*) follows each of the expressions below.**

> things that may help make a town more <u>attractive to</u> visitors.
> – they're always <u>popular with</u> tourists.
> <u>instead of</u> the music festival, I'd choose the local cooking.

ashamed capable conscious familiar fed up in connection in need in place in relation in response in terms in view informed involved (have) nothing to do obliged obsessed prepared required sensitive sort supposed the trouble with regard

2 **For each of these sentences written by exam candidates, choose the correct preposition (A, B, C or D).**

1 Sometimes it was a stressful job because I was responsible .... many people.
A to **B** over **C** for **D** upon

2 I didn't enjoy the show because it was aimed .... young teenagers.
A at **B** to **C** over **D** below

3 I'm writing to you on behalf .... my husband.
A for **B** by **C** off **D** of

4 My younger brother goes to the same university as me, so I keep an eye .... him.
A on **B** over **C** to **D** about

5 Living at home with your family is a bit easier compared .... your first year living on your own.
A by **B** to **C** of **D** on

6 The teacher would like to have a word .... you.
A to **B** for **C** at **D** with

Part 1

3 **Look at the exam task. Answer these questions.**

1 How many words are missing?
2 How many possible words are there for each gap?
3 What do these words have in common?

4 **Quickly read the title, the example and the text without filling in any gaps. Decide what the text is about. Then do the exam task.**

Quick steps to Part 1

- For each gap, decide what kind of word, e.g. adjectives, the four options are.
- Study the words either side of the gap, underlining any dependent prepositions.
- Try each word in the gap, checking whether it fits the grammar of the sentence.

Exam task

For questions **1–8**, read the text below and decide which answer (**A**, **B**, **C** or **D**) best fits each gap. There is an example at the beginning (**0**).

Example: 0 A set **B** held **C** made **D** kept

The Battle of the Oranges

The centuries-old Battle of the Oranges is **(0)** .....B..... every February in the Northern Italian city of Ivrea. The local citizens are divided into nine teams whose task is to **(1)** .... their neighbourhood against others, who ride around in horse-drawn carts throwing oranges at them.
Oranges, **(2)** .... to the fruit thrown in similar events elsewhere, are both heavy and hard, which **(3)** .... inevitably to minor injuries. Spectators are allowed in the streets where the battles take place, but in **(4)** .... of the risks involved they wear bright red hats in order to **(5)** .... them from the teams.
Visitors are not permitted to throw fruit and participants are not **(6)** .... to target those in red hats, either. The **(7)** .... is, however, that when a quarter of a million kilos of oranges are being thrown around it's almost impossible to avoid getting covered in orange pulp and **(8)** .... a bruise or two. It is, though, wonderful fun.

	A	B	C	D
1	**A** challenge	**B** prevent	**C** defend	**D** oppose
2	**A** associated	**B** contrasted	**C** related	**D** compared
3	**A** results	**B** leads	**C** causes	**D** produces
4	**A** view	**B** account	**C** mind	**D** sight
5	**A** identify	**B** recognise	**C** regard	**D** distinguish
6	**A** approved	**B** tolerated	**C** supposed	**D** obliged
7	**A** trouble	**B** fate	**C** case	**D** matter
8	**A** aching	**B** suffering	**C** hurting	**D** wounding

5 **Tell another student about a carnival or special event in your country. In what ways is it similar or different to the one in Ivrea?**

Exam tip

Read the completed text and check that it all makes sense.

Part 1 essay

Page 118

1 Which of these linking expressions do we use in an essay for:

1 the first point
2 more points
3 the final point
4 the conclusion?

First of all, For another thing, For one thing, In the first place, Lastly, Next, On balance, To conclude,

2 Look at the exam task instructions and answer these questions.

1 What is the situation and the topic?
2 Who will read your essay?
3 What question must you answer?
4 What points must you include?
5 What must you add to those points?

Exam task

In your English class you have been talking about the advantages and disadvantages of taking holidays near home rather than travelling abroad. Now, your English teacher has asked you to write an essay.

Write an essay using all the notes and give reasons for your point of view.

Is it better to have holidays near home rather than travel abroad?

Notes

Write about:

1 which is cheaper
2 which is better for the environment
3 your own idea

Write your **essay** in **140–190** words. You must use grammatically correct sentences with accurate spelling and punctuation in an appropriate style.

Exam tip

Always plan your essay, but don't try to write a draft. There won't be time in the exam to write the essay twice.

3 Read the model essay and answer these questions.

1 Which kind of holiday does the writer say is better?
2 Which paragraph covers each of the points?
3 Which addition links, e.g. *firstly*, are used?
4 What other addition links do you know?

Some people believe we should not travel long distances for our holidays; that we ought to spend our free time in our own country, enjoying the local countryside. I, however, disagree.

To begin with, budget flights and package holidays enable ordinary people to travel to exotic locations that previous generations could only have dreamt of visiting. Inexpensive student railcards also make it possible to take trains to exciting international destinations. In fact, it often costs less to travel abroad than at home.

Secondly, green holidays in distant countries are now widely available. Much of the journey can be done by ship, train or bus. Once there, accommodation may be in tents or in country houses that use little energy, with local travel by horse, by bicycle or on foot.

Finally, it is natural for young people to want to see more of the world, meet people in different cultures and understand the problems that other societies face. They cannot do this by staying in their hometown.

To sum up, I am absolutely convinced that holidays abroad are positive experiences that can be both economical and environmentally friendly.

4 Read the essay again and find formal expressions that mean the same as these words and expressions (1–7).

1 shouldn't
2 though
3 places
4 cheap
5 you can do
6 can't
7 I'm quite sure

Quick steps to Part 1 essay

- Read the question or statement in the instructions and decide what your opinion is.
- Write in a fairly formal style if the intended reader is a teacher.
- Connect your points with addition links.

5 Follow the exam task instructions and write your essay.

6 When you have finished, check your work as in Unit 1 Writing Exercise 5 on page 13.

4 Getting creative

1 **The people in the photos all work in the arts. What do they do? Use some of these words.**

abstract artistic camera operator cast costume designer director lyrics perform portrait producer rehearse role scene script set shoot solo soundtrack studio

2 **Discuss these questions.**

1 In what ways are the people in the four photos similar? In what ways are they different?
2 Which of their jobs would you like to do? Why?

Part 6

3 **Look at the exam task, but not at options A–G. Quickly read the text and answer this question.**

What advice does the writer give to people who want to work in films?

A avoid working on cheaply made films
B get to know lots of people in the film industry
C concentrate on only one aspect of filmmaking
D don't try to get your films shown at film festivals

4 **Read the first paragraph of the text. Answer these questions. Then do the exam task.**

1 Which of options A–G has a time expression that links it to *less than two years ago*?
2 Which words in the option you chose above link to *break into the industry*?

Quick steps to Part 6

- Look quickly at sentences A–G, choosing any that clearly fit particular gaps.
- When choosing one of the sentences A–G, make sure that verbs and nouns agree in tense, person or number with the main text.
- Underline any vocabulary links, grammatical links and linking expressions in the main text and/or sentences A–G.

Exam task

You are going to read an article written by a woman who became a film director two years after leaving film school. Six sentences have been removed from the article. Choose from the sentences **A–G** the one which fits each gap (**1–6**). There is one extra sentence which you do not need to use.

A This breakthrough at such important events and locations helped me make a name for myself and introduced me to agents.
B Disappointments like those teach an important lesson: just because you're working today, it doesn't mean you'll be working tomorrow.
C As I was a mature student and classroom learning didn't really appeal, a course with that kind of approach suited me perfectly.
D In my experience, trying to enter the film industry in that way is rarely successful.
E You might find that experimenting with film-crew roles like these stimulates your interest and talent.
F During that time I have been lucky enough to land an agent, work on various sets in a range of roles and have my own projects in development.
G So if you can afford to give up a few days to help them out, it's a great way to try different things and meet people.

Exam tip

When you have chosen all your answers, read the complete text. Does it all make sense? Have you chosen a letter for every question?

4

Lights, camera ... and actions

to becoming a successful filmmaker

by Krysten Resnick

Do you dream of making an Oscar-winning movie? Many people go into the film industry in search of glamour, only to be disappointed. You could be spending 12 hours outside in the freezing rain on one project, or 14 hours struggling to solve a problem on another. It is hard work, but also incredible fun. People often ask how I managed to break into the industry, given that I graduated from film school less than two years ago. **1** ______ So what steps should you take if you are serious about becoming a filmmaker?

By the time I began film school, I'd already had a bit of experience on set doing trainee camera work, and even working as an extra. I chose to go to the Met Film School in London because it focused on the practical nature of filmmaking, putting a camera in your hands on the very first day. **2** ______ Film school gave me the opportunity to learn how a production worked, try out different crew roles and, ultimately, attempt to tell the stories I wanted to tell. However, the most important thing it gave me was a network of creative and inspiring fellow graduates.

You need to put yourself out there. The makers of student and low-budget films, for instance, are often looking for people to lend a hand. **3** ______ The film and television industry is quite a small world and if you land a job and work hard, people will often ask you to do another job ... and probably another.

Help your friends turn their passion into projects, and they'll do the same for you. When I was in film school, I wrote, directed and produced a short film called *Benny and Jack's Flying Machine*, which a group of student friends helped me to make. We had no money, little time, but a whole lot of passion. The film premiered at Toronto International Film Festival Kids and was screened at various festivals and venues, including the Museum of Modern Art in New York. **4** ______ It was a key turning point in my career.

Knowing how all the departments work helps you become a better filmmaker. Take opportunities to try out different things such as writing scripts, designing sets or recording sound. **5** ______ Shoot a music video for a friend's band. Try making a commercial. Take on a corporate or editing job. It's all part of the experience and will help you to become a better storyteller.

For every film festival you make it into, two more will say no. Projects will look promising, but can fall flat. **6** ______ But if you work hard and love what you do those things will shine through your projects. Be as helpful and as useful as you can, make sure people want to work with you and come to rely on you, and make yourself indispensable.

Phrasal verbs with *on*

5 **Look at these verbs in the text. What does each one mean?**

1. focused on (line 10)
2. take on (line 30)
3. rely on (line 35)

6 **Complete the sentences with phrasal verbs. Use the correct form of these verbs + *on*.**

base carry count depend keep jump ~~log~~ play sit turn

1. I'll ......log on...... to my computer to find out more about the composer of that music.
2. During the concert, somebody from the audience .... the stage.
3. I don't know where the theatre is, so I asked them to wait for me, but they just .... walking.
4. The special effects in a movie often .... the film's budget.
5. There are some comfortable armchairs to .... at that art gallery.
6. The concert was supposed to finish at 10.30, but they .... until after midnight.
7. Mid-way through the play there was an interval and all of the lights ....
8. The play is .... a female scientist from the 1950s.
9. The singer thanked his fans. 'You're fantastic and I know I can always .... your support,' he said.
10. I've been listening to a new album on my phone, but the first song .... playing twice, it's really annoying.

Listening

1 **Do you ever read or listen to reviews of songs or concerts? Why? / Why not?**

Quick steps to Part 4

- Quickly read the instructions. These may include information such as the main speaker's name, occupation or hobby, and the setting, e.g. a radio interview.
- For each question, study the stem only and underline the key words. When you listen, think of an answer in your own words.
- Choose the option (A, B or C) most like your answer.

Part 4

2 06 **Look at the exam task instructions and read question 1. Then listen to the first part of the recording and answer these questions.**

1. Which expressions have similar meanings to the key words *become*, *critic* and *must*?
2. Which is the correct answer (A, B or C)? Why?
3. Why are the other two answers wrong?

3 07 **Look at the stem of questions 2–7 and underline the key words. Then listen and do the exam task. When you hear the recording, listen for expressions with similar or opposite meanings to these words.**

Exam task

You will hear part of an interview with a music critic called Leo Clemson. For questions **1–7**, choose the best answer (**A**, **B** or **C**).

1 Leo says that to become a music critic you must
A be a talented singer or musician.
B spend a lot of time doing research.
C have a degree in literature or journalism.

2 How did Leo start out as a critic?
A He got help from experienced critics.
B He worked for a local newspaper.
C He wrote reviews without being paid.

3 How did Leo first get his music reviews published?
A He looked at the social media pages of other reviewers.
B He contacted the agents of well-known musicians.
C He sent his CV to the editors of a lot of music magazines.

4 In Leo's opinion, what does a critic most need to do to be successful?
A make lots of contacts in the music industry
B develop a writing style that people will like
C stay up to date on developments in music

5 Leo believes his greatest professional weakness is
A being too sensitive to criticism of his work by other reviewers.
B feeling uncertain that what he has written is fair.
C taking too much notice when people praise his work.

6 Which aspect of his work does Leo dislike?
A being alone during the day
B having arguments with his editor
C having to work late in the evenings

7 What appeals most to Leo about the idea of becoming a magazine editor?
A He would meet famous singers and musicians.
B He would earn a bigger salary.
C He could select articles for publication.

Exam tips

- Remember that the questions follow the order of the information that you hear, and each part of the recording relates to a particular question.
- Make sure you have chosen only one of the options (A, B or C) for each of questions 1–7. Then check your answers are correct.

Verbs followed by *to* + infinitive or *-ing*

Page 104

1 Look at extracts a–f from the recording in Listening. Answer these questions.

1 Which verbs are followed by *to* + infinitive, and which by *-ing*?
Example: a *need + to + infinitive*
2 Which verb can be followed by either *to* + infinitive or *-ing*? Does the meaning change?

a Some say you need to be a graduate.
b The number of positive comments posted on my site started to grow.
c I started earning something from it.
d The editor agreed to take me on.
e I do, though, miss having colleagues to chat with.
f And who wouldn't enjoy doing that?

2 Decide which of these verbs are followed by *to* + infinitive, and which by *-ing*.

appear avoid bother dislike expect finish get round to imagine insist on keep (on) learn manage mind offer promise refuse seem suggest tend threaten want

3 Match the sentence halves and explain the difference in meaning.

1 a I regret saying that **b** I regret to say that	**i** your application to join the Drama school has been declined. **ii** your performance in the play was terrible.
2 a We stopped talking to **b** We stopped to talk to	**i** our friends in the street last night. **ii** our friends because they didn't invite us to the party.
3 a I won't forget meeting **b** I won't forget to meet	**i** my favourite actor last year. **ii** you at the cinema later.
4 a I'll remember going to **b** I'll remember to go to	**i** that concert for many years. **ii** the school concert on Thursday!
5 a I went on watching **b** I went on to watch	**i** the women's match after the men's final had ended. **ii** the game for about half an hour.
6 a He tried working in fashion **b** He tried to work in fashion	**i** but he never managed to get a job. **ii** but he earned very little money.

4 Correct the mistakes in the sentences written by exam candidates.

1 He was preparing for an interview so I agreed helping him.
2 My friend suggested to buy them a microwave as a wedding present.
3 I forgot asking you what time the party starts.
4 It was my first job and I remember to be very nervous.
5 I don't mind to show you around the town.
6 You will disturb people if you carry on to talk in the cinema.

5 Complete the news story with the *to* + infinitive and the *-ing* form of the verbs in brackets.

Cinema audiences still rising

The latest cinema audience figures, which appear **(1)** .... (show) an increase of 12 per cent on the same period last year, seem **(2)** .... (indicate) that the economic downturn has not stopped people **(3)** .... (go) to watch their favourite films. Film critic Nick Kaminski says: 'These days people are trying **(4)** .... (spend) less money, and as an evening out at the cinema is much cheaper than, say, going to a restaurant, many of them are choosing **(5)** .... (see) a film rather than have a meal out. I expect the figures will keep on **(6)** .... (rise).'

6 Work in pairs. Ask your partner about the following:

- a film they particularly remember seeing
- a film they don't want to see
- a film they regret missing
- a film they must remember to see

7 Tell your partner about a film you have enjoyed watching. Use as many verbs as you can from Exercises 1–3.

Speaking

Too and enough

Page 104

1 Complete extracts a–e from the recording in Listening on page 32 with *too* and *enough*. Then answer the questions below.

a I was .... unknown to get anywhere.
b I worry about my tendency to get a bit .... upset.
c Probably .... many to mention.
d I have doubts about whether I've been objective .... in a particular review.
e There aren't really .... opportunities to talk to her.

1 Does *too* go before or after adjectives and adverbs? Does it mean the same as *very*?
2 Does *enough* usually go before or after adjectives and adverbs? What about nouns?
3 Can *too* and *enough* be followed by *to* + infinitive, or the *-ing* form of the verb?

2 Correct the mistakes in these sentences written by exam candidates.

1 I don't like shopping on Saturdays because there are too much people everywhere.
2 I'm too much lazy to walk to work.
3 We didn't come to the party as we had some too bad news.
4 Since I started my new job, I don't have leisure time enough.
5 Here are too narrow streets, so driving can be stressful.
6 If you don't go to bed enough early, you will be tired the next day.

3 Look at the examples. Then rewrite sentences 2–5 using *too* and *enough* with *for* in the same ways.

1 I can't watch films on this computer because it is so slow.
This computer is too slow for me to watch films on.
This computer isn't fast enough for me to watch films on.
2 The DVD was so expensive that I couldn't buy it.
3 It was so dark that we couldn't see what was going on.
4 I couldn't finish my project this week because there were so many meetings.
5 The hotel was so noisy that I couldn't sleep last night.

Part 4

Page 136

Quick steps to Part 4

- Support your opinions by giving reasons and examples.
- Listen carefully to what your partner says, adding to their ideas or encouraging them to say more.

4 Put these expressions into four groups: 1 *Asking for opinions*, 2 *Asking for reasons*, 3 *Giving reasons*, 4 *Giving examples*.

because … for example … for instance …
for one thing … like … so … such as …
Why do you think so? What's your opinion?
What do you think? Is that because … ?
The main reason is that … Could you tell me why?
What are your feelings about this?
Any particular reason? How do you feel about … ?

5 08 You will hear two strong students, Raffaele and Anna, practising Part 4. Which of questions 1–6 does the teacher ask? Which student do you think does this part of the Speaking test better? Why?

1 How important do you think it is to have a lot of free time?
2 Do you think hobbies are more fun with other people than on your own? Why? / Why not?
3 If you had more free time, what would you do with it? Why?
4 Which are the most popular hobbies where you live? Why?
5 Which do you prefer: indoor or outdoor hobbies? Why?
6 Do you think people will stop reading books in the future? Why? / Why not?

6 08 Listen again and tick the expressions in Exercise 4 that Anna uses.

Exam tip

The questions in Part 4 are not written down, so you need to listen to the examiner carefully.

7 Work in a group of three: one 'examiner' and two 'candidates'. The examiner asks the candidates some of the questions in Exercise 5. The candidates answer, using some of the following:

- expressions from Exercise 4
- verbs followed by *to* + infinitive and *-ing*, e.g. *tend, enjoy*
- *too* and *enough* to give reasons

Present perfect

Page 105

1 Look at these extracts from the recording in Speaking and answer the questions.

> I've been thinking of doing that for years.
> I've just downloaded some onto my phone.
> It looks exciting but I haven't tried it yet.
> I've been getting headaches since I started there last month.
> I've already begun taking a break every half hour.

1 Which tense is used for something:
   a that happened in a period of time that is finished?
   b that started changing or developing in the past and is still happening now?
   c that started in the past and is permanent or has a result now?

2 Match the underlined words with uses a–e.
   a for something that has happened sooner than expected
   b to say how long something has been happening
   c for an event that is expected to happen
   d to say when something that is happening started
   e for something that happened a short time ago

2 Correct the mistakes in these sentences written by exam candidates.

1 I have been studying here since two months.
2 I'm learning to play the drums for one year now.
3 I'd like to tell you more about what I've done last week.
4 I'll call you later; the lesson has ended yet.
5 I already have finished the book; it was so interesting.
6 We've waited for over an hour. Did you miss the train?

Part 4

3 Look at the exam task example. Answer these questions.

1 What adverb is used in the second sentence instead of *since*?
2 What change is there in verb form?
3 Which word is not needed in the second sentence?
4 Which two parts of the answer do you get marks for?

Quick steps to Part 4

- Decide whether the word in capitals is a noun or verb, for example, and what often goes with it, e.g. an adverb.
- Look at any verb in the second sentence to see whether you need a singular or plural noun in your answer.
- Use no more than five words. Contracted forms like ***I'd*** or ***it's*** count as two words, except ***can't*** – which counts as one.

4 Do the exam task. Note down the changes you make.

Exam task

For questions **1–6**, complete the second sentence so that it has a similar meaning to the first sentence, using the word given. Do not change the word given. You must use between two and five words, including the word given. Here is an example (**0**):

Example:

0 It's ages since I last saw Julia.
SEEN
I HAVEN'T (or HAVE NOT) SEEN JULIA FOR ages.

1 We can't be sure we'll make any money from this film.
COUNT
We can't .... any money from this film.

2 That crossword was so difficult that I couldn't complete it.
TOO
That crossword was .... me to complete.

3 For years I'd meant to tidy up the attic and I finally did it.
ROUND
For years I'd meant to tidy up the attic and I finally .... it.

4 The president's speech began at eight o'clock and it's still going on.
TALKING
The president .... eight o'clock.

5 You must continue to practise until you can play that tune well.
KEEP
You must .... until you can play that tune well.

6 I can't wear those boots because they're so small.
ENOUGH
Those boots aren't .... wear.

Exam tips

- If more than one answer is possible, give only one of them.
- When you have finished, remember to check all your answers for correct grammar and spelling.

Part 2 review

» Page 122

1 Look at the exam task and answer these questions.

1. Who will read your review?
2. What should it contain?
3. How many words must you write?

Exam task

You see this notice in an international English-language magazine.

Have you read a good novel recently?

If so, would you like to write a review of it? Include information on the setting, story and main characters, and say whether you would recommend the book to other readers.

Write your **review** in **140–190** words.

2 Read the model review and answer these questions.

1. Match the headings a–d with the four paragraphs of the review.
   - **a** conclusion and recommendation
   - **b** comments on various aspects of the book
   - **c** introduction and setting
   - **d** outline of the story and main characters
2. Is the review written in a style that is quite formal or very informal? Give examples.
3. Find words in the review that mean the following:
   - **a** things that happen in the story (noun)
   - **b** moves along quickly (adjective)
   - **c** completely holds your attention (adjective)
   - **d** can make you believe they are real (adjective)
   - **e** makes you admire it (adjective)
   - **f** subjects of a book, film, play, etc. (noun)
   - **g** that makes it difficult to relax (adjective)
4. Does the reviewer recommend the book to other readers? If so, in which sentence?

The Sugar Glider

Rod Neilsen's novel *The Sugar Glider* is an adventure story set in Australia, moving from the modern coastal city of Brisbane to the wild uninhabited interior.

When their small aeroplane crashes in the outback, pilot Don Radcliffe and his teenage daughter Judy quickly realise it was no accident. They discover, too, that the plane was carrying an illegal cargo. They then face a struggle to survive in the desert as a criminal gang tries to find that cargo – and them. It is a struggle in which Judy soon finds herself having to take the lead.

The plot is well constructed and as the story develops it becomes fast-paced and quite gripping. The main characters, particularly Judy, are convincing, and for such a short book there is an impressive mixture of themes that range from dishonesty, greed and selfishness, to courage, loyalty and respect for indigenous cultures.

This is a book I could not put down, and I read it right through in a few hours. If you enjoy a tense thriller which is quick and easy to read, I suggest you choose this one.

3 **Which of these descriptive adjectives usually have a negative meaning?**

absurd bizarre breathtaking delightful dreadful exceptional fine moving mysterious outstanding poor predictable remarkable slow-moving superb tremendous

4 **Which of these expressions do we use to recommend something, and which to say not to do something?**

My advice is to avoid this … and instead …
This … is really worth … because …
This is one of the best … I have ever …, so I suggest …
I would advise everyone to … a better … than this, such as …
Anyone who likes … will really enjoy this …

Quick steps to Part 2 review

- Think about who your readers are and what they want to know.
- Make a plan that includes description, explanation and conclusion.
- Try to include some interesting facts and lively comments.
- Recommend or advise readers against the subject of your review.

5 **Write your own book review. Include some descriptive adjectives.**

6 **When you have finished, check your work as in Unit 1 Writing Exercise 5 on page 13.**

Exam tip

Always make sure your writing style is consistent throughout the review.

5 Making your way

1 **Look at these photos. Answer these questions.**

1. What skills do you think are required for each of these jobs?
2. Which people (a–d) do you think are more likely to have these skills when they grow up? Why?
   a an elder child
   b a middle child
   c a youngest child
   d an only child
3. Check the meaning of the phrase 'sibling rivalry' and give some examples of this behaviour.

Part 7

2 **Read the exam task instructions and the title of the text, and look at its layout. Answer these questions.**

1. What is the topic of the text and how many parts are there?
2. Who are the people?
3. What kind of information do you need to find?

3 **For each of questions 1–10, underline (or note down) the key words as in the example (1).**

4 **Do the exam task. As you read, look for words, phrases and sentences that express the same ideas as the key words in the questions. Underline the words, phrases or sentences that tell you the right answers.**

Quick steps to Part 7

- You don't have to begin by reading the whole text. You may find it helpful to read the questions first, then scan each part of the text.
- Before you make your mind up about an answer, read the question again and look carefully at the evidence in the text.
- For some questions, you may be able to choose more than one option. If so, there will be extra spaces next to these questions.

Exam task

You are going to read an article about possible effects of birth order on four people's careers. For questions **1–10**, choose from the sections (**A–D**). The sections may be chosen more than once.

In which section does the writer mention someone who

is glad to have changed job?	**1**	
complains about not earning enough money?	**2**	
is aware of sometimes being too self-critical?	**3**	
often spent more time with friends than family?	**4**	
would like to become the boss?	**5**	
can't remember ever being treated like a child?	**6**	
is able to persuade others?	**7**	
developed self-confidence while still a child?	**8**	
claims to be good at making deals?	**9**	
is said to have a good sense of humour?	**10**	

5 **Are you an eldest, middle, youngest or only child? In what ways do you think that has had an effect on your childhood, your personality and your choice of career? Why?**

Exam tip

Make sure you have put a letter in every space.

How birth order can influence career choices

A an eldest child

Research scientist Amelie recalls that her parents would spend more time with her than with her younger brother and sister, having conversations with her as though she were an adult. 'They also took it for granted that I'd make it in whatever field I entered, and at quite an early age some of that must have had an influence on me,' she says. The eldest may be expected to look after siblings, which can help develop leadership qualities, although Amelie's main professional aim has always been to be the best in her branch of science. This desire to succeed, possibly created by early parental pressure, can turn into perfectionism, which also has its downside. 'It sometimes bothers me that I have to get things absolutely right, feeling that otherwise people will think less of me as a person,' she says. A lot of scientists, rock stars and astronauts were eldest children.

B a middle child

During childhood, the middle one may take on the role of peacemaker between quarrelling siblings, and can become quite a skilled negotiator. They also, however, sometimes feel they are being ignored at home so they build lots of relationships outside it. 'I've always had an active social life,' says Erin. 'In business I somehow always manage to reach agreement with others, and that has helped my career really take off.' Erin's ultimate ambition is to run the company, although that once seemed highly unlikely: 'Unlike my sister, I didn't go to university, and that really affected my confidence. I shouldn't have worried though: at 18 I had a little luck when a local firm took me on as a trainee, and since then I've already received a few promotions plus salary increases.' Middle children often become politicians, sportspeople or nurses.

C a youngest child

The 'baby' of the family, lacking the size to avoid getting pushed around, may use intuition and charm instead, so people often take to them. 'I suppose I've always been good at talking people into things, and that certainly makes life easier,' says Louis. People also sometimes regard the youngest as something of a comedian and in this Louis is no exception. They tend to prefer the outdoor life – their numbers include famous explorers – so it is perhaps unsurprising that Louis feels more comfortable since taking up his current role of travelling reporter than he was in the local radio station studios. They are also likely to be the lowest-earning, perhaps lacking their elder siblings' driving ambition, though that is not something which particularly concerns Louis, who firmly believes 'life is for living'. Those born last sometimes go into sales, set up small businesses or compose music.

D an only child

An only child gets lots of parental attention and lives in an entirely adult world without any sibling rivalry – but always as the junior family member. 'I'm close to my parents,' says Matteo, 'but I've always had friends too.' They are often encouraged to study hard and develop artistic skills. Although theories about them having difficulty socialising with other children were long ago disproved, many do seem suited to working alone. 'I did well at school,' Matteo says, 'and my dad was confident that one day I'd be a senior executive, but the funny thing was I always knew I'd do something completely different. I love painting, and although it has its disadvantages – I've recently had to take out a loan just to get by – I'm my own boss and there's nothing I'd rather do.' Only children tend to do well in any career, but particularly in art.

Phrasal verbs with *take*

6 Match these phrasal verbs in the text with meanings 1–6.

take on (B)	take off (B)	took on (B)
take to (C)	taking up (C)	take out (D)

1 start doing (a job)
2 employ
3 start to like
4 obtain, from a bank or insurance company, for example
5 suddenly start to be successful
6 accepting (a responsibility)

7 Complete the sentences with phrasal verbs. Use the correct form of *take* and a suitable adverb particle.

1 As many people in the department are off sick, I am having to .... more work.
2 At first I didn't really .... the new teacher, but I really like her now.
3 Simona has .... a new assistant. She seems a lot more relaxed now that she has someone to help her.
4 The new menu has really .... since we began offering more vegetarian options.
5 Our new house has a lot of outdoor space, so I've decided to .... gardening.
6 If you travel abroad it's a good idea to .... insurance in case you have an accident.

Listening

1 **Look at the photos. Which do you think are the advantages of each of the following after you leave school? Why?**

a learning while you work
b going to university
c starting your own business

2 09 **Complete the text with these words. Then listen to check your answers.**

academic apprenticeship Bachelor's graduate Master's postgraduate secondary self-employed thesis trade traineeship undergraduates

Young people leaving UK **(1)** .... schools have a number of options. They can go into paid employment or become **(2)** ...., working independently and perhaps setting up their own business. Alternatively, they can do an **(3)** .... with a firm lasting between one and six years, which involves doing paid work while learning a **(4)** ...., often manual work, or a profession such as accounting. Or else they can consider doing a much shorter **(5)** .... that is unpaid but provides valuable work experience. Those who go to university usually do a **(6)** .... degree course, which normally lasts three or four years. At this stage students are known as **(7)** .... When they successfully finish their first degree, students **(8)** .... and may then go on to do a **(9)** .... course such as a **(10)** .... degree. For most students, the highest **(11)** .... achievement is to obtain a doctoral degree by writing a **(12)** .... based on research.

Part 2

3 **Look at the exam task instructions and answer these questions.**

1 What is the topic of the recording?
2 Why do you think Sofia chose to do that job?

4 10 **Read exam questions 1–10. What kind of word, e.g. object, person, number, do you need for each question? Then listen and do the exam task.**

Quick steps to Part 2

- Try to predict what you will hear by reading the instructions and the sentences.
- The first time you listen, write your answer lightly in pencil, in case you want to change it later.

Exam task

You will hear a woman called Sofia Nielson talking about her job as a designer of plastic models. For questions **1–10**, complete the sentences with a word or short phrase.

Exam tip

You usually have to write one or two words, but sometimes you may need to write three, e.g. ***check-in desk***.

My job: making models

As a small child, Sofia most enjoyed making models of ______ **1** with plastic bricks.

Sofia thought about studying ______ **2** at university.

Sofia decided not to go to university because of the experience her ______ **3** had.

Sofia had to make a model of a ______ **4** when applying for a job at a toy company.

Sofia believes it was her ______ **5** that got her the job.

Sofia believes the ability to work in a ______ **6** is also essential.

Sofia often tells people that ______ **7** are the most enjoyable models to make.

Nowadays, Sofia likes to spend time ______ **8** in the evenings.

Sofia started working for her current employer ______ **9** ago.

To become a project manager, Sofia will have to improve her ______ **10** skills.

Grammar

Future forms

a b

Page 106

1 Look at these sentences a–f about Sofia Nielson from Listening and match them with uses 1–6. What is the name, e.g. future simple, future continuous, of each of these future forms?

a Hopefully, she'll be working as a project manager in the future.
b By December she'll have been there for three years.
c She's meeting her line manager next week.
d Her next project starts in March.
e She's going to talk to her on Monday.
f It will probably take her a lot of time and effort to learn leadership skills.

1 for a definite future arrangement with someone
2 for an action in progress in the future
3 for a decision about the future or a prediction based on evidence
4 for a prediction, something that's not certain or a sudden decision
5 for a future event fixed by a timetable or schedule
6 for something that will be finished before a particular time

2 Which of these sentences written by exam candidates contain mistakes? Correct the mistakes. In some cases more than one answer is possible.

1 On the ticket it says that my train is leaving at 17.30 on Wednesday.
2 The new manager is meeting the staff later today.
3 I would like to be more sociable and possibly go on holiday in June because I've just finished my course by then.
4 I also know Spanish and German quite well, which I believe are going to help me a great deal.
5 I'll tell you all about it, when we meet again.
6 I'm sorry but I can't come to the seaside in August because I'll go camping with my friends in the mountains then.
7 Visiting you in July is just perfect because the schools will have closed and I will already have sat my exams.
8 I need some new running shoes. I think I will have gone to the shopping centre on Saturday.

3 In pairs, ask and answer these questions using future forms. Use full sentences.

1 When / you do / your homework?
A When are you going to do your homework?
B I'm going to do it tonight.
2 Where / you spend / your summer holidays?
3 Where / you meet your friends / next weekend?
4 On which day / the next photography course / start?
5 By what age / you think / you / bought your first home?
6 What pet / you think / you have?
7 Where / you probably live / five years from now?

Noun suffixes: *-ant, -er, -ian, -ist, -or*

4 Match these suffixes with groups 1–5 to form words for jobs, then write each word. What spelling changes are needed for some of the words in each group?

-ant -er -ian -ist -or

1 music, politics, electricity, history, mathematics
2 deal, lecture, bank, philosophy, research
3 novel, guitar, economics, physics, psychology
4 assist, attend, consult, account, serve
5 invent, operate, inspect, investigate, invest

5 Look at these pairs of nouns. In each case, which means 'the person who gives something', and which means 'the person who receives something'?

employee/employer examinee/examiner
interviewee/interviewer
payee/payer trainee/trainer

6 What do we call somebody who:

1 participates in something?
2 instructs other people?
3 works in chemistry, or studies it?
4 presents a TV show?
5 specialises in something?
6 works in a library?
7 survives an accident?
8 drives a motor vehicle?
9 supplies something?
10 seeks refuge from a disaster?

Countable and uncountable nouns

Page 107

1 Look at these extracts from the text in Reading and Use of English on page 39 and complete the rules with the words *countable nouns* and *uncountable nouns*.

I had a little luck
a local firm took me on as a trainee
I've already received a few promotions
may use intuition and charm instead
they build lots of relationships outside it
an only child gets lots of parental attention

1 We can use *a* or *an* with singular .... We can use (*a*) *few, many* or *a lot of / lots of* with them in the plural.
2 We can't use *a* or *an* with .... and there is no plural. We can use (*a*) *little, much* or *a lot / lots of* with them.

2 Correct the mistakes in these sentences written by exam candidates.

1 I often use public transports, instead of driving.
2 I got many information about this issue from the internet.
3 I have a big room, in a good location, but I don't like the old furnitures.
4 It was a short phone call because I didn't have many news to tell her.
5 On my course I have to do a lot of practical works.
6 He asked if I could give him a few money.
7 Computer memories are small these days, so there isn't space to install a lot of softwares.
8 I like to read or go for long walks when I have a spare time.
9 Unemployments are increasing, because of automation.
10 I would like to get a better job, but I have very few experience, so I am doing a course part-time.

3 Are these nouns usually countable or uncountable? Write phrases with six of them.

Example: a little knowledge

advice agreement association career certification commerce communication construction discovery earnings homework information knowledge location obligation opportunity production relaxation research responsibility technology

Part 1

Page 128

4 11 You are going to hear two very strong students, Julie and Max, doing Part 1. The first time you listen, tick the topics that the examiner asks them about.

a home
b music and cinema
c education and work
d social media
e family
f leisure activities

5 11 Listen again. How do Julie and Max use these words and phrases? Which are countable, and which uncountable?

advertising chemistry course construction fitness overtime pleasure research degree spare time

Quick steps to Part 1

- Be confident and speak loudly enough for the examiners and your partner to hear you.
- Listen to the examiner and your partner speaking to each other. This will help you get used to their voices.

6 Work in pairs. Ask and answer these questions.

1 How well do you think you'll do in your next exams?
2 What are you going to do when you've finished your studies?
3 Do you think you'll use English a lot in your job? Why? / Why not?
4 What kind of studies or work do you think you'll be doing in three years' time?
5 What are you going to do when you next have some free time?

Exam tip

Don't try to make a speech that you prepared earlier! It may not answer the question asked, and it wouldn't sound natural.

7 Tell your partner how well you think they answered the questions in Exercise 6. Be polite and give helpful advice.

1 **Complete the sentences with the correct form of the words in brackets. Use suffixes, and plural forms where necessary.**

1 I'm studying to become a .... (biology); I think it's a fascinating subject.
2 I've started a new job in management and I have a lot of .... (responsible).
3 We have introduced a new system to increase .... (produce).
4 We always ask the .... (interview) what his or her main strengths are.
5 For many young people, finding well-paid .... (employ) is difficult.
6 Some .... (employ) give their staff more holidays than others.
7 She gave me some really good .... (advise), and now I have my dream job.
8 Some people say there is too much .... (advertise) on television.
9 My parents are both .... (politics)!

Part 3

Quick steps to Part 3

- If the missing word is a noun, decide whether it's countable or uncountable. If it's countable, does it need to be plural?
- Make sure that the word you have written makes sense in the sentence as a whole.

2 **Look at the exam task. Quickly read the title and the text, without filling in any gaps for now. Does the writer recommend working in an office?**

3 **Look at the example (0). Answer these questions. Then do the exam task.**

1 What kind of word (noun, adjective, etc.) is *know*?
2 What kind of word is needed for the gap?
3 What do you need to add to it?
4 Is *knowledge* countable or uncountable? Does it need a final *-s*?

Exam tip

Make sure the completed text makes sense, and you have spelt all the words correctly.

Exam task

For questions **1–8**, read the text below. Use the word given in capitals at the end of some of the lines to form a word that fits in the gap in the same line. There is an example at the beginning (**0**).

Working in an office

Why work in an office? To begin with, because you get support from bosses and colleagues, and you can acquire useful **(0)** KNOWLEDGE from them too. Whether you're working in a government department or a **(1)** .... company, you also learn how to interact positively with fellow **(2)** .... For many people, one of the most **(3)** .... effects of that is building friendships that can last a lifetime.
Of course, office work has its disadvantages. Among any group of people working closely together **(4)** .... sometimes arise, and frequent **(5)** .... by colleagues can make it hard to concentrate on work. Also, there isn't the **(6)** .... of working from home, where you are often free to choose your own working hours.
Overall, though, you're likely to be quite a bit more **(7)** .... when you're working closely with others, and being part of a team has an **(8)** .... major advantage: there's always someone you can have lunch with.

(0)	**KNOW**
(1)	**COMMERCE**
(2)	**EMPLOY**
(3)	**BENEFIT**
(4)	**TENSE**
(5)	**INTERRUPT**
(6)	**FLEXIBLE**
(7)	**PRODUCE**
(8)	**ADDITION**

Part 2 formal letter of application

» Page 120

1 Look at the exam task and answer these questions.

1 Which organisation placed the advertisement?
2 What kind of job is advertised?
3 What does the work involve?
4 What three requirements are there?
5 Who must you write to, and in what style?
6 What must you aim to do in your letter?

Exam task

You have seen this advertisement in an English-language newspaper.

International Student Fair requires staff

The International Student Fair helps people choose the right college or university, and we are looking for assistants for this year's Fair. Duties will include giving directions and offering advice.

- Do you like helping people?
- Do you have experience of choosing a place of study?
- Are you willing to work evenings?

If so, apply to the organiser, Ms Evie Ross, saying why you think you are suitable for the job.

Write your **letter of application** in **140–190** words in an appropriate style.

Quick steps to Part 2 formal letter of application

- Say why you're writing and where you saw the advertisement.
- Make sure you deal with all the points in the advertisement.
- Vary the expressions you use. For example, instead of using ***I can*** all the time, say ***I believe I am capable of***.
- Write in complete sentences, where possible using passive verb forms, formal linkers and longer words.
- Don't use conversational expressions, abbreviations or contracted forms, and try to avoid using phrasal verbs.

2 Read the model letter. Which phrases and sentences does the writer use to do these things?

1 begin and end the letter formally
Example: Dear Ms Ross, Yours sincerely,
2 give a reason for writing
3 say how he heard about the job
4 answer each of the questions in the advertisement
5 ask about pay and conditions
6 describe any relevant experience
7 say what he has sent with the letter
8 offer to give the reader more information
9 state availability for interview

Dear Ms Ross,

I would like to apply for the post of assistant at this year's International Student Fair, as advertised in the newspaper on 2 January.

I am aged 19 and in my second year of a mechanical engineering course. Before deciding on City College, I looked at the advantages and disadvantages of many academic institutions, and I therefore feel capable of offering advice to young people who are at that stage now.

The work sounds extremely interesting. Could you please tell me how much I would be paid, and whether training would be necessary?

I would be available to work evenings as all my lectures are in the afternoons and consequently, I can study in the mornings.

I have always enjoyed assisting others and last year I worked as a volunteer at a book fair.

Details of this, plus personal details including qualifications, are shown in my curriculum vitae, which I enclose.

If you need any further information, please do not hesitate to contact me. I would be able to attend an interview any morning.

Yours sincerely,

Jonas Meyer

3 Plan your own letter to Ms Ross. Make notes about how you will answer the three questions and how you will convince her of your suitability for the job. Then decide how many paragraphs you are going to use and which points will go in which.

4 Write your letter, following your plan. You can use some of the formal expressions from Jonas's letter, but you should give different details about yourself and ask different questions.

Exam tip

Never begin your letter *Dear Manager* or *Dear Organiser*. If you know the name, use ***Dear Mr*** or ***Dear Ms*** (their surname). If the name isn't given in the exam task, use ***Dear Sir*** or ***Madam***.

6 Setting the pace

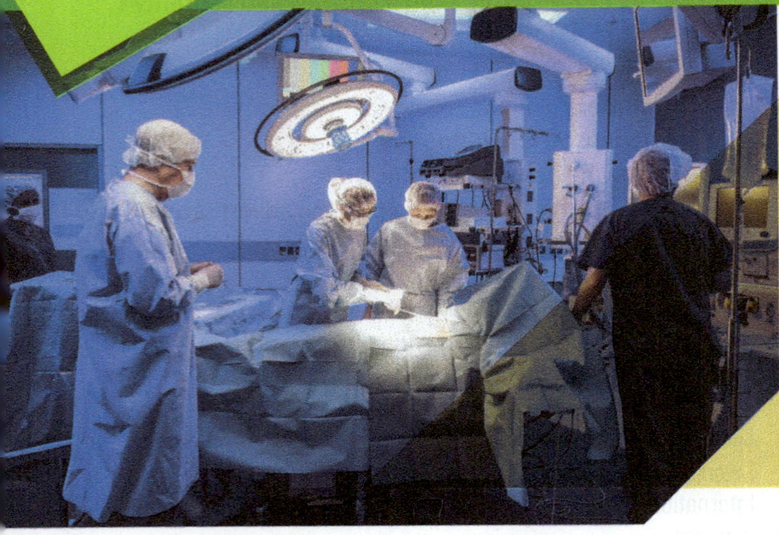

Medical vocabulary

1 **Put these words into the correct groups: a) people, b) injuries and illnesses, c) treatments.**

ache bandage bruise disease fever fracture graze infection injection medicine nurse operation pain patient plaster prescription specialist sprain stitches surgeon tablets temperature thermometer wound

2 **Make sure you know the meanings of these expressions, then explain the differences between them.**

1 *cure*, *heal* and *treat*
2 *health care* and *mental health*
3 *recovery* and *well-being*
4 *psychological* and *therapeutic*

3 **Use words and phrases from Exercises 1 and 2 to say what is happening in each of the photos. Then talk about the treatment you received when you last had a minor illness or injury. How long did it take you to get better?**

Part 5

Quick steps to Part 5

- Remember that questions 1–6 normally follow the order of information in the text.
- Look at options A–D after you've read what the text says. Otherwise the wrong answers might mislead you.
- You don't need to understand everything in the text to answer the questions, so don't spend a lot of time on words or phrases you don't know.

4 **Quickly read the text. Then, for each of questions 2–6, find the relevant part of the text. Draw a line in pencil with the question number next to it, as in the example for question 1.**

5 **Do the exam task on your own. Find the answer to each question by looking at the part of the text that you have marked.**

Exam task

You are going to read an article about the health benefits of being near water. For questions **1–6**, choose the answer (**A**, **B**, **C** or **D**) which you think fits best according to the text.

1 What do we learn about Kelly in the first paragraph?
A She wanted to take up sailing.
B She wanted to get a better job.
C She decided to leave her country.
D She felt she had to live by the sea.

2 What did Kelly realise by the end of her stay on the coast of Ireland?
A The academic research she had read was correct.
B She had been wrong to doubt the benefits of rural life.
C Living there had enabled her to make a full recovery.
D She could never be happy living so far from other people.

3 What is suggested about spending time in countryside areas?
A It is less beneficial than being close to water.
B There are no health benefits unless there is water nearby.
C There is no evidence that it improves people's health.
D It is always healthier than being in urban green zones.

4 What does 'one of the best ever' in line 37 refer to?
A a health benefit of blue space
B a particular academic study
C a feeling of happiness
D a natural environment

5 The writer suggests that the easiest way to feel better is by
A taking an interest in art.
B regularly going to the coast.
C using mobile phones far less.
D living quite close to the sea.

6 What does Kelly suggest in the last paragraph?
A Everybody relaxes when they are by the sea.
B Travelling frequently to the seaside can be stressful.
C Spending time next to a river is as good as being near the sea.
D The only way to feel any better is to live on the coast.

Exam tips

- Look for evidence that your answer is right, and that any references to the other three options are wrong.
- Make sure you have answered every question. For any you aren't sure about, cross out the options you know are wrong and then choose from the rest.

6 **Do you agree that being next to water makes people feel better? Why? / Why not?**

Blue spaces:

why time spent near water is the secret of happiness

By Elle Hunt

After the sudden loss of a close relative, Catherine Kelly heard the call of the sea. She was in her 20s and had been working as a geographer in London away from her native Ireland. She spent a year in Dublin with her family, then accepted an academic position on the Irish west coast, near Westport. 'I thought: "I need to go and get my head cleared in this place, to be blown away by the wind and nature."'

Kelly bought a little house in a remote area and surfed, swam and walked a three-mile-long beach twice a day. 'I guess the five or six years that I spent there on the wild Atlantic coast just healed me, really.' She didn't understand why that might be until some years later, when she started to see scientific literature that proved what she had long felt to be true: that she felt much better by the sea. For the past eight years, Kelly has been based in the British seaside resort of Brighton, researching 'outdoor well-being' and the therapeutic effects of nature – particularly of water.

In recent years, stressed-out people from urban areas have been seeking peace and quiet in green spaces, for which the proven positive impacts on physical and mental health are often cited in arguments for more inner-city parks and accessible woodlands. The benefits of 'blue space' – the sea and coastline, but also rivers, lakes, canals, waterfalls, even fountains – are less well publicised, yet for at least a decade the science has confirmed that being by water is good for body and mind.

Spending time near water – especially the sea – is associated with many positive measures of physical and mental well-being, from higher levels of vitamin D to better social relations. 'Many of the processes are exactly the same as with green space – with some added benefits,' says Dr Mathew White, a senior lecturer at the University of Exeter and an environmental psychologist with BlueHealth, a programme researching the health and well-being benefits of blue space across 18 (mostly European) countries.

An extensive study on happiness in natural environments – to White's mind, 'one of the best ever' – asked 20,000 37
smartphone users to record their sense of well-being and their immediate environment at random intervals. Marine and coastal regions were found by some distance to be the happiest locations, with responses approximately six points higher than in a continuous urban environment. The researchers said it was similar to 'the difference between attending an art exhibition and doing housework'.

Although living within 1 km of the coast – and to a lesser extent, within 5 km – has been associated with better general and mental health, it seems that making frequent visits is key. 'We find people who visit the coast, for example, at least twice weekly tend to experience better general and mental health,' says Dr Lewis Elliott, also of the University of Exeter and BlueHealth. 'Some of our research suggests around two hours a week is probably beneficial, across many parts of society.' Even sea views have been associated with better mental health.

'People work with what they have,' says Kelly. When she lived in London, she would head for the River Thames when she had a spare ten minutes 'and think things over'. Then, four times a year, she would go to Brighton 'and the benefits would keep me going for the next few months – so I didn't get into a place of being overwhelmed or stressed'. She adds: 'To go to the coast means taking it easy. It could be lying on a beach or somebody handing you a cool drink. For somebody else, it could be a wild, empty shoreline. But there is this really human sense of: "Oh, look, there's the sea" – and the shoulders drop.'

Listening

Part 1

1 **Look at the introductory sentence and question in the example below. Underline the key words and answer these questions.**

1 What's the focus, e.g. opinion, topic, purpose?
2 Who's talking to whom?
3 Where?
4 Why?
5 When?

Example:
You hear two friends talking about a sporting event.
Which sporting activity have they just watched?
A cycling
B running
C swimming

2 **Match options A–C in the example with photos 1–3, which show the three stages of a triathlon race.**

3 12 **Listen and choose the best answer (A, B or C).**

Quick steps to Part 1

- Quickly read the first line of each question. Decide what the situation is and how many speakers you will hear.
- Before the recording is played, think of words connected with those in the question. For example: ***Why ... ? – because, so, as, reason, result.***
- You may hear words from all three options, but be careful: in two cases, the speaker is saying something else.
- Once the recording finishes and you have chosen your answer, forget about that question and focus on the next one.

4 12 **Listen again. Why is your answer correct? Why are the other two options wrong?**

5 **Look at questions 1–6 in the exam task. In each case, underline the key words. Question 1 has been done for you. Then answer as many of the questions from Exercise 1 as you can.**

6 13 **Now listen and do the exam task.**

Exam task

You will hear people talking in six different situations. For questions **1–6**, choose the best answer (**A**, **B** or **C**).

1 You hear a woman talking on the phone about a hospital.
What does she say about it?
A She received excellent medical treatment there.
B She can visit a relative there whenever she wants.
C She has enjoyed working there from the start.

2 You hear a man talking about a marathon he has just run.
How does he feel now?
A disappointed that the distance he ran took him so long
B relieved that he was able to complete the race
C embarrassed that he had to stop running

3 You hear two people talking about colds.
What do they agree about?
A how to avoid catching a cold
B how to treat a cold
C how long a cold normally lasts

4 You hear a woman leaving a message for a doctor's receptionist.
What does she want to do?
A make an appointment for a child
B cancel an appointment
C postpone an appointment for herself

5 You hear part of a radio programme about sportspeople.
What is the man's attitude to professional footballers?
A They have to play too many matches.
B They should retire at the age of 30.
C They are all paid too much money.

6 You hear a man talking about his local rail service.
What does he think of it?
A The trains aren't frequent enough.
B The trains too often arrive late.
C The tickets are too expensive.

Exam tip

Make sure you have answered all the questions. If you can't decide which of options A–C is right, cross out the one you are sure is wrong and guess.

Phrasal verbs with *up*

1 **Look at these extracts from the recording in Listening. What do the phrasal verbs mean?**

If I'd had to **give up** then I wouldn't have been the only one.
Still, I'm sure it'll **clear up** soon.
I **grew up** round here.

2 **Complete the sentences with the correct form of these verbs. Then match the phrasal verbs you have made with meanings a–j.**

come dig eat heal run speak speed split tidy use

1 Your dinner is getting cold, so .... up!
2 If we don't change our way of life, we'll .... up all the Earth's resources.
3 If we have a party, can you help to .... up afterwards?
4 The music is really loud, I can't hear you. Can you .... up, please?
5 The athlete had to .... up to win the race.
6 My aunt and uncle .... up after 30 years together!
7 Although her injuries had .... up quickly, she still felt nervous in the car.
8 I dropped my wallet, but luckily a man saw it and .... up to hand it back to me.
9 When they started building the new apartment block, they .... up some ancient ruins and they had to suspend construction.
10 The Champions League Final .... up next month. I can't wait!

a separated completely
b talk more loudly
c go faster
d finish your food quickly
e getting nearer in time
f brought to the surface
g approached quickly
h got completely better
i put everything where it belongs
j completely finish

Relative clauses

Page 107

3 **Look at these pairs of sentences and answer the questions.**

1 **a** For the first time I attended a lecture which was interesting.
b For the first time I attended a lecture, which was interesting.
Who had never attended a lecture before? Who had only attended boring lectures before?

2 **a** My brother who is a teacher works there. (defining relative clause)
b My brother, who is a teacher, works there. (non-defining relative clause)
Who has only one brother? Who has more than one brother?

3 **a** The match which I saw was very close.
b The match, which I saw, was very close.
In which sentence could we leave out *which*? Why?

4 **Look again at the sentences in Exercise 3 and answer these questions.**

1 Which kind of relative clause, defining or non-defining, gives essential information?
2 Which kind gives extra information?
3 Which kind uses commas? Where?

5 **Join these pairs of sentences with non-defining relative clauses. Use *who, which, when, where* and *whose*, adding commas where necessary.**

1 Emily's novel was successful. It was set in a school.
Emily's novel, which was set in a school, was successful.
2 Rafael Nadal has won many championships. He is very popular.
Rafael Nadal, ... championships.
3 The World Cup was held in Russia in 2018. France won.
In 2018 .... won.
4 The two cyclists were brothers. They were in an accident.
The two cyclists .... an accident.
5 Kate won an Oscar. Her mother had also been a famous actor.
Kate .... an Oscar.
6 Everyone in the theatre was excited. The play was about to start.
In the theatre .... excited.

6 **Correct the mistakes in these sentences written by exam candidates by either replacing the relative pronoun or adding commas where necessary. Then underline the word(s) in each sentence that the relative pronoun refers to, as in sentence 1.**

1 I've chosen to study two languages, whose are Portuguese and Italian.
2 You should visit in June, where the weather is usually nice.
3 I don't like people which are unkind to their friends.
4 We went to Bondi Beach which is a famous spot in Sydney.
5 The wallet belonged to a man who name was Giacomo.
6 There is a new gym which we can do spin classes.
7 Anna who is keen on painting saw some brilliant artwork in the gallery.

Speaking

Sports vocabulary

1 **Match the sports in box A with the places in box B.**

A

athletics baseball basketball boxing cycling diving football golf gymnastics hockey ice skating motorcycling rugby sailing skiing snowboarding squash surfing tennis

B

course court gym pitch ring rink sea slope track

2 **What do we call people who take part in these sports? Use *do*, *play* or *go* and a defining relative clause.**

Examples:

Someone who plays football is a footballer.
A person that does gymnastics is a gymnast.
A skier is someone who goes skiing.

3 **Say what sportspeople do with these objects. Which ones have you worn, used or kicked?**

ball bat board club gloves helmet racket skates skis

Example:

A footballer kicks a (foot)ball.

Agreeing and politely disagreeing

4 14 **Listen to these extracts from the recording in Listening question 3, and practise saying them with the same intonation.**

Yes, I know what you mean.
I'm not so sure. I think it's more likely …

5 15 **Complete expressions a–f with these words. Then listen to check your answers.**

agree feeling just know so what

Agreeing

a I think ...., too.
b Yes, I .... with that.
c That's .... what I was thinking.

Politely disagreeing

d Perhaps, but .... about … ?
e Well, my own .... is …
f I don't .... about that.

Part 3

Page 134

6 16 **Look at the exam task instructions and listen to students Nico and Eva doing the task. Answer these questions.**

1. Which sport do they agree is not very dangerous?
2. Which sport do they agree is one of the most dangerous?
3. Which other sport does Nico suggest as the most dangerous?
4. Which other sport does Eva think is the most dangerous?

7 16 **Listen again. Which expressions from Exercise 5 do Nico and Eva use? Number them in the order you hear them.**

Exam task

Now I'd like you to talk about something together for about two minutes.
Here are some sports that can be dangerous.
You now have some time to look at the task.
Now talk to each other about **what can happen to people who do these sports if they aren't careful.**

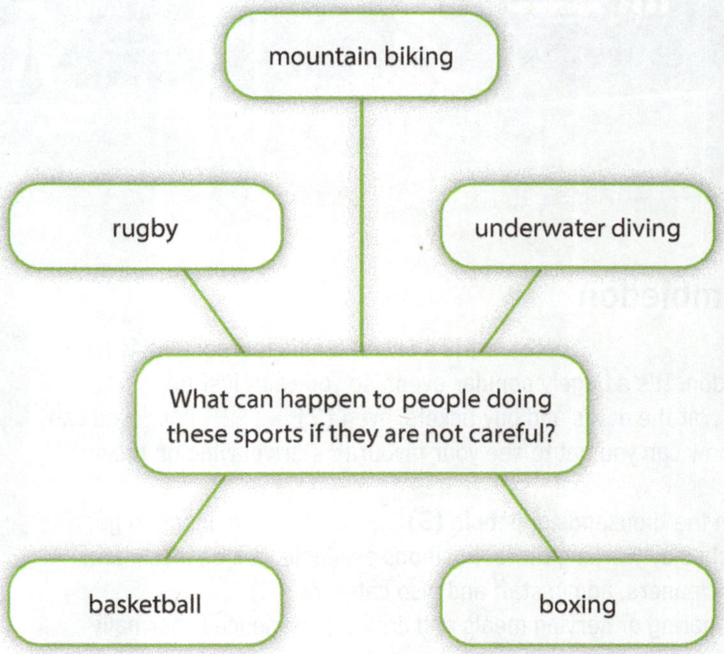

Thank you. Now you have a minute to decide **which two are the most dangerous sports.**

Quick steps to Part 3

- Begin the discussion by saying something like: ***Would you like to start, or shall I?***
- Talk about each thing in turn, giving reasons for your opinions.
- Don't try to get through all the things too quickly.

8 **In pairs, do the same exam task as Nico and Eva. Use expressions from Agreeing and politely disagreeing.**

9 **Compare your decision(s) with other pairs.**

Exam tip

Remember you can agree or disagree with what your partner says, but you must always be polite.

Reading and Use of English

1 **Imagine a major sporting event is going to be held in your country next summer. Discuss these questions.**

1. What jobs might be available?
2. What could be the advantages and disadvantages of doing this kind of work?

2 **Without filling in any gaps, quickly read *A job at Wimbledon* to find out how the text answers the questions in Exercise 1.**

Part 2

3 **Do the exam task.**

Quick steps to Part 2

- For each question, look at the context and decide what kind of word, e.g. phrasal verb, relative pronoun, is needed.
- Look closely at the words either side of the gap for more clues.
- Remember that gaps may have more than one possible answer, but you must only give one.

Exam task

For questions **1–8**, read the text below and think of the word which best fits each gap. Use only one word in each gap. There is an example at the beginning (**0**).

Example: 0 WHICH

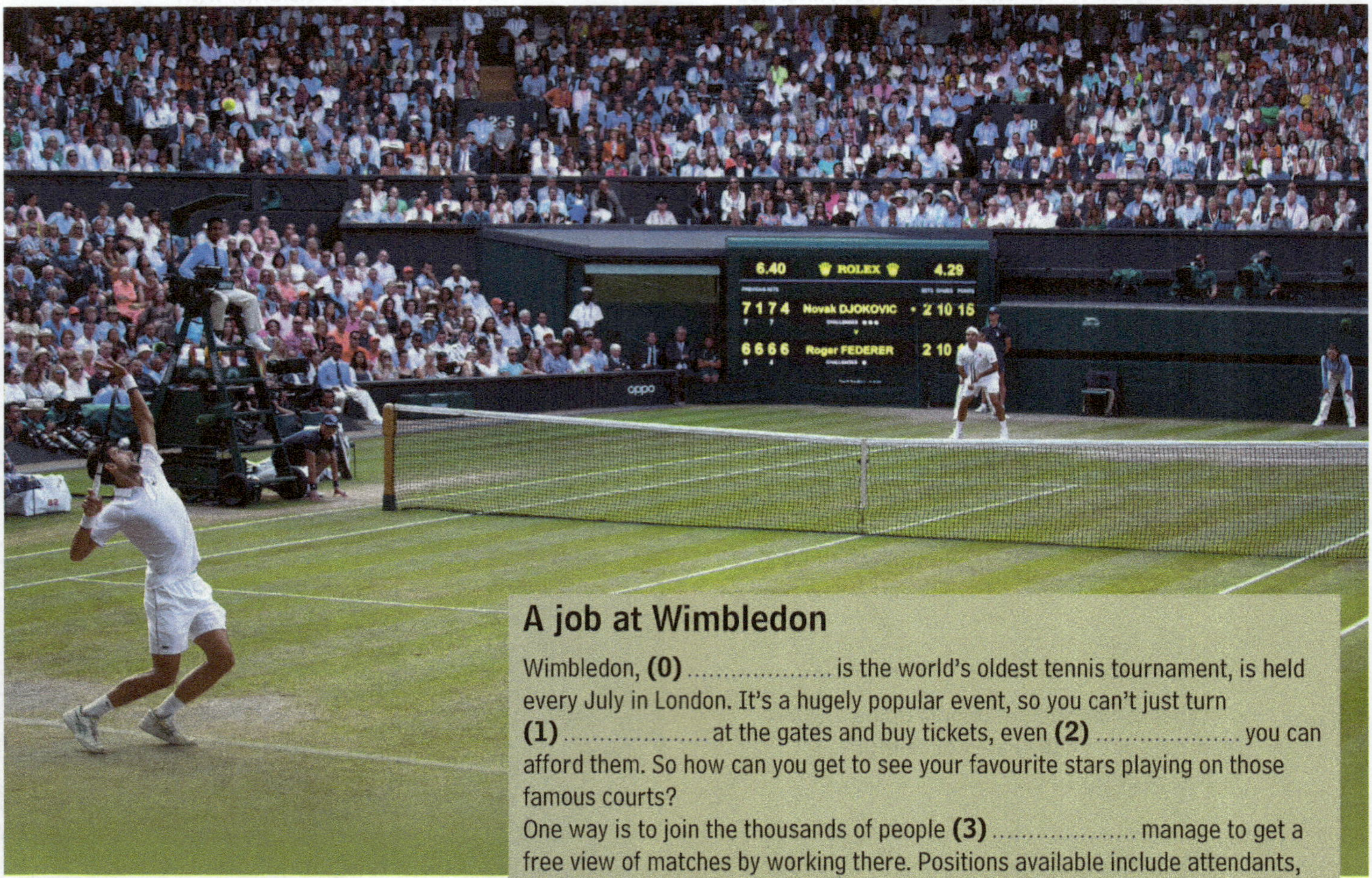

A job at Wimbledon

Wimbledon, **(0)** .... is the world's oldest tennis tournament, is held every July in London. It's a hugely popular event, so you can't just turn **(1)** .... at the gates and buy tickets, even **(2)** .... you can afford them. So how can you get to see your favourite stars playing on those famous courts?

One way is to join the thousands of people **(3)** .... manage to get a free view of matches by working there. Positions available include attendants, security officers, cleaners, admin staff and also caterers, **(4)** .... duties involve preparing or serving meals and drinks. Experience is normally required.

For younger tennis fans, by **(5)** .... the most exciting opportunity is to become a ball boy or girl, known as BBGs. Their job is to collect loose tennis balls and give them to the players, **(6)** .... interfering with play in any way. BBGs are aged 15 **(7)** .... average and have to be available from February, **(8)** .... their highly intensive training begins.

Exam tip

Pencil in your answers on the question paper, then check your answers to make sure the completed text makes sense. Remember to fill in the answer sheet or your answers won't count!

Purpose links

Page 109

1 Look at Purpose links on page 108. Then choose the correct option in these sentences. Sometimes both may be possible.

1. We've extended the deadline *in order that / so as to* more applications can be processed.
2. You should buy good-quality running shoes *in order not to / so that you don't* damage your feet when you run the marathon.
3. Josh took his suitcase to the office *in order to / so that* he could leave for his holiday straight after work.
4. I joined a book club *so that / to* make new friends.
5. There's a train strike tomorrow, so *in order to / in order that* avoid delays, you should leave early.
6. *So as not to / So that I didn't* forget my appointment, I set a reminder on my phone.
7. We moved closer to the city *so as to / so that* see our grandchildren more often.
8. I put the medicine on a high shelf *so that / so as* the children couldn't reach it.

2 In pairs, ask and answer these questions using purpose links.

Why do some people:

1. buy big TV screens?
   Example: *to / in order to / so as to watch sports* or *so that / in order that they can watch sports*
2. go to the gym?
3. go to the supermarket?
4. want to learn a new language?
5. work part-time?
6. play team sports?

Part 2 letter

Page 120

3 Look at the exam task and answer these questions.

1. What kind of text have you received?
2. Who wrote it and what are they planning to do?
3. What do they want you to do?
4. Do they mainly use formal or informal language? Give examples.

Exam tip

The style of language in the text you have received can help you decide how formal or informal your reply should be.

Exam task

You have received a letter from an Irish penfriend, Linda. Read this part of the letter and then write your letter to Linda.

> I'm really looking forward to spending my summer holidays in your country – and to seeing you! As you know, I always try to keep quite fit. So can you give me some tips on the sports I could do in your town while I'm there? Write back soon,
>
> Linda

Write your **letter** in **140–190** words. Do not write any addresses.

Quick steps to Part 2 letter

- Put the opening (e.g. ***Dear Jenny***), the closing (e.g. ***Best regards***) and your own name on separate lines.
- Don't use the same expression too often. For example, instead of repeating ***please tell me***, say ***I'd like to know*** or ***can you let me know***.

4 Read Sam's letter and answer the questions.

1. Which paragraph deals with: a) indoor sports, b) sports they can do together, c) outdoor sports?
2. What examples can you find of: a) informal language, b) relative clauses, c) purpose links?

> Hi Linda,
>
> Thanks very much for your last letter. I'm fine, and I'm glad to hear you're well, too.
>
> I'm sure you'll have a great time here. There are lots of sports you can do in the countryside, such as hill-walking or mountain-biking, as well as water sports like rowing and sailing on the lake. It will be too cold for swimming, though.
>
> If you'd rather go to a sports centre there's a really good one which has facilities for things like squash and basketball, and an Olympic-size pool where they play water-polo. Now that really is good exercise: I tried it once and I was exhausted after about ten minutes!
>
> Actually, it'd be nice if we could both do the same sports so that we have more time together. I sometimes go ice skating – would you like to try that? Or how about playing tennis? If so, I'll need to book ahead to make sure we get a court.
>
> Anyway, let me know what you'd like to do and I'll make some arrangements.
>
> Bye for now,
>
> Sam

5 Plan your letter. Think about the topic and your reader, and the number of paragraphs and writing style you will need.

6 Write your letter. When you have finished, check your work as in Unit 1 Writing Exercise 5 on page 13.

7 Feeling the heat

1 **Answer these questions about the photos, giving reasons. Which kind of food:**

1 is better for your health?
2 is better for the environment?
3 do you prefer to eat?

Part 6

2 **Look at the exam task instructions and read quickly through the text, ignoring sentences A–G for now. Do the scientists believe they can change people's eating habits?**

Quick steps to Part 6

- When you first skim through the main text, decide what each paragraph is about.
- Look for expressions that indicate examples, explanations, comparisons, and adding or ordering of points.
- Look for reference words such as ***this*** or ***they*** both in sentences A–G and in the main text.

3 **Look at sentences A–G. Reference words and linking expressions in A and B have been underlined. Underline similar words in sentences C–G.**

4 **Do the exam task, using the underlined words as clues. Look for similar words in the main text, as well as vocabulary linkers.**

Exam task

You are going to read an article about the benefits to the environment of healthy eating. Six sentences have been removed from the article. Choose from the sentences **A–G** the one which fits each gap (**1–6**). There is one extra sentence which you do not need to use.

A But this is the first study to consider both together in detail.
B In view of this, the scientists hope more detailed information will help these consumers make better buying decisions.
C These limitations on research make it difficult to study the direct effects on health of eating specific foods.
D This sudden improvement in many of these people's health is also having a positive effect on the environment.
E In contrast, eating red and processed meat causes the most ill health and pollution.
F It was also many times worse than pulses such as peas, beans or lentils.
G But the researchers disagree, saying that replacing all of it with plant-based food makes the biggest difference.

Exam tip

Read the complete text, including the sentences you have chosen for gaps 1–6. Does it all make sense? Make sure you have chosen one letter for every question. Then check your answers.

Healthy diet means a healthy planet

Damian Carrington

Eating healthy food is almost always also best for the environment, according to the most sophisticated analysis to date. The researchers said poor diets, often containing too much fatty food, sugar and salt, threaten society by seriously harming people and the planet, for instance through the greenhouse gases created by cattle farming.

The analysis assessed the health and environmental impacts of 15 foods common in western diets and found fruit, vegetables, beans and wholegrains were best for both avoiding disease and protecting the climate and water resources. **1** ____ There were a small number of foods that went against this trend. Fish is generally a healthy choice but has a bigger environmental footprint on average than plant-based diets. High-sugar foods, such as biscuits and fizzy drinks, have a low impact on the planet but are bad for health.

The effect of bad diets on health in rich nations is well known, as is the need to cut western meat consumption in order to tackle climate breakdown and other environmental crises. **2** ____ Michael Clark at the University of Oxford, who led this research, said: 'Continuing to eat the way we do threatens societies, through serious ill health and degradation of Earth's climate, ecosystems and water resources. Choosing better, more sustainable diets is one of the main ways people can improve their health and help protect the environment.'

Some farming groups argue that only intensively produced meat is seriously damaging to the environment. **3** ____ 'How and where a food is produced affects its environmental impact, but to a much smaller extent than the type of food chosen,' Clark explained.

Marco Springmann, also part of the study team, said: 'We now know that mainly plant-based diets are much healthier and more sustainable than meat-heavy diets. But sometimes there is still confusion among people about what foods to choose.' **4** ____ The researchers are currently working on new types of food labels to see if providing facts on health and environmental impacts changes their selection of food.

The research assessed plant-based foods, refined grains and wholegrain cereals, sugar-sweetened drinks, and animal-based foods. Using data from other studies on the diets and health outcomes of tens of millions of people, they calculated the health impact of eating one extra portion of each food on heart disease, stroke, type 2 diabetes and cancer. The environmental harm for each food, from greenhouse gases to water use to pollution, was calculated relative to a portion of vegetables. Producing unprocessed red meat had the highest impact for all these environmental indicators. **5** ____

The researchers said food with medium environmental effects or not significantly associated with ill health, such as refined grain cereals and dairy products, could help improve health and reduce environmental harm if they replaced foods such as red meat.

Professor Tim Benton at the Chatham House think tank said that if reasonable guidelines defining healthy and sustainable diets were produced, and followed, the world would be in a better place. According to Benton, strictly controlling people's diets over many years for scientific study is impractical. **6** ____ Despite this, he said, the weight of evidence was now significant. 'Our existing agricultural economy is destroying our ability to deal with climate change and also destroying our public health,' he said.

5 **Find words or phrases in the text that mean the following. The paragraph number is in brackets to help you.**

a advanced, using the latest techniques (1)
b effects on someone or something (2)
c the amount eaten (3)
d process of spoiling or destroying (3)
e causing little or no environmental damage (3)
f not chemically treated to improve its taste (6)
g gases that make the Earth's atmosphere heat up (6)
h treated to make it pure (6)
i group of experts (7)
j advice on how to do something (7)

6 **Do you think many people would change their eating habits if they knew more about the environmental impact of their diet? Why? / Why not?**

Listening

1 **Match the words in box A with the words in box B to form expressions that describe environmental issues. Which of these are good for the environment, and which are harmful?**

A

animal carbon climate fossil global industrial melting oil renewable solar

B

change conservation footprint fuels ice caps power resources spills warming waste

2 **Match these words with the photos. How do you think people in each place will be affected by climate change? Use expressions from Exercise 1.**

Arctic coastal desert mountainous tropical

Part 3

3 **Look at the exam task instructions, underlining the key words, and options A–H. What will the five people be talking about?**

4 **Underline the key words in each of options A–H. Note down some expressions with similar meanings to these words.**

Example: *A floods – water, sea, river*

5 **Look at this sentence spoken by Speaker 1. Is D the correct option? Why? / Why not?**

If the flames had come any closer our homes would've been destroyed.

6 17 **Now listen and do the exam task.**

Quick steps to Part 3

- Underline the key word(s) that say what you must do, e.g. ***choose from the list (A–H) what each speaker feels is currently their biggest problem***.
- Wait to hear everything the speaker has to say before you answer a question.
- Be careful if you hear words from an option, but with different grammar, e.g. a conditional.

4

5

Exam task

You will hear five short extracts in which people from different parts of the world talk about how climate change is affecting their villages. For questions **1–5** choose from the list (**A–H**) what each speaker feels is currently their biggest problem. Use the letters only once. There are three extra letters which you do not need to use.

A Floods have damaged buildings in the village.
B Farmers have had to start growing different crops.
C People have been left without electricity.
D Houses have been burnt down by forest fires.
E Some people have had to leave their homes.
F Air pollution has increased to dangerous levels.
G Some houses have been covered in sand.
H There has recently been too much rain.

Speaker	Answer	
Speaker 1		1
Speaker 2		2
Speaker 3		3
Speaker 4		4
Speaker 5		5

Exam tips

- Each time you choose an answer, cross it out lightly in pencil and then focus on the other options.
- Make sure you have chosen a letter for each of questions 1–5 and check your answers.

Grammar

Conditionals 1–3

Page 109

a b

1 **Look at these extracts from the recording in Listening. In each case, say which verb forms are used and answer the corresponding questions.**

a If we don't take urgent action we'll lose it (the Great Barrier Reef) forever.
b Our village would be flooded if the sea level rose by a metre.
c The whole building would have burnt down if she hadn't been at home.

a Will they definitely lose it? Is it likely or unlikely that they will take urgent action?
b Is the sea level likely or unlikely to rise by a metre in the near future? Is their village likely to be flooded?
c Was she at home? Did the whole house burn down?

2 **Match the sentence halves.**

1 If the river had risen any higher,
2 If the desert had a rainy season,
3 If people stopped using single-use plastic,
4 Unless it stops raining,
5 If the storm doesn't stop soon,

a the picnic will be cancelled.
b the oceans would be much cleaner.
c there won't be any flights home.
d it would be possible to live there.
e it might have flooded the city.

3 **Correct the mistakes in these sentences written by exam candidates.**

1 If I had time, I would have drive you to the station.
2 If I were you, I will see a doctor.
3 If I would live near my work, I would prefer to go by bicycle.
4 If I would have known you were coming, I would have waited for you.
5 If the climate keeps changing, we would have only two seasons.
6 Honestly, if I had more money, I would have buy a new house.

4 **Use the given conditional form to complete the questions. Then work in pairs and ask your partner the questions.**

1 If it .... (rain) this weekend, what .... (you do)? (first conditional)
2 If the summers where you live .... (become) much hotter, what .... (you do)? (second conditional)
3 If .... (you be able) to live in a different country, ... (you prefer) to live somewhere with a hotter or cooler climate? (second conditional)
4 What .... (you do) if bad weather .... (prevent) you going on holiday? (third conditional)

Mixed conditionals

Page 109

5 **In these extracts from the recording in Listening, second and third conditional forms are mixed. Answer the questions.**

a If we hadn't planted so many trees, our homes would be buried under sand by now.
b It (a power failure) wouldn't have happened if we had underground cables here.

1 Which part of a and b refers to the present or to a permanent situation? Which refers to the past?
2 In a, did they plant trees? Are their homes now buried under sand?
3 In b, did the power failure happen? Do they have underground cables there?

6 **Use mixed conditionals to complete the second sentence so that it means the same as the first.**

1 The low temperatures in Finland didn't bother me because I used to live in Iceland.
The low temperatures in Finland might have bothered me if ....
2 You're not cold now because you brought your coat.
If you hadn't brought your coat
....
3 I started my new job last week, so I couldn't go skiing with my friends.
If I hadn't started my new job last week, I
....
4 We polluted the air for many years, so now the climate is changing.
The climate wouldn't be changing now if we
....
5 Your bill is so high because you wasted so much electricity.
Your bill wouldn't be so high if
....
6 I didn't bring an umbrella because I didn't check the weather forecast.
If I had checked the weather forecast,
....

7 **Work in pairs. Imagine these situations and tell your partner about them, using mixed conditionals.**

1 You were offered a job in another country, with a different culture and climate. What would you have had to get used to?
2 You're a student from another country. How would your life be different?

Comparative forms

Page 110

1 Study these example sentences and complete the summary with the words given.

a The new buses go as fast as the old ones, and they use fuel more efficiently than other types of transport in the city.
b The hotel is more popular in June than in May, but less popular than in August.
c The capital city isn't so polluted as in the 1990s, though the air in other towns in the country is worse than it was then.

as   less   so   than

When we make comparisons, we use **(1)** .... after the adjective or adverb. To say two things are the same we put **(2)** .... both before and after it. To say one thing is less than another we use *not as* or *not* **(3)** ...., or we can put **(4)** .... before the adjective or adverb.

2 Complete the second sentence so that it means the same as the first sentence.

1 Solar energy is much more environmentally friendly than other energy sources.
Other energy sources are
much less environmentally friendly than solar energy.

2 These people seem to be happier than those.
Those people seem to be
....

3 Individuals are no less responsible than big businesses for protecting our environment.
Individuals are just as
....

4 Small towns have more success dealing with environmental issues than large cities.
Large cities deal with environmental issues
....

5 Both these ideas for saving energy are sensible.
The first idea for saving energy is
....

6 Travelling by train or bus is better for the environment than travelling by car.
Travelling by car
....

Part 2

Page 130

Quick steps to Part 2

- Compare the scenes by using adjectives and adverbs with ***more/less ... than*** and (***not***) ***as/so ... as***.
- If you can't think of the word for something, explain it in English. Say, for example: ***It's the place where ...***
- Speak at normal speed until the examiner tells you it's time to stop.

3 Look at photos 1 and 2 on page 97. Which of these features is in each photo?

boots   dam   electricity   equipment
helmets   high-vis jackets   mountains/hills
roof   solar panels   solar power

4 Look at the instructions for Exam tasks 1 and 2. What does each candidate have to do?

5 In pairs, do exam tasks 1 and 2. Then change roles and repeat the task.

Exam tip

At home, practise speaking for a minute about pairs of photos, for example, in a magazine or on the internet. Time yourself, or ask a friend to!

Exam task 1

Candidate A: It's your turn first. Look at photographs 1 and 2 on page 97. They show two ways of producing cleaner energy. Compare the photographs, and say what you think the people are doing.

Candidate B: Which source of energy is more widely used where you live?

Exam task 2

Candidate B: Look at photographs 3 and 4 on page 98. They show people who are travelling a long distance. Compare the photographs, and say why you think the people have decided to travel in these ways.

Candidate A: Which of these ways of travelling do you think is better for the environment?

6 Did both of you do the two things you were asked to do during your long turn? Do you think you did them well? Why? / Why not?

Reading and Use of English

Phrases with *in*

1 Match the underlined phrases with meanings a–h.

1 The plan to improve the rail system is in progress.
2 In all, there were 20 volunteers on the project.
3 A decision regarding the proposal for new cycle lanes will be made in due course.
4 In practice, the new regulations have done little to reduce waste.
5 Rising temperatures will do damage in the long term.
6 Employees should play a part in reducing waste.
7 Next month there will be a meeting about how to make our school more eco-friendly. In the meantime, please email any suggestions you have.
8 Sadly, the future of the project is now in doubt.

a over a period of time continuing far into the future
b be involved in
c at a suitable time in the future
d happening or being done now
e the total number
f uncertain
g the real situation is that
h in the time between two events

2 Complete the text using phrases with *in* from Exercise 1.

A plan to set up a paper recycling scheme is **(1)** .... at our college, enabling everyone to **(2)** .... reducing the amount of paper thrown away. **(3)** ...., it means that special bins will be placed at various points in the school, and the paper collected will, **(4)** ...., be sent for recycling. The original plan was to have a bin outside every room, which would have meant over 90 **(5)** .... by the end of this term. That number, though, must now be **(6)** .... because of the cost, and there are unlikely to be that many until the end of next year. **(7)** ...., it will require just a short walk to the nearest collection point. Perhaps the move towards paperless offices will one day reach colleges like mine, so that **(8)** .... the bins may not be needed at all.

Part 4

3 Look at the exam task example. What kind of grammatical changes have been made? Which words get marks?

4 Look quickly at questions 1–6 and decide what main changes you should make. Then do the exam task.

Quick steps to Part 4

- Decide whether you must change the grammar, the vocabulary, or both.
- Include all the information from the first sentence in your answer, without anything added.

Exam task

For questions **1–6**, complete the second sentence so that it has a similar meaning to the first sentence, using the word given. Do not change the word given. You must use between two and five words, including the word given. Here is an example (**0**):

Example:

0 We all played worse in the second half of the basketball match so we lost.
IF
We would've won IF WE HAD (or WE'D) ALL PLAYED BETTER in the second half of the basketball match.

1 Wholegrain rice is better for you than white rice.
SO
White rice isn't .... wholegrain rice.

2 I was late for my appointment because I went by car.
HAVE
If I hadn't gone by car I .... time for my appointment.

3 The plan to prevent flooding has been delayed and it may not succeed now.
DOUBT
The plan to prevent flooding has been delayed and its .... now.

4 As plane tickets aren't so expensive as train tickets, people prefer to fly.
MORE
People wouldn't prefer to fly if plane tickets .... train tickets.

5 I strongly agree that waste should be reduced.
FAVOUR
I'm strongly .... waste.

6 Eating red meat is worse for the environment than eating chicken.
NOT
Eating chicken .... for the environment as eating red meat.

Exam tip

Make sure your spelling and grammar are correct.

Contrast links

» Page 111

1 Choose the correct option.

1 *Even though / Despite* the storm had passed, many flights were cancelled or delayed.
2 Some changes are easy to make, *nevertheless, / whereas* others need more time and effort.
3 The north of the country is very cold in winter. *In contrast, / While* the south is quite mild.
4 *On the other hand, / Despite* the heavy rain, the event went ahead as planned.

Part 1 essay

» Page 118

2 Look at the exam task instructions and answer these questions.

1 What is the situation?
2 Who will read your essay?
3 What is the topic?
4 Do you agree with the statement?

Exam task

Your English class has done a project on the subject of the environment. Now, your teacher has asked you to write an essay.
Write an essay using all the notes and give reasons for your point of view.

We are not doing enough to protect our world.

Notes
Write about:
1 the harm we are doing to the environment
2 what we are doing to save the environment
3 your own idea

Write your **essay** in **140–190** words. You must use grammatically correct sentences with accurate spelling and punctuation in an appropriate style.

3 Read the model essay and answer these questions.

1 Is the answer about the right length, and in a suitable style?

2 Which paragraph contains the following?
  a the writer's own opinion
  b arguments against the statement
  c a reference back to points already made
  d a general comment on the topic
  e arguments for the statement

3 Find examples of the following:
  a contrast links
  b addition links
  c conditional forms
  d comparative forms

Nowadays, everybody is talking about the need to save the planet. Despite this, the problems are getting worse all the time, so maybe we should do more than just talk about them if we really want to make a difference.

Firstly, we use more energy and create more waste than ever before. For instance, we drive to the supermarket to buy imported goods wrapped in plastic, and fly halfway round the world for our holidays. In addition, global warming is destroying rainforests, rivers and ice caps while we, in contrast, keep cool by using air conditioning.

On the other hand, we are now trying to lead a greener way of life. For example, we produce much of our energy from wind and solar power, we can take fast trains instead of planes, and people now recycle rubbish and unwanted household items.

Nevertheless, these measures alone are insufficient. I believe we should change our lifestyle completely, for instance, by becoming vegetarian, buying far fewer manufactured products, and travelling much less. And unless richer nations give up making constant economic growth their objective, our planet will in the long term face disaster.

4 Think about the following to get some ideas for your essay.

- environmental problems you have heard or read about
- how countries are trying to protect the environment
- what ordinary people are doing to try to help

5 Look at the Quick steps and plan your essay.

Quick steps to Part 1 essay

- Decide how many paragraphs you will need and put your ideas under headings. Include one or two sentences about each of the notes you are given. In a short introductory paragraph, comment generally on the topic.
- Connect your points with contrast links such as ***whereas***.
- Use a suitable expression such as ***in my view …*** to give your own opinion.

6 Write your essay. When you have finished, check your work as in Unit 1 Writing Exercise 5 on page 13.

Exam tip

Try to use your own words – not those in the notes.

8 Moving ahead

Communications vocabulary

1 **Answer the questions about these forms of communication.**

blogging emailing file sharing instant messaging posting on social media texting tweeting video calling

1 Which of them are becoming more popular, and which less popular?
2 Which do you use? Why?

2 **Compound nouns are formed from two words that function together as a noun, e.g. *backup, laptop, webcam*. Match the words in box A with the words in box B to form compound nouns. Which compound nouns do you associate with a computer, which with a mobile phone, and which with both?**

A

book broad data desk hash hand key pass ring smart touch web

B

band base board mark phone screen set site tag tones top word

3 **What changes has the internet made to people's lives? Do you think all of these changes have been positive? Why? / Why not?**

Part 5

4 **Quickly read the text. Do you think the writer believes that bookshops have a future?**

Quick steps to Part 5

- To answer a question about the meaning of a word or phrase, look for an explanation in the text, or for words with a similar or opposite meaning.
- For questions like *What does 'this' refer to?*, study everything before and after the reference word in that part of the text.

5 **Look quickly at the questions. Which focus on:**
a) the meaning of a particular phrase, and
b) a reference word?

6 **Do the exam task on your own.**

Exam task

You are going to read an article about a bookshop. For questions **1–6**, choose the answer (**A**, **B**, **C** or **D**) which you think fits best according to the text.

Exam tips

- Use only the information in the text to choose your answers, not your own knowledge or opinions.
- Remember to check that you have chosen one answer for every question.

7 **Would you rather buy books online or go to a bookshop? Why?**

The bookshop and the tweet

A local bookshop, which failed to sell a single book in a day for the first time in its 100-year history, has been 'completely overwhelmed' with orders after its Twitter post went viral. Robert Sansom, who has worked at the Petersfield Bookshop in Hampshire for 13 years, posted a tweet about their slow day, saying: 'Not a single book sold today. £0.00.' The shop assistant shared a link to the store's website and begged its customers to take advantage of the bookshop's 25 per cent discounts.

The message was retweeted by thousands of book lovers, including science-fiction author Neil Gaiman, who shared the post with his 2.8 million followers. Following Neil's tweet, messages came in from around the world accompanied, in many cases, by an order request. The bookshop's social media account gained 1,100 new followers in just 15 hours, and attracted over £1,000 worth of online orders. Robert, who runs the shop's social media account, said: 'Somebody we have a connection with at the bookshop has a vague connection with Neil Gaiman, and sent
16 it to him, and then everything started'.

'I couldn't believe it,' said Robert. 'It's been a real 'kindness of strangers' story. The number of likes and retweets started going up right before my eyes; it was as if it was animated. I had messages and one order request after another coming in from all over the world, and eventually I had to stop replying to messages at two o'clock this morning.' In a further tweet the next day, he described how a man who'd spent his whole life in Petersfield came into the shop for the first time ever after a friend in California, USA suggested he do so right away.

None of the staff could remember a single day when they hadn't sold a book before. Robert said: 'We're used to having slow days, especially in January and February, which are always notoriously bad. But yesterday was very strange. It was very stormy, so most people were staying in.' He went on: 'We had a few come in and browse, but nobody was really in the buying mood. It got to about an hour before closing time and we realised we hadn't taken a single penny all day.' Even so, they weren't too concerned. Naturally, they would have preferred to make a sale, but essentially their attitude was 'these things happen'.

Figures released recently by the Booksellers Association indicate that the number of independent bookshops in the UK and Ireland has grown steadily over the last three years, from 868 to 890. At a time when so many famous names are disappearing from the high street, it would seem that
38 bookshops are bucking the trend.

Petersfield Managing Director John Westwood said: 'I believe in this industry, but online ordering has hit us hard. I've had to sell my flat to keep the store in business, and most evenings sleep on a camp bed in the shop. We have lots of big plans for the future, on how to expand and grow, we just need to get there first.' Westwood added that the response has been 'overwhelming, astonishing; a very emotional experience'. '… everyone has been so supportive,' he said. 'Books are special things and nothing beats going into a bookstore. Seeing them, touching them, smelling them – it is a special place.'

1 Why did Sansom send the tweet about the bookshop?

A to tell customers how long ago the shop was founded
B to let customers know that they are unable to take any more orders
C to encourage people to purchase books at reduced prices
D to show that nowadays most people buy books online

2 What does 'it' in line 16 refer to?

A an order for a book
B the bookshop's social media account
C a message from an author
D a tweet from Sansom

3 What does Sansom say about Gaiman retweeting his message?

A He had difficulty coping with the massive international response to it.
B He was amazed that a customer came all the way from the US after reading it.
C He was surprised to see an online animation of what had happened on social media.
D He noticed that it only created interest in the bookshop abroad.

4 What was the staff's reaction to the day without any sales?

A They were angry with people who treated the shop like a library.
B They were disappointed but they accepted the situation.
C They weren't bothered because they had expected it.
D They were surprised because sales generally had improved.

5 What does 'bucking' mean in line 38?

A working out
B going against
C keeping up with
D turning down

6 How does Westwood describe his feelings in the final paragraph?

A amazed to realise he's just a small part of a huge community
B confident the bookshop's new owners will make it successful again
C worried that the number of book readers is declining so quickly
D sad that the bookshop may soon have to close down

Listening

Science and technology vocabulary

1 **Test your knowledge of science and technology by filling in the gaps with these words.**

atom breakthrough cell discovery element electronics energy gas graphics images information innovations invention liquid living solid substances

Science and Technology Quiz

1. The ………………… of electricity, which led to the ………………… of the light bulb, was a huge ………………… in scientific knowledge.
2. Chemistry is the study of ………………… and how they react or combine with each other.
3. Recent ………………… in IT have led to greatly improved ………………… on our screens, such as 3-D ………………… .
4. Oil is a …………………, steam is a …………………, and copper is a …………………
5. An ………………… is the smallest unit that an ………………… can be divided into, and a ………………… is the smallest unit of a plant or animal.
6. Biology is the study of ………………… things.
7. Technology has many branches, for example, biotechnology, ………………… and ………………… technology.
8. Physics is the study of matter and …………………, and their effect on one another.

2 18 **Listen to check your answers to the quiz.**

3 **How important do you think it is for young people to be interested in science and technology? Why?**

Exam tip

After listening, make sure the completed sentences make sense, with no spelling or grammar mistakes.

Part 2

Quick steps to Part 2

- When the answer is a number, take care with other numbers you may hear that don't answer the question.
- Use figures in your answers, for example *40* instead of *forty*.
- For each question, the speaker will say something that indicates the answer is coming soon.

4 **It is easier to recognise numbers you hear if you are familiar with their pronunciation. How are these numbers pronounced?**

31st 1989 (year) 463 3.55 12th 60%
⅓ 12,300 35° 22nd 2015 (year) ¾

5 **Look at questions 1–10 in the exam task. Which focus on numbers? What kind of number is it in each case?**

6 19 **Listen and do the exam task.**

Exam task

You will hear a film industry journalist called Ariana Torres talking about the use of computer technology in films. For questions **1–10**, complete the sentences with a word or short phrase.

Ariana's first memory of CGI is of seeing [1] in a film when she was a child.

In early [2], Ariana was particularly impressed by the use of CGI in a film for the first time.

Ariana particularly likes the way CGI has made [3] to the action more spectacular.

Ariana wonders whether making actors look much [4] is really about saving money.

Ariana supports the use of CGI to [5] a film without the original actor.

Ariana believes filmmakers should always get the [6] if they want to bring back actors using CGI.

One famous actor banned any commercial use of their image for [7] after their death.

To develop young actors' careers, Ariana suggests creating [8] for films.

Ariana accuses some filmmakers of not paying enough attention to [9] because of CGI.

Ariana praises CGI for bringing her favourite [10] to the screen.

Passive forms

Page 112

1 Underline the passive verbs in this extract from the recording in Listening, and complete the rule below.

> Their every emotion and facial expression is generated by computer and this cannot be described as authentic.

The passive uses a form of the verb **(1)** .... followed by the **(2)** ....

2 Rewrite these sentences in the passive. Then match them with uses of the passive a–e.

1. Someone has taken my laptop!
2. Finally, you add hot water.
3. You must wear a helmet on the construction site.
4. A very young boy won this year's literature competition.
5. People say that electricity is the most important invention.

- **a** polite rules and requests
- **b** what people in general believe, expect, etc.
- **c** when we don't know who did something
- **d** if the object is more important than the subject
- **e** describing a process

3 Which of these sentences written by exam candidates contain mistakes? Correct the mistakes.

1. When I was in primary school, I used to be teaching English every day.
2. The internet has invented in the 20th century.
3. The work is be done right now to improve the system.
4. Their vision is said to have improved a little.
5. You will be ask to help with the new project.
6. The room wasn't ready when we arrived because it was being cleaning.
7. It is thought that smiling improves your mood.
8. Electricity had invented many years before then.

4 Replace the underlined active verbs with passive forms. Use *by* only where necessary.

When **(1)** you warm a meal up in a microwave oven, **(2)** the food absorbs radio waves and these are converted into heat. While **(3)** it is cooking the meal, only the food gets hot. So when **(4)** it has heated the food up, the dish, glass or plastic container will still be relatively cool, as **(5)** these materials will not have absorbed the radio waves. This means that **(6)** we can describe microwaving as quite an efficient use of electricity. Although **(7)** we often think of the microwave as a fairly modern appliance, in fact **(8)** someone invented it back in 1945. The first microwaves were huge, nearly two metres high, but **(9)** restaurants were already using them in the 1950s. Within 20 years manufacturers were producing much smaller models, and by 1975 **(10)** they had sold over a million in the USA alone.

5 Which of these do you think is the most useful household appliance? Without saying which, use passive verbs to tell your partner about it and see if they can guess. Say where and when you think it was invented, how it is used, and how you think its job will be done in the future.

air conditioning | cooker | dishwasher | electric heater | electric iron | freezer | fridge | toaster | vacuum cleaner | washing machine

6 Use passive verbs to complete the second sentence so that it means the same as the first sentence. There's no need to use *by*.

1. Scientists believe there is water on that distant planet.
   It is believed that there is water on that distant planet ....
2. We hope there will be an update soon.
   It ....
3. The students know the test is difficult.
   The test ....
4. We think the company has made great progress in waste management.
   The company ....
5. Nowadays, people expect cafés and restaurants to have wi-fi.
   Nowadays, cafés and restaurants ....
6. There are reports that the new network will be ten times faster than the old one.
   It ....

7 Work in pairs. Think about recent news stories and tell your partner about three things that are said to have happened. Give more information, using *It is reported that* …

Speaking

Articles

» Page 113

1 Complete the rules with *the*, no article and *a/ an*.

1. We use .... with singular countable nouns mentioned for the first time, with people's jobs and some expressions with numbers.
2. We use .... when we mention something again or it is common knowledge, when there is only one of something, with superlatives, inventions, types of animal, musical instruments, and certain groups of people, e.g. *the young, the unemployed*.
3. We use .... when we talk in general and in the plural, with abstract nouns, or with sports, certain illnesses and some expressions following *to*, such as *work*, *bed* and *school*.

2 Correct the mistakes in these sentences written by exam candidates.

1. Some people think internet is the most important modern invention.
2. I still haven't recovered from a flu.
3. I enjoy reading about royal family.
4. I think cycling is best way to get there.
5. There was ten per cent decrease in sales last year.
6. I wanted to tell you, I've found the really useful new app.
7. I am better at playing the violin than playing piano.
8. I am accountant in Japan.

3 (20) Fill in the gaps with *a*, *an* or *the*, or leave the gap blank if no article can be used. Then listen to students Hannah and Anton to check your answers.

Hannah: For me, by far **(1)** .... most interesting subject when I was at **(2)** .... school was **(3)** .... physics. I particularly remember a lesson about the invention of **(4)** .... steel back in **(5)** .... 19th century. I think that was when I decided I wanted to be **(6)** .... engineer.

Anton: I remember **(7)** .... one I really enjoyed was **(8)** .... music. I was quite good at **(9)** .... piano and my ambition then was to become **(10)** .... professional musician. I certainly had plenty of **(11)** .... enthusiasm, but I also needed **(12)** .... patience, which at that age I didn't have at all.

Part 4

» Page 136

Quick steps to Part 4

- Think of at least two points to make in reply to each of the examiner's questions.
- If you don't know any facts about the topic, give your opinion.
- Encourage the other candidate to say more. Ask questions like ***What's your opinion?***

4 (21) Listen to Hannah and Anton practising Part 4. How many points do they each make? Then listen again. Which of these expressions do they use to add more points?

and also ...
and then there's ...
and what's more, ...
and not only that, ...
and there's another thing, ...
apart from that,
... as well as that,
... even better, ...
just as importantly, ...
worse still, ...

5 In pairs, ask and answer this Part 4 question: *Many people believe everyone should study science at school. What do you think?* Add some of these points to your own ideas, and introduce them with expressions from Exercise 4.

harder than some other subjects
memorising facts and figures
not enough practical work
poorly equipped laboratories
some lessons can be boring
can lead to a good job
developing thinking skills
good science teachers
interesting experiments
learning practical skills

6 In groups of three, choose four of these questions and think of as many ideas as you can for each.

- How well is science taught at school?
- Do you think it's true that anyone can be good at science if they study hard? Why? / Why not?
- Which branches of science would you like to study? Why?
- What kinds of job in science sound interesting? Why?
- What was the most important invention last century?
- Do you think that time travel would be a good thing or a bad thing? Why?

7 Work as an 'examiner' and two 'candidates'. The examiner asks the candidates the questions chosen in Exercise 6. The candidates discuss the answers together as fully as they can. The examiner then comments on how well they have done.

Exam tip

Look at the examiner to answer his or her questions, but at your partner when you are talking together.

Collocations

1 **Match the verbs in box A with the nouns in box B to form collocations.**

A

attach browse carry out charge
prove run store undo

B

a change (you have made) a mobile phone
data (on a hard disk) a program
an experiment a theory
a file (to an email) websites

2 **Choose the correct word (A, B, C or D). Which word(s) in the sentence does each form a collocation with?**

1 Sometimes Lana's voice is very .... and I struggle to hear her.
A faint **B** pale **C** dull **D** faded

2 Your computer is very slow; you might need to close some of the ....
A bookmarks **B** hardware **C** networks
D applications

3 When everyone has finished, I will .... the answers on the screen.
A display **B** extend **C** present **D** spread

4 My PC .... again, and I lost all the work I hadn't saved.
A collapsed **B** crashed **C** scratched
D folded

5 Eleven .... twenty-four is two hundred and sixty-four.
A plus **B** for **C** times **D** from

6 The problem was caused by a .... of poor communication and human error.
A connection **B** composition **C** combination
D conjunction

7 I'm going to ask the IT department to look at my computer as I think there's a ....
A insect **B** worm **C** pest **D** bug

Part 1

Quick steps to Part 1

- Prepare by noting collocations, e.g. ***scientific discovery***, in your vocabulary notebook.
- Look for collocations formed by words before or after the gap.

3 **Which animals *hibernate* in winter? Quickly read the text. How does it answer the question in the title?**

4 **The example answer forms a collocation with *sense*. Underline words that may collocate with gaps 1–8. Then do the exam task.**

Exam task

For questions **1–8**, read the text below and decide which answer (**A**, **B**, **C** or **D**) best fits each gap. There is an example at the beginning (**0**).

Example: 0 A do **B** be **C** make **D** have

Is human hibernation possible?

As winter is our least favourite season, maybe it would **(0)** .... sense just to sleep through it? Many animal **(1)** ...., including bears, bats and squirrels, do it, so why not humans?
The problem is that human body temperature varies only a few degrees around 37 °C, for instance, when someone has a **(2)** .... fever, and any bigger change can put their life in serious **(3)** .... However, cooling is increasingly being used in hospitals, especially when **(4)** .... major injuries, and these techniques may eventually be extended to other uses.
It would certainly make travel into **(5)** .... space more practical by **(6)** .... reducing the amount of food astronauts would have to take with them. One crew **(7)** .... would stay awake while the others hibernated during much of the journey. Better **(8)** ...., we might one day simply take a pill on Earth and then wake up on a distant planet, but that day is probably a long way off.

	A	B	C	D
1	**A** breeds	**B** species	**C** tribes	**D** kinds
2	**A** deep	**B** strong	**C** heavy	**D** high
3	**A** risk	**B** danger	**C** threat	**D** harm
4	**A** treating	**B** healing	**C** curing	**D** mending
5	**A** longer	**B** wider	**C** outer	**D** further
6	**A** highly	**B** extremely	**C** largely	**D** greatly
7	**A** member	**B** agent	**C** colleague	**D** employee
8	**A** even	**B** still	**C** so	**D** than

Exam tips

- Writing in the example word can help you understand the text when you read it through.
- Read through the complete text, making sure that everything makes sense with the missing words added.

Reason and result links

1 Complete the sentences with these words. Which expressions are quite formal?

account because consequently owing reason result since therefore view why

1 As a .... of the increasing demand, several new factories were opened.
2 Electric cars produce fewer greenhouse gases, that is .... they are better for the environment.
3 It would take years to reach even the nearest stars, ... to their huge distance from Earth.
4 It may be difficult to access certain programs on .... of a bug in the computer.
5 Nowadays, mobile phones have very sophisticated cameras. ...., most people do not own a traditional camera.
6 Many people have to travel for work. For this ...., many companies provide their employees with laptops.
7 .... the technology is so new, we don't yet know how it will be used.
8 In .... of the fact that there are more forms of communication nowadays, you might expect it to be easier. Unfortunately, this is not always the case.
9 The cost of some electronic goods has gone up, ... of increases in taxes.
10 Many people use their mobile device to navigate, ... very few people know how to read a map.

Part 2 article

Page 124

2 Look at the exam task and answer these questions.

1 Who will read your article?
2 Why should you write it?
3 What two things do you have to do?

Exam task

You see this announcement in an international magazine.

> What is the most important piece of technology you have?
>
> Write us an article about it, saying why it is so important to you and how it could be improved. The writer of the best article will win a prize.

Write your **article** in **140–190** words.

3 Read the model article and answer these questions.

1 Is the style very formal or very informal – or somewhere in between? Give some examples.
2 Which paragraphs describe the good things? Which mention problems and suggest improvements?
3 How are readers encouraged to start and continue reading? What are they asked to think about at the end?
4 Find the following:
   a reason or result links
   b lively expressions
   c passive verb forms

Lost without my laptop

I couldn't imagine a world without laptops. I use mine at home every day and it's also my main link to the outside world. And since it's so small it goes everywhere with me.

As an engineering student I need to do lots of research. As a result, I spend hours online searching for information, and later I key in my assignments. Although I stay in most evenings, I'm never lonely because of all the ways I can keep in touch with friends: email, instant messaging, Skype and Facebook. Without my laptop, my life would crash.

Wonderful though laptops are, technology moves on and that is why they could be even better. For instance, they can't always be connected to mains electricity, and for that reason more powerful batteries are needed.

Looking further ahead, perhaps one day we'll be interacting with our laptops just by thinking, rather than through a keyboard, touchpad or mouse. Then we could store our thoughts, analyse them or even send them to other people.

Quick steps to Part 2 article

- Write in an entertaining way that will hold your readers' interest, using some lively expressions.
- Give reasons for your opinion, and possibly also examples.
- Use linking expressions, such as ***on account of*** and ***in view of***.
- Get readers to think about what you have written by making the ending interesting.

4 **Think about these questions to get some ideas for your article.**

1 Which piece of technology do you know something about?
2 What will interest your readers about this topic?
3 Have you had any interesting experiences with this technology?
4 How might this technology change in the future?

Exam tip

Prepare for this task by reading articles in English in magazines or online.

5 **Write your article. When you have finished, check your work as in Unit 1 Writing Exercise 5 on page 13.**

9 Breaking news

1 **Discuss these questions.**

1. What is a social media influencer?
2. Which famous ones have you heard of? How did they become popular? How do they interact with their followers?
3. What do you think are the advantages and disadvantages of being famous on social media?

Part 7

2 **Read the exam task instructions, and look at the title and layout of the text. Answer these questions.**

1. What is the topic?
2. How many people are there?
3. Is there one long text or a number of shorter, separate texts?

Quick steps to Part 7

- Look for the parts of the text that express the same idea as the questions, not the same words.
- Be careful with questions that say the same as the text, but are about someone else in a different section.
- As you go through the questions, cross out those you have already answered so that you don't keep looking at all of them.

3 **Underline the key words in questions 1–10. Then do the exam task, looking for parts of the text that express the same ideas as those words.**

Exam task

You are going to read a magazine article about someone who used to be a social media influencer. For questions **1–10**, choose from the sections (**A–D**). The sections may be chosen more than once.

In which section does the writer mention

wishing she had made a change sooner.	1
feeling unable to resist the pressure to buy something.	2
big brands no longer trusting influencers.	3
people being able to identify with their favourite influencers.	4
the need to avoid being too sensitive.	5
the competition among influencers becoming tougher.	6
being delighted by a statistic.	7
the need to consider the possible effects of products on consumers.	8
the mistake of thinking becoming an influencer is an easy way to make money.	9
increasing investments in influencers by companies.	10

Exam tip

Make sure you have answered all the questions, and that any alterations you have made are clear. Remember that in the exam you will need to rub out any answers you want to change.

A Eight years ago I became an influencer, helping to shape people's attitudes via social media platforms including YouTube and the then relatively new app Instagram. I gave honest reviews of products I felt people might be interested in buying and the number of my followers steadily grew. When I realised I had my first 10,000 followers I was over the moon. They shared the same thoughts and feelings I was having, and it led to people like me building enormous, loyal followings as social media boomed. We were 'the new stars of web advertising'. Big business was quick to spot our marketing potential, and soon we were receiving free samples and fees in return for promoting their products. That was not something I'd foreseen, but it was certainly welcome. Many people have since said they wish they'd got into influencing back in those early days.

B I felt I'd found the ideal occupation although it's a myth that it's a get-rich-quick job. It involves putting in long hours, especially on research into products, images and platforms. I had to be absolutely sure about the quality of everything I put my name to as the influencer has a duty of care to people who trust them enough to make purchases based entirely on their recommendations. Setting up photos and shooting videos take ages, and you need to study a wide range of competitors' posts and images. Annoyingly, I found some of them so convincing I ended up becoming a customer myself. You also have to choose your platforms carefully, as something that may work well on, say, Twitter, might not be so successful elsewhere. And, of course, you need to be sensitive to constructive comments from your followers, making changes to your content where necessary to help and protect them.

C With 2.4 billion users a month on Facebook, 1.8 billion on YouTube and a billion on Instagram, the number of consumers on social media is huge and the potential market for influencers is, too. Even so, it gradually became smaller as more and more people entered it, driving down the rates brands paid because many new influencers would work for less money, or even nothing at all. Eventually we found ourselves working harder and harder for ever-decreasing returns. At around the same time, fake social media accounts started selling likes and followers, harming the reputation of influencers in general and ultimately leading to major organisations losing faith in us completely. At that point I ought to have realised it was time to move on, but I stuck with it for another year before finally deciding I'd had enough.

D Do I miss it? Not really. These days I'm working full-time in marketing, earning a decent salary in a large company. Followers sometimes get in touch to say they're missing me and I appreciate that, but I won't go back to influencing. However, I've just seen a rather worrying statistic: apparently, a third of under-18s want to be YouTubers, compared to just over 10% wanting to be doctors or nurses. So, if it really does appeal, my advice is to become a micro-influencer, with just a few thousand followers who you communicate with frequently about a particular brand. That's what interests the remaining companies most. Stay one step ahead of your competitors but don't spend too much on new clothes or designer furniture in an attempt to improve the look of your photos and videos: concentrate on the product. And finally, report any abuse immediately but don't let negative but well-meaning comments get you down.

4 **Find words or phrases in the text that mean the following:**

1 very pleased about something (A)
2 quickly became successful (A)
3 notice (A)
4 expected to happen (A)
5 commonly believed but false idea (B)
6 able to make you believe that something is true or right (B)
7 helpful or useful (B)
8 no longer trusting (C)
9 with good intentions (D)
10 make you feel unhappy or depressed (D)

5 **Look at the reported speech below, then find the direct speech in the text above.**

1 She explained that eight years earlier she'd become an influencer.
2 She said she'd given honest reviews of products.
3 She declared that at that time she was working full-time in marketing.
4 She insisted she wouldn't go back to influencing.
5 She mentioned she'd just seen a rather worrying statistic.

6 **Would you like to be a social media influencer? Say why or why not.**

Listening

Media vocabulary

1 **Which of these words and phrases do you associate with: a) television and radio, b) newspapers and magazines, c) online media, d) all of a–c?**

biased broadcasting commercials downloads episode fake news go viral the headlines network objective platform podcast pop-up ads the press propaganda publication remote control streaming tabloids trending topics

2 **How many kinds of TV programme can you name? Which of these do you often watch? Which do you never watch? Why?**

Examples: *chat shows, reality TV shows*

3 **What do these TV people do? Which job would you most like to do? Why?**

camera operator editor interviewer investigative journalist news reporter newsreader presenter producer scriptwriter set designer

Part 4

4 **Look at the exam task instructions. Answer these questions.**

1 What kind of extract will you hear?
2 Who will you hear?
3 What is the likely topic?

5 22 **Look at the stem of questions 1–7 and for each one note down the kind of information you need to listen for, e.g. opinion, activity. Then listen and do the exam task.**

Quick steps to Part 4

- Study the instructions, and think about who and what you will hear.
- Quickly read the stem of each question, underlining important words, and decide what kind of information you will need to listen for.

Exam task

You will hear a radio interview with Max Davidson, an expert on the role of social media in news reporting. For questions **1–7**, choose the best answer (**A**, **B** or **C**).

1 Max works as
A an author of books about the media.
B a researcher for politicians.
C a journalist on a magazine.

2 Why did Max take an interest in the topic of 'fake news'?
A He had been the victim of a false report.
B So many people were talking about it.
C A politician admitted to him that he had told lies.

3 Max believes newspapers are less popular than they used to be because
A reporters more often fail to tell the truth.
B the press is now owned by a small number of individuals.
C more people prefer to seek the truth for themselves.

4 What, according to Max, causes the greatest anger online about TV news?
A stories that may or may not be entirely true
B the running order of the stories in the programmes
C stories that they choose to include or leave out

5 Max says it is a mistake to think that
A almost everything that happens is now being recorded.
B traditional media reporting is slower than that of social media.
C photos and video can be relied on to show reality.

6 Max is particularly critical of the techniques now used in
A filming news.
B reporting comments.
C news photography.

7 Max believes that in the future
A it will be impossible to know which news is true and which is false.
B there will still be a need for journalists.
C all news information will be controlled by governments.

Exam tips

- Remember the answers are in the same order as the questions, so if you miss an answer, keep listening and move on to the next question.
- Make sure you have answered every question. Then check your answers.

Reported speech

a b

Page 114

1 23 **Rewrite these sentences in the actual words used in the recording in Listening. Then listen again to check your answers.**

a **She** said **that** morning she had with **her there** in the studio Max Davidson, who had taken a special interest in the role of social media.
b He said he had done **his** undergraduate degree in journalism.
c He said that as the amount of available data was increasing all the time, it wouldn't be easy.

2 **Look at the verbs in the sentences in Exercise 1. How do these tenses change in reported speech?**

present simple present perfect present continuous past simple *will* future

3 **How have the words in bold in the reported speech changed in Exercise 1? Think of other words that change in the same ways.**

4 **Change the sentences to reported speech. In which sentence does the tense stay the same?**

1 'I watched the match at my girlfriend's house last night,' Joey said on Monday.
2 'I don't want to play this game now,' said Luigi.
3 'I'm leaving as soon as my sister gets here,' Emma told me over the phone.
4 'I've always wanted to be on the show, and next week I will be,' said Paul.
5 'Later this evening I'll be meeting my favourite singer,' my sister said.
6 'I'd been working in entertainment ever since I left school,' Julia told the presenter.

5 **Change these questions from the recording in Listening into reported speech. Then answer the questions.**

Do you think the press are becoming less popular?
What angers people most about it?

1 The interviewer asked Max …
2 He asked Max …

How do we form reported questions? What do we add to reported *yes/no* questions?
Check your answers in the Grammar reference on page 114.

6 **Complete the sentences with these reporting verbs.**

admit apologise offer suggest tell

1 Leena ...suggested... that we should watch TV.
2 Pete .... to lend me his copy of the DVD.
3 The mother .... the little boy to say sorry.
4 I .... for losing the tickets.
5 He .... that he was wrong.

7 **Put the reporting verbs from Exercise 6 into the correct group, a, b, c, d or e. Some verbs can go into more than one group. Then do the same with these verbs.**

advise decide deny explain insist invite order persuade promise recommend refuse remind threaten warn

Verbs followed by:

a *to*: ......offer......
b object + *to*: ....
c *-ing*: ....
d (*that*) + clause: ....
e preposition + *-ing*: ....

8 **Complete the second sentence so that it has a similar meaning to the first sentence, using the word given. Do not change the word given. You must use between two and five words, including the word given.**

1 'Don't forget to do your homework,' the teacher said to us.
REMINDED
The teacher .... our homework.

2 'Would you like to come to the party, Jo?' said Rosa.
INVITED
Rosa .... come to the party.

3 'I won't help you if you are rude to me,' my sister said to me.
REFUSED
My sister .... if I was rude to her.

4 'I didn't eat the last cookie,' James said when I asked him.
DENIED
James .... the last cookie.

5 'Let's take the bus home,' said Martin as we left the office.
SUGGESTED
Martin .... home as we left the office.

6 'I don't think you should go there on your own,' Lorna's mother said.
AGAINST
Lorna's mother .... there on her own.

Speaking

Keeping going

1 24 **Listen to student Carlota comparing photos A and B and saying how the people might feel. Which of points 1–8 does she mention?**

1 what's happening
2 where it's happening
3 how the people feel
4 why they feel like that
5 their ages
6 their clothes
7 their hairstyles
8 people in the background

2 24 **Listen again. Which expressions does Carlota use to add points?**

A

B

3 **Work in groups. Look at photos C and D, and note down as many similarities and differences as you can.**

4 **Work in pairs. Take it in turns to discuss photos C and D. Compare the photos and say how the people might feel. When your partner has finished, tell them how long they were speaking.**

C

D

Part 2

Page 130

5 **Look at the instructions for exam tasks 1 and 2. What does each candidate have to do? Make a list of points you can include when you speak.**

6 **In pairs, do the exam tasks. Add as many points as you can to make sure you keep talking for a full minute.**

Quick steps to Part 2

- Don't talk for less than a minute. You can't get good marks if you don't say enough.
- Remember that in the exam you will see the question written above the photos.

Exam task 1

1

2

In this part of the test, I'm going to give each of you two photographs. I'd like you to talk about your photographs on your own for about a minute, and also to answer a question about your partner's photographs.

Candidate A, it's your turn first. Look at photographs 1 and 2. They show **people protesting**. I'd like you to compare the photographs, and say **why you think the people have decided to do this.**

Candidate B, **which of these kinds of news story interest you? Why?**

Exam task 2

3

4

Candidate B, look at photographs 3 and 4. They show **people watching public events.** I'd like you to compare the photographs, and say **how you think the people watching these events feel.**

Candidate A, **do you ever watch public events like these? Why? / Why not?**

7 **Change roles and repeat exam tasks 1 and 2.**

8 **Did you both talk for a full minute? Discuss this with your partner.**

Exam tip

Imagine you are describing the <u>similarities</u> and <u>differences</u> in the photos to somebody who can't see them.

Reading and Use of English

Noun suffixes

1 Look at the underlined nouns in these extracts from the recording in Speaking. Answer these questions.

a another kind of entertainment
b another difference is the professional photographers are mostly middle-aged men
c the explanation is that they are working
d they have happy expressions on their faces
e their appearance is different

1 What verb is each noun formed from?
2 What suffix does each noun have?
3 Are there any other spelling changes?

2 Form nouns from these verbs and write them in groups a–e. Which require extra spelling changes?

arrange contribute disappear exist expect identify intend introduce maintain prefer recommend require vary

3 Use suffixes to correct the mistakes in these sentences written by exam candidates.

1 He didn't come to work for a week and didn't give an explain.
2 I saw the advertise for the job online.
3 They are just suggests, but I think they will help you.
4 You can do the course if you meet the requires.
5 As an employee I was expecting to get a reduce in the price.
6 I think we need to work together on the solves.

4 Complete the sentences with these nouns. Say which verb or adjective each noun is formed from.

choice depth heat height proof

1 Viewers have a ....choice..... between a variety of streaming services. (verb: ....choose.....)
2 With all the studio lights on, the .... makes air conditioning necessary. (adjective: ....)
3 The film crew used a drone to film from a .... of 200 metres. (adjective: ....)
4 The documentary is about people in prison, but there is no .... that they did the crimes. (verb: ....)
5 They filmed the fish at a .... of 6,000 metres. (adjective: ....)

Part 3

Quick steps to Part 3

- Note words with prefixes and/or suffixes you see when you are reading in English.
- When you look up a new word, note any prefixes and/or suffixes you can add and how these affect its meaning.

5 Quickly read the text. Decide how the writer answers the question in the title. Then do the exam task.

Exam tips

- Look out for internal spelling changes when forming a word, e.g. ***long – length***.
- Remember to make sure the text makes sense and that you have made all the necessary changes to the words.

Exam task

For questions **1–8**, read the text below. Use the word given in capitals at the end of some of the lines to form a word that fits in the gap in the same line. There is an example at the beginning (**0**).

Example: 0 APPEARANCE

Has streaming replaced live TV?

Before the **(0)** .... of streaming services like Netflix on our screens, for the ordinary **(1)** .... there was little alternative to whatever programmes the TV channels decided to show, normally with breaks for **(2)** .... at regular intervals. **APPEAR** / **VIEW** / **COMMERCE**

Nowadays, we have a far wider **(3)** .... of films and series, as streaming gives us the **(4)** .... to watch what we want, when we want. The streaming providers also make it easy for us to find movies and shows we may like by studying all our **(5)** .... and watching history, and then creating lists of personalised **(6)** .... for us. **CHOOSE** / **FLEXIBLE** / **PREFER** / **RECOMMEND**

But live TV still has its advantages. For instance, you can usually find a particular show on one channel or another, but it might not be **(7)** .... on your country's streaming service, or be unavailable because one of its **(8)** .... owns the rights. So television is likely to be around for quite some time yet. **ACCESS** / **COMPETE**

1 **Complete the underlined expressions with these words and phrases.**

carried out challenge conclusion purpose recommendation step sum

1. This report makes the .... that local residents should receive free theatre tickets.
2. In ...., I believe that a new theatre will bring more advantages than disadvantages to the town.
3. The next .... will be to ask residents what their preference would be.
4. To .... up, it is clear that leisure facilities need more investment.
5. A key .... is the limited number of experienced employees.
6. A survey was .... which showed that many people disapproved of the project.
7. The .... of this report is to describe the plans for developing tourism in the town.

Part 2 report

Page 126

2 **Look at the exam task and answer these questions.**

1. Who is your report for?
2. Why do you need to write it?
3. What information should you give?
4. What question do you have to answer?

Exam task

A group of English-speaking people are planning to visit your town next winter. You have been asked to write a report about the television and radio there, and say which kinds of programme you think the group might enjoy watching and listening to.

Write your **report** in **140–190** words.

3 **Read the model report and answer these questions.**

1. How many paragraphs does the writer use?
2. Do the title and the headings tell the reader what to expect?
3. Is the report written in a formal, a neutral or an informal style?
4. What recommendation(s) does the writer make?
5. Find examples of the following:
   a. expressions similar to those in Exercise 1
   b. linking expressions
   c. reported speech

The media for visitors

Introduction

The aim of this report is to inform visitors about the media here, and to suggest which types of programme may appeal to them.

What's on television

There are 24 channels, all of which show a variety of programmes ranging from sports and soaps to quiz shows and chat shows. They can be streamed with wi-fi. In addition, channels such as CNN and the BBC are available via cable TV.

What's on the radio

There is a wide range of radio stations offering music, drama, comedies, sports commentaries, news bulletins and weather forecasts. All are available on your phone via free apps.

Programmes of interest

Many tourists have said they enjoyed the sports, nature and arts programmes on TV, while most films and drama series can be watched in English by changing the language in the television menu. Radio, too, has a lot to offer, and I strongly recommend the wonderful 24-hour music stations.

Conclusion

To sum up, there is plenty to enjoy on TV and radio here, even if you do not understand our language. And listening to it is an excellent way to learn it.

Quick steps to Part 2 report

- Decide what your readers will want to know.
- Make notes on any facts you know about the subject and any personal experience you may have.
- Think of a good title that tells readers about the content.
- Plan your report, including recommendations and suggestions at or near the end.
- In your first paragraph, say what the aim of your report is.
- Write in an appropriate style for your readers.

4 **Get ideas for your report by thinking about these questions.**

1. What do you know about your national TV and radio?
2. Is wi-fi widely available?
3. Which programmes do you enjoy?
4. Which kinds of programme might your visitors enjoy?

Exam tip

Use paragraph headings to make your report clearer.

5 **Write your report. When you have finished, check your work as in Unit 1 Writing Exercise 5 on page 13.**

10 Shopping around

Clothing and shopping vocabulary

1 **Find pairs of adjectives with opposite meanings used to describe clothes.**

Examples: *bright – dark*

~~bright~~ casual clashing cool ~~dark~~ fake formal genuine loose matching patterned plain simple smart sophisticated tight unfashionable untidy

2 **Which of the adjectives in Exercise 1 form adverbs that can be used with *dressed* in phrases such as *smartly dressed* or *a smartly dressed woman*?**

3 **Describe the people and clothes in the photo.**

4 **Make sure you understand the words in *italics*. Then discuss these questions.**

1 Which celebrities do you think wear the most *stylish outfits*?
2 How far do you think people's clothes *reflect* their personalities?
3 Do you prefer comfortable *items of clothing*, or fashionable ones?
4 How important to you is it that clothes have *designer labels*?
5 What styles and colours of clothes *suit* you best?
6 What do you like to buy in the *sales*?

5 **For each sentence, explain the difference between the expressions in italics. Some are opposites, others are not.**

1 Size 38 is currently *out of stock*, but we have a size 40 *in stock*.
2 If it's *a bargain* I'll buy it, but if it's *poor value for money* I won't.
3 No, I don't want to *exchange* the item. Please send me *a refund*.
4 A week after their new style of shirt *was launched*, it *was sold out*.
5 Instead of buying *brand new* clothes I now prefer *pre-owned* garments.
6 Customers are making fewer clothes *purchases*, so the store must increase *sales* of other items.
7 *Budget* online stores offering low prices have made many high-street shops *uncompetitive*.
8 *Consumers* should take care if buying from *dealers* in second-hand goods.
9 The new line in jeans was so popular that *shopkeepers* soon ran out and asked their *suppliers* for more.
10 I used to buy *the latest* fashions but now I like to wear *vintage* clothes from the 1990s.

Part 6

Quick steps to Part 6

- Look for ideas, opinions or events that develop through the main text.
- Look for language clues, such as reference words and plural and singular nouns, before you decide on each answer.

6 **Quickly read the exam task instructions and the main text. In which order does the writer make these points about vintage clothes?**

a what 'vintage' is
b famous brands reacting to the trend
c not always high quality
d recently becoming popular
e disadvantages of buying them
f linked to the rise of internet shopping

7 **Underline the words and phrases in B–G that may provide clues. A is done for you.**

8 **Do the exam task, using the words you underlined to help you.**

Exam tips

- Don't choose an option just because it contains the same word, number or name as a particular paragraph.
- Make sure that the completed text makes sense and that you've chosen a letter for all the answers.

9 **Discuss the questions, giving reasons.**

1 Would you wear vintage clothes?
2 Which decade's fashions do you find most attractive?

Exam task

You are going to read an article about the rise in sales of fashionable second-hand clothes. Six sentences have been removed from the article. Choose from the sentences **A–G** the one which fits each gap (**1–6**). There is one extra sentence which you do not need to use.

IS BUYING VINTAGE CLOTHING THE MOST ECOLOGICAL WAY TO SHOP?

by Ellie Violet Bramley

As consumers become increasingly aware of the environmental impact of fast fashion, they are looking for a more sustainable way to shop. Could buying second-hand be the answer?

A study shows that last year 64% of British women were willing to buy pre-owned pieces compared with 45% three years ago – and it is thought that by 2028, 13% of the clothes in women's wardrobes are likely to be second-hand. Yet until fairly recently, according to one online shop owner, people were still dismissive of used clothing. **1** And that, crucially, includes the massive shift to online buying that has rapidly brought it to a much wider audience.

Apart from an increased awareness of sustainability, vintage fashion neatly fits into the wider mood of today's Instagram age. **2** So what better way to stand out from them than to wear clothes few others are likely to own? Vintage sceptics who may have been put off in the past by thoughts of searching through piles of old clothes in bargain basements may be persuaded by the ability to buy online. 'The popularity of online vintage shops is great for those who don't have access to everything a city such as New York has to offer,' says Gabriel Held, described by Vogue as 'Instagram's most celebrated vintage dealer'.

Perhaps unsurprisingly, however, opening up the market with numerous online shops has meant less quality control. Held sees 'a lot of very ordinary used clothing being marketed as vintage. Something doesn't have to be 20 years old to be considered vintage, but, for me, if it's not true vintage, then it should be something extraordinary.' **3** For some, the latter means any era up to the early 80s, while others consider it to be clothing that is more than 20 years old.

Virginia Bates, whose Notting Hill vintage store attracted the likes of Naomi Campbell and Donatella Versace, used to stock items from the end of the 19th century. Her definition of vintage runs 'up to the 1920s, 30s, a bit of 40s, occasionally 50s. **4** I would never have sold anything made then because I was there, I was wearing it.' But, as she says: 'With another generation coming up, the 60s is the equivalent of what I thought of as antique when I opened my shop.'

Not content to sit back and watch others profit from their vintage items, some luxury labels are relaunching decades-old designs from their own past. **5** This was entirely due to the attention it was getting in the vintage fashion market. In February, Italian fashion house Fendi brought back its most famous one from the same era – luxury resale website Vestiaire Collective had seen a 558% increase in its sales since January last year.

Of course, for some, buying vintage will never feel quite right. 'It's really not my thing,' says Bates. There are obvious risks. **6** Also, sizing can vary from country to country. 'But at the end of the day it doesn't really matter: the most important thing is that it's recycled – it encourages people not to go out and buy more.'

A This point about quality shows just how difficult it is to distinguish between second-hand and vintage.

B For example, shoppers have to be careful to look out for holes, moths and rips before buying an item.

C I don't consider the decade which followed that to be vintage.

D Now, by contrast, it is not just acceptable – it's cool and completely in line with current fashion trends here.

E Last year, for instance, Dior brought back its 1999 Saddle handbag.

F Other such stores then announced that they, too, would soon be stocking vintage items.

G This is one where authenticity and originality – not being seen in the same outfit as anyone else – are highly prized.

Adverbs of manner and opinion

Page 115

10 **Find the adverbs *increasingly, crucially, rapidly, neatly* and *unsurprisingly* in the first four paragraphs of the text. Notice their position in the sentence.**

11 **Correct the mistakes with adverb position in these sentences written by exam candidates.**

1. I enjoy the summer months more because I like very much doing sports outdoors.
2. I'm attending lessons because I want to speak well English.
3. I had read carefully the instructions.
4. I will send very quickly an email to rearrange the meeting.
5. I don't like cars, so I have naturally a bicycle.
6. I didn't unfortunately pass my driving test.

Listening

1 🔊 25 **Complete the text with these words. Then listen to check your answers.**

brand catalogue checkout debit debt guarantee mall off on offer trolley

I always try to get everything I need for the week down at the shops and supermarket at the big shopping **(1)** .... on the outskirts of town. At the supermarket, I fill up my **(2)** .... with my favourite items of food, sometimes choosing a different **(3)** .... from the one I usually buy if it happens to be **(4)** ...., for instance, 'Buy 2 and get 1 free', or '20% **(5)** ....'. At the **(6)** .... I normally pay cash or by **(7)** .... card rather than by credit card, as I don't want to get into **(8)** .... by spending more than I can afford. Sometimes I call in at one of the other shops to buy something for the house, though for a big item I usually look it up in the online **(9)** .... first. I always check it has a good **(10)** .... in case anything goes wrong after I've bought it.

2 **Say what you think is happening in the photo, using words from Exercise 1.**

Part 3

3 **Look at the exam task. What will all the people be talking about?**

Quick steps to Part 3

- Listen for ideas similar to those in sentences A–H, not just words or phrases.
- Remember it isn't necessary to understand every word that all five speakers say.
- Don't forget that three of sentences A–H aren't needed.

4 🔊 26 **Underline the key words in sentences A–H and think of expressions with similar or opposite meanings. Then listen and do the exam task.**

Exam task

You will hear five short extracts in which people are talking about shopping malls in their town. For questions **1–5** choose from the list **(A–H)** what each speaker says about their local mall. Use the letters only once. There are three extra letters which you do not need to use.

A I prefer to buy items online at home and then collect them at the mall.
B I regret spending too much money while I was there.
C I always find it easy to park my car there.
D I don't think there are enough places in public areas to sit down.
E I've noticed that the restaurants sometimes get too crowded.
F I like to have things I buy there sent to my house.
G I think it's a good place for people who don't have much money to spend.
H I think its popularity is declining because fewer people go out shopping these days.

Speaker 1		1
Speaker 2		2
Speaker 3		3
Speaker 4		4
Speaker 5		5

Exam tips

- If you think you may have answered one question incorrectly, make sure that it hasn't led to other mistakes.
- Make sure you have answered all the questions.

Wish and *if only*

Page 116

1 Look at these extracts from the recording in Listening and answer the questions.

a I wish some people would park more sensibly.
b I wish there were more benches.
c I wish I hadn't bought those luxury armchairs.

1 Which sentence expresses regret about the past?
2 Which sentence expresses a desire for change in the future, in this case something annoying that other people do?
3 Which sentence refers to a present situation we would like to be different?
4 In which sentence(s) could you use *If only* instead of *I wish*?

2 Correct the mistakes in these sentences written by exam candidates.

1 I wish you were at the party last Saturday.
2 We all wish scientists can find a vaccination.
3 I wish I didn't buy white trainers; they're already dirty.
4 As soon as he started talking about politics, I wished I didn't invite him for dinner.
5 If only I would have known you were allergic to shellfish, I wouldn't have made this dish.
6 I wish you came on the trip; it won't be the same without you.
7 I wish you will spend more time with me.
8 I wish I have decided to wear a coat.

3 What would you say in these situations? Write two sentences for each, using *wish* or *If only*.

1 You saw a shirt on offer on Friday, but when you went to buy it on Monday it had gone.
I wish I'd bought the shirt on Friday. If only I hadn't waited until Monday.
2 You bought a jacket in a shop, but then saw the same jacket on sale for less in the market.
3 You're in the supermarket on a Saturday morning, but it's crowded and there are long queues.
4 The sales start tomorrow, but you don't feel very well so you won't be able to go.
5 Your brother keeps borrowing your things without asking you first.

Causative *have* and *get*

Page 116

4 Study these example sentences and answer the questions.

a We're going to get the car cleaned.
b She had her dress made to measure.
c Yesterday I had my bike stolen.

1 When we use *have* or *get* like this, do we do something ourselves?
2 Do we use *have* or *get* when something unpleasant is done to us?
3 What form of the verb do we use after *have* or *get* + noun (or pronoun)?

5 Complete the sentences with the correct form of *have* or *get* and these verbs.

clean cut deliver repair test waste

1 It would have cost too much to .... the car .... so we bought a new one.
2 I'm tired of .... my time .... by customers who don't really want to buy anything.
3 I .... my hair .... if I can get an appointment.
4 I bought a vintage wedding dress. I must .... it .... before the wedding.
5 He has been complaining about his vision; he should .... his eyes ....
6 Sometimes I like to order my dinner on the app and .... it .... to my house.

6 Imagine you have a personal assistant. Say what you would have done for you.

Example: *I would have my schedule managed by my assistant.*

Parts 3 and 4

Page 134

1 27 **Complete the summary with these expressions. Then listen to check your answers.**

Right, we're agreed.
Well, are we both in favour of this one?
Which do you think would be best?
Let's leave it at that.
OK, those are the ones we'll go for.
So, which shall we choose?
Let's just agree to disagree.
Shall we go for those two, then?

To bring the conversation towards a conclusion, you can say **(1)** .... or **(2)** ...., and to try to reach a decision you can use expressions such as **(3)** .... or **(4)** .... If you both decide on the same one or ones, say something like **(5)** .... or **(6)** ...., but if you can't reach a decision, just say to your partner **(7)** .... or **(8)** ....

Quick steps to Part 3

- To keep the conversation going, say ***What about this one?*** or ***Let's go on to the next one*** to your partner.
- Remember that you have a full minute to make a decision together.

2 **Read the exam task instructions. How many things do you have to look at? What two things do you have to do?**

3 **Work in groups of three: one 'examiner' and two 'candidates'. The examiner reads the instructions to the candidates, then lets them talk for two minutes. The candidates listen to the examiner's instructions, then have one minute to do the task together. Include some expressions from Exercise 1 at the end of your conversation.**

Exam tip

Don't talk too long without letting your partner speak, or you may lose marks.

Exam task

I'd like you to talk about something together for about two minutes. **Some people say that online shopping is better than buying things in shopping centres and other people disagree. Here are some ideas** and a question for you to discuss. You now have some time to look at the task. Talk to each other about **whether online shopping is better than buying things in shopping centres.**

Now you have a minute to decide **which two are the most important reasons for your decision.**

Quick steps to Part 4

- You can ask the examiner to repeat a question by saying, for example: ***Sorry, I didn't catch that***, or ***Could you repeat that, please?***
- Show interest in what the other candidate is saying. For example, nod, or say *Yes* or *Right*.

4 **Stay in your groups for Speaking Part 4 and do the task.**

Exam task

Examiner: Ask both candidates three or four questions from this list.
Candidates: Discuss the examiner's questions with your partner, thinking of as many ideas as you can for each and giving full answers.

- Do you think it's true that online shopping has reduced shop sales? Why? / Why not?
- Why is it important to compare prices before buying something?
- Is it always better to go shopping with someone else? Why? / Why not?
- Do you think people too often buy things they don't really need? Why? / Why not?
- Which are the most popular shops where you live? Why?
- What do you most wish you could afford to buy? Why?
- Some people say that we won't need shops any more because one day we'll buy everything online. What do you think?
- Do you think it's better to buy things in small shops than in big supermarkets and department stores? Why? / Why not?
- Some people say it's never a good idea to borrow money in order to buy something. Do you agree? Why? / Why not?

5 **Change roles so that the examiner becomes a candidate, and repeat Exercises 3–5.**

Phrasal verbs with *out*

1 Use the context to work out the meaning of each of the underlined phrasal verbs.

1. They're my favourite jeans, even though they've got holes in I don't want to throw them out!
2. We'll be out of petrol if we don't find a garage soon.
3. I've been to three different supermarkets but they've all run out of pasta.
4. Our cat stays out at night, unless it's very cold.
5. I don't want to order a new phone online because I want to try it out first.
6. I don't often take out money from the bank because I use contactless.
7. The sale is so popular that they will sell out of most items in a few hours.
8. Very cheap clothes can often turn out to be poor quality.

2 Complete the sentences with the correct form of these verbs + *out*.

back breathe cross rush shut wear

1. When you're ill you .... germs.
2. I saw a man fall off his bike outside my house, so I .... to help him.
3. If you make a mistake, ... it .... and then write the correct word.
4. I get really angry when people .... of agreements they have already made.
5. I left my key in the house and now I'm ....
6. I've just been to the gym for the first time in weeks; now I'm ....

Part 4

3 Look at the exam task example and note down the grammatical changes that have been made in the answer.

4 Look quickly at questions 1–6 and decide what the focus of each question is. Then do the exam task.

Quick steps to Part 4

- If you can't give the whole answer to a question, write as much as you can. You might get one mark.
- Write only the missing words and the key word on your answer sheet, not the whole sentence.

Exam task

For questions **1–6**, complete the second sentence so that it has a similar meaning to the first sentence, using the word given. Do not change the word given. You must use between two and five words, including the word given. Here is an example (**0**):

Example:

0 I need to get someone to take my photo today.
HAVE
I need to ....HAVE MY PHOTO TAKEN........ today.

1 It's a pity we don't have any money left.
RUN
I wish we .... money.

2 I'm tired of that company sending me advertisements all the time.
WISH
I .... send me advertisements all the time.

3 It's a shame I didn't see that bargain in the sales.
ONLY
If .... that bargain in the sales.

4 I shouldn't have put those vintage clothes in the bin.
THROWN
I wish I .... those vintage clothes.

5 It was a real shock when the bank blocked my credit card.
HAD
It was a real shock when I .... by the bank.

6 Ethan regrets not completing that financial deal.
BACKED
Ethan wishes he .... that financial deal.

Exam tips

- Part 4 carries more marks than Parts 1–3 of Paper 1, so you may want to spend a little more time on key-word transformations than those other three parts.
- Make sure all your completed sentences make sense, and that you haven't made any spelling mistakes or used too many words.

Extreme adjectives

1 **You can make your writing more lively by using extreme adjectives. For example, instead of *interesting*, we might say *fascinating*. Match the adjectives in box A with the more extreme adjectives in box B.**

A

angry big bright pleasant silly strange suitable surprising

B

absurd bizarre breathtaking delightful furious ideal massive vivid

2 **Which of these extreme adjectives mean 'very good', and which mean 'very bad'?**

disgraceful dreadful exceptional fine outstanding severe stunning superb tremendous

3 **Complete the sentences with extreme adjectives from Exercises 1 and 2. In some cases more than one answer is possible.**

1 I was .... when I saw my sister wearing my new dress.
2 He often wears ties with .... colours, whereas I wear plain ones.
3 I find it quite .... that two peppers cost less than one.
4 I really enjoy helping people choose clothes that make them feel good, so working in a department store is my .... job.
5 We enjoyed our stay, particularly because of the .... view from our room.
6 I don't go to that shop any more because of the .... service.
7 There is a .... weather warning this weekend.
8 There are some .... clothes in that shop, but they are far too expensive.

Part 1 essay

Page 118

4 **Look at the exam task instructions and answer these questions.**

1 What is the situation?
2 What do you have to do?
3 Which points must you include?
4 Do you agree with the statement?

Quick steps to Part 1 essay

- Read the essay question and notes carefully to understand what you need to write about. Underline the key words.
- Remember you must write about the two points in the notes as well as your own idea.
- Make sure your ideas are relevant to the essay question and remember to include an introduction and a conclusion.

Exam task

In your English class you have been talking about the advantages and disadvantages of buying things online rather than getting them in the shops. Now, your English teacher has asked you to write an essay.

Write an essay using **all** the notes and give reasons for your point of view.

Shopping online is better than going to the shops. Do you agree?

Notes

Write about:

1 which is cheaper
2 which is easier
3 your own idea

Write your **essay** in **140–190** words. You must use grammatically correct sentences with accurate spelling and punctuation in an appropriate style.

5 **Read the model essay and answer these questions.**

1 Does the writer agree or disagree with the statement? In which paragraph?
2 Which paragraph discusses each of notes 1, 2 and 3? What reason is given in each case?
3 Which of the following does the writer use?
 a addition links **b** contrast links **c** adverbs of opinion or manner **d** extreme adjectives **e** causative *have*

Nowadays, more and more people are buying items online rather than in the high street, supermarket or shopping mall. Increasingly, websites are replacing department stores as places to shop. Not everyone, however, welcomes this change.

Going to the shops with friends is fun, and you can always try on clothes before you buy. On the other hand, being able to select from a massive range of products while sitting comfortably at home is an enormous advantage, as is having your purchases delivered.

Some people worry their purchases may arrive late, or even not at all. Also, any faulty items have to be returned by post. But you can often track goods from the supplier to your home, and a growing number of stores offer free return shipping.

There are certainly many excellent discount stores, and tremendous reductions can be obtained during the sales or on Black Friday. Online, though, you can find outstanding bargains from all over the world, with the added advantage that the sellers are open 24/7.

In conclusion, online shopping can be more convenient and less expensive, offering a far wider choice than traditional shops.

6 **Plan and write your essay. When you have finished, check your work as in Unit 1 Writing Exercise 5 on page 13.**

Exam tip

Use a wide range of vocabulary in your essay in order to improve your mark.

UNIT 1

1 Complete the sentences with the present simple or present continuous form of the verbs in brackets.

1 My friends .... (usually eat) at home, but this evening they .... (have) dinner in a restaurant.
2 This winter, I .... (stay) at a ski resort and I .... (work) in a local restaurant.
3 Hi Alex, I .... (wait) to see the doctor now, but there .... (seem) to be a delay.
4 The train .... (arrive) on time every morning, but we .... (always get) to work late!
5 Natalie .... (be) quite annoying. She .... (always complain) about something.
6 I still .... (have) a house in the mountains, but I .... (not stay) there very often.
7 This far north, it .... (get) dark very early at this time of year, so I .... (think) of spending the winter in Australia.

2 Add a prefix or suffix to these words and complete the sentences.

artist caution energy greed honest optimism polite

1 Luca always eats all of the biscuits. He's really ....
2 It's .... to take things from a shop without paying for them.
3 Alexia is so ....; her paintings are on display in the local gallery.
4 If someone helps you, it's .... not to say 'thank you'.
5 Paola is usually quite ...., but she doesn't feel like doing sports today.
6 You should be .... in crowded places; make sure your bag is fastened properly.
7 I'm feeling really ....; I'm sure we're going to win the game!

3 Complete the sentences with the correct form of the words in brackets.

1 Jane is quite .... (predict). She has the same thing for lunch every day.
2 I thanked my friends for being so .... (sympathy) when I had to go into hospital.
3 It's .... (reason) to expect people to do all your work for you.
4 The walk to the beach wasn't very .... (challenge) because it was all downhill.
5 It was .... (thought) of you to forget to buy her a birthday present.
6 To succeed in business, you have to be .... (decision) and not keep changing your mind.

4 Read the text below. Use the word given in capitals at the end of some of the lines to form a word that fits in the gap in the same line.

As houses and flats in cities become	
ever more expensive, even young	
people with **(1)** .... careers	**SUCCESS**
are sometimes finding that the only	
(2) .... solution is to move	**PRACTICE**
back in with their parents. When	
they decide to do this, the so-called	
'boomerang generation' are grateful	
for the **(3)** .... of their	**GENEROUS**
parents but sometimes they don't fully	
appreciate the **(4)** .... effect	**EMOTION**
of returning to the place where they	
grew up. As adults, they may find it hard	
to accept comments on what they wear	
or how they spend their free time, and	
their behaviour can become a little	
(5) .... They may accuse	**CHILD**
their parents of being **(6)**	**BOSS**
and eventually this can sometimes lead	
to silly **(7)** .... To avoid this,	**ARGUE**
both sides need to be **(8)**	**RESPECT**
of the other. The parents shouldn't	
forget that their children are now	
grown-ups, that for instance it is no	
longer **(9)** .... to tell them	**REASON**
what time they have to be home at	
night. The young adults, for their part,	
can greatly improve matters by being	
(10) .... around the house,	**HELP**
by tidying, cooking and cleaning rather	
more often than perhaps they did as	
teenagers.	

Now go to Practice Extra Unit 1

UNIT 2

1 Choose the correct options to complete the text.

Working as a waiter

It was three years ago, while I **(1)** *spent / was spending* a year abroad, that I first **(2)** *got / was getting* a job in a restaurant. I **(3)** *never worked / 'd never worked* as a waiter before and with so much to learn about the job I **(4)** *found / used to find* it quite hard during the first few weeks. I was on my feet all day and by the time my shift **(5)** *finished / had been finishing* at 10.30 pm my arms **(6)** *had ached / were aching* from carrying heavy plates all evening. There were also one or two other waiters who made my job even more difficult. One of them often **(7)** *was arriving / used to arrive* late and then, to make matters worse, he **(8)** *would disappear / had disappeared* somewhere every 15 minutes or so to check his phone. But once I **(9)** *was working / 'd been working* there for a while things gradually started to improve. I **(10)** *realised / was realising* that if I needed more cash I could work overtime, and I liked the fact that – unlike in many occupations – I could forget all about the job once I **(11)** *used to leave / 'd left* my place of work. I also had some fantastic co-workers, who **(12)** *would help / had helped* me out when I needed a break or if I **(13)** *didn't use to feel / wasn't feeling* well.

So I have some good memories of my time working there. When my contract finally ended I was glad I **(14)** *'d had / was having* the chance to make some great new friends, and I knew that while I **(15)** *was working / would work* there I acquired skills that in the future would enable me to work in any town or city I liked: anywhere there are restaurants.

2 Correct the mistakes in the fixed phrases.

1 As soon as Lara and Tim saw each other, it was love at first heart.
2 Sadly, I lost company with Lucas when he went to live in Australia.
3 Elisa is worried and she doesn't look at all on ease.
4 I know you're missing your family, so I'll stay and keep you companion.
5 It broke Josef's feelings when his girlfriend ended their relationship.
6 The boss depends on you, so don't let him leave you for granted.
7 Carl is always making stupid jokes and it keeps on my nerves.
8 I don't want to see anyone. Please go away and leave me only.

3 Complete the sentences with these words.

amazement eventually long meantime moment once

1 We're very early for our flight, so in the .... let's have a drink.
2 .... I'd climbed over the hill, I could finally see the finish line.
3 I looked up at the desert sky and, to my ...., I saw snow starting to fall.
4 .... the waiter brought our coffees, after we'd been waiting for over half an hour.
5 The .... I first saw Carmen, I knew we would get married.
6 The garden looked terrible, but before .... we were making good progress.

4 Complete the crossword with words from Unit 2.

Across
2 a person who judges (food)
7 quantity of food for one
8 something which is easy and simple
9 part of a meal or a container for serving food

Down
1 newly prepared or obtained (especially fruit)
3 type/style of cooking
4 original, not copied
5 clean and sanitary
6 unhealthy, fast (food)
7 (food) is sold or displayed in

Now go to Practice Extra Unit 2

UNIT 3

1 Complete the sentences with the correct form of the modals and verbs in brackets.

1 You .... (must / hit) your brother's computer, or you'll break it!
2 I'm not sure when Julia was going. She .... (may / leave) on Saturday.
3 We left on our bikes at the same time, but Ethan arrived before me. He .... (must / ride) very fast.
4 You .... (should / spend) all your pocket money on sweets! Now you can't buy that doll.
5 Laura is away in Switzerland all winter. You .... (can / see) her here yesterday!
6 Jan isn't answering the phone. He .... (might / take) his phone with him.
7 I made a lovely three-course dinner for Steve, but he felt ill so hardly ate anything. I .... (need / cook) so much.

2 Complete the second sentence so that it means the same as the first sentence. Use modal verbs.

1 It isn't necessary to check in if you already have a boarding pass.
If you already have a boarding pass, you don't ....
2 There's a possibility of heavy snow later today.
Later today it ....
3 I'm sure that David went home early.
David ....
4 It wasn't necessary to go to the meeting yesterday so I finished off some work at my desk.
I finished off some work at my desk because I ....
5 It was compulsory for passengers to wear seatbelts on the coach.
Passengers on the coach ....
6 It's a pity you didn't have breakfast before you set off.
Before you set off, you ....
7 It's possible that courier had the wrong address.
The courier ....

3 Decide which answer (A, B, C or D) best fits each gap.

1 I'm going on a long bus .... from Singapore to Kuala Lumpur.
A trip **B** travel **C** voyage **D** journey
2 We went .... around the lake and then through the woods.
A hiking **B** travelling **C** touring **D** hitchhiking
3 Although it's more expensive, the train is the most effective .... of transport.
A way **B** means **C** method **D** system
4 I am .... certain that he knows the way to the museum.
A slightly **B** quite **C** extremely **D** rather
5 I have had a very productive week, and I am now ahead of ....
A timetable **B** forecast **C** schedule **D** programme
6 Some tour .... can organise amazing holidays for even the smallest budgets.
A dealers **B** supervisors **C** operators **D** controllers

4 Fill in the gaps with suitable prepositions.

Blog

This week I'm in south-west Spain, at the Jerez Fair, a festival popular **(1)** .... both local people and visitors from around the world. I was already familiar **(2)** .... the Seville April Fair, so this year I came to Jerez instead **(3)** .... going there again. Compared **(4)** .... Seville this is a much smaller city, but in terms **(5)** .... the fantastic things to see and do it's very similar, and it has the same sort **(6)** .... exciting atmosphere, too. Something that makes it really attractive **(7)** .... visitors is that you can go into just about any of the big tents here: you're not obliged **(8)** .... belong to any particular family or club. So if you're capable **(9)** .... it, you can spend the whole night dancing and eating until the sun comes up. After a long weekend here, I'm definitely in need **(10)** .... a good long sleep!

Now go to Practice Extra Unit 3

UNIT 4

1 Complete the second sentence so that it has a similar meaning to the first sentence, using the word given. Do not change the word given. You must use between two and five words, including the word given.

1 The last time Bruce sang here was 20 years ago.
SUNG
Bruce .... 20 years.

2 Marta took up football last summer.
BEEN
Marta .... last summer.

3 Nathan was determined to pay for dinner.
INSISTED
Nathan .... dinner.

4 I should have gone to that party.
REGRET
I .... to that party.

5 Unfortunately, the heating in that theatre regularly breaks down.
KEEPS
Unfortunately, the heating in that theatre ....

6 That mountain is so difficult to climb, only the most experienced climbers can do it.
TOO
That mountain is ...., except the very best.

2 Put the words in the correct order to form questions. Then write your answers in full sentences.

1 have / the cinema / you / how many times / to / been?
2 been / how long / you / English / learning / have?
3 the TV / watching / the last hour / you / been / have / for?
4 spoken / you / to / just / your teacher / have?
5 lunch / yet / your / had / have / you?

3 Complete the questions with the *to* + infinitive or the *-ing* form of the verbs in brackets. Then answer these questions about yourself.

1 What kind of films do you enjoy .... (watch)?
2 Is there anything you've tried .... (do) recently, but failed?
3 What mustn't you forget .... (take) to your English lesson next week?
4 Is there anything you regret .... (not do) last year?
5 What have you managed .... (do), even though it was difficult?
6 What do you most dislike .... (study) in your English lesson?
7 Which other language would you like to learn .... (speak)?
8 Which song do you first remember .... (hear) when you were a child?

4 Complete the crossword with words from Unit 4.

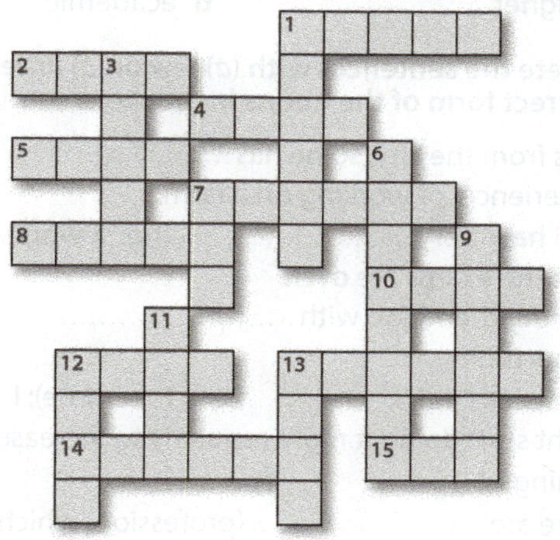

Across

1 short part of a film or play
2 played to an audience
4 painting, book, piece of music, etc.
5 of very high quality
7 marvellous
8 subject of a book
10 all the things which happen in a story
12 photograph, or picture in a film
13 person who reviews books, films, etc.
14 words of a song
15 pop concert (informal)

Down

1 words of a film or play
3 place where music is performed
6 holding your attention completely
7 place where a film is recorded
9 causing strong feelings
11 of very low quality
12 performed by one person only
13 all the actors in a film or play

Now go to Practice Extra Unit 4

UNIT 5

1 Decide which answer (A, B, C or D) best fits each gap.

1 The .... at this university are extremely interesting.
A classes B lectures C talks D speeches

2 My mother has a .... in physics from Cambridge University.
A title B degree C grade D mark

3 My .... gave a talk at the economics seminar I attended.
A tutor B trainer C coach D consultant

4 After I .... from university I took a gap year and went travelling.
A qualified B graduated C educated D succeeded

5 You must take a gondola ride to explore the city and .... all the sights.
A take on B take out C take in D take to

6 I'm having trouble finding a job since finishing university, partly because firms aren't .... new graduates.
A taking up B taking over C taking off D taking on

7 When I was an 18-year-old ...., I was excited about my first year in higher education.
A postgraduate B master C bachelor D undergraduate

8 After Carlos left .... school, he started work in a restaurant and now he is training to become a chef.
A higher B academic C secondary D superior

2 Complete the sentences with (a) *few* or (a) *little* and the correct form of the nouns in brackets.

1 Joe's from the city, so he has little experience (experience) of working on a farm.
2 We'll have very .... (homework) to do once the exams are over.
3 It's a dead-end job with .... (opportunity).
4 Last week I did .... (overtime); I might start doing it more regularly to increase my earnings.
5 There are .... (profession) which are as rewarding as medicine.
6 We have done .... (research) into the problem and we think we have found a solution.

3 Choose the correct option.

1 Here are your tickets for Wednesday. Your train *is leaving / leaves / will have left* at 9.30.
2 The train left at 4 pm; it's 6 pm and we're still two hours away! I *will travel / will have been travelling / will be travelling* for four hours by the time we arrive.
3 You can sit in Tina's chair while she's away. She *won't mind / isn't going to mind / wouldn't have minded.*
4 *I'm helping / I'll help / I'm going to help* you make dinner if you like.
5 I can't come to the party because *I'm seeing / I'll see / I see* a film at the cinema tonight.
6 This time next week *I'll hike / I'll be hiking / I'm hiking* around Lake Tahoe.

4 Use the word given in capitals at the end of some of the lines to form a word that fits in the gap in the same line.

Choosing a future

At 16 I had no idea what I wanted to do in life. I
was a good **(1)** .... so naturally, like **GUITAR**
so many other teenagers, I dreamt of becoming a
professional **(2)** .... But even at **MUSIC**
that age I realised that was unlikely ever to happen.
Becoming an **(3)** .... of a big **EMPLOY**
firm didn't appeal to me, and neither did taking
out an enormous **(4)** .... to go to **LEND**
university, with no guarantee at all that after my
(5) .... I would actually get a good **GRADUATE**
job. So in the end I decided to set up my own online
business, working from home.
The work, which often keeps me busy seven days a
week, was very **(6)** .... at first, but **DEMAND**
the business is starting to become quite
(7) .... and I now feel it was the **PROFIT**
right **(8)** .... to go it alone. **DECIDE**

Now go to Practice Extra Unit 5

UNIT 6

1 Complete the crossword with words from Unit 6.

Across
1 place where football is played
3 place where people run
7 person who goes sailing
9 pain over an area of the body
11 person who cares for ill people
12 dark area on skin caused by injury
14 place where tennis is played
16 person being treated by a doctor
17 place where golf is played

Down
2 object worn by a rider
4 person who does athletics
5 broken bone
6 injury caused by twisting
7 the ability to see
8 person who rides a bicycle
10 injury, such as a cut
12 piece of equipment used by a baseball player
13 place where people go skiing
15 place where people do boxing

2 Complete the sentences with relative pronouns, adding commas where necessary. In which of your answers could you leave out the relative pronoun?

1 In 2000, ...when.......... I was born, very few people ....who/that.......... lived in my village did any sports.
2 This finger, ... is a funny shape, is the one .... I fractured.
3 Mark is the boy .... father gave a lecture on climate change .... was really interesting.
4 That's the library .... students .... study business and economics normally go.
5 He's the footballer .... was injured in the accident .... I was telling you about.
6 The estate agent .... I spoke to said the house has been sold, ... is disappointing.

3 Read the text below and think of the word which best fits each gap. Use only one word in each gap.

Eating and drinking well for exercise

Anyone **(1)** .... aim is to get fitter and stronger needs to have a healthy, varied diet.

When you exercise, your body **(2)** .... up more energy, **(3)** .... means you need to eat more food. In **(4)** .... to provide that extra energy, you should eat plenty of rice, bread, pasta, fruit and vegetables. It's best, though, not to have a large meal less than three hours before exercising **(5)** .... that you avoid any stomach ache.

There may be times **(6)** .... you are exercising that you start to feel tired for no apparent reason, and it may be because you're becoming dehydrated. In **(7)** .... words, you don't have enough water in your body. So **(8)** .... not to suffer from this, you should drink more water than usual before, during and after exercise. Don't wait until you feel thirsty!

4 Complete the second sentence so that it has a similar meaning to the first sentence, using the word given. Do not change the word given. You must use between two and five words, including the word given.

1 I believe Grace and her boyfriend aren't together any more.
UP
Grace and her boyfriend ...., I believe.

2 Erica spent her childhood in Rome, but lives in Milan now.
GREW
Erica, ... in Rome, lives in Milan now.

3 Mike got the vaccine to avoid getting sick.
SO
Mike got the vaccine .... get sick.

4 The boy refused to collect the rubbish lying on the ground.
WAS
The boy refused to pick .... lying on the ground.

5 Some people say they're busy so that they don't have to help.
IN
Some people say they're busy .... to help.

6 At our local hospital there is a heart specialist called Dr Valentine.
WHOSE
At our local hospital there is a heart specialist .... Dr Valentine.

Now go to Practice Extra Unit 6

UNIT 7

1 **Read the text below and think of the word which best fits each gap. Use only one word in each gap.**

The weather in 2050

One of the main effects of global warming is that there will be more extreme weather events such as hurricanes, heatwaves and rainstorms (1) .... at present. In wetter parts of the world it will rain (2) .... heavily than now, while in dry or desert areas there will be even (3) .... rain than there is now. Although the increase in temperatures in regions such as the Caribbean or East Asia will probably not be (4) .... great (5) .... elsewhere, other places are likely to heat up (6) .... more quickly. By 2050, London is expected to be (7) .... warm (8) .... present-day Barcelona, while Madrid and Rome, with predicted summer temperature increases of 6.4 °C and 5.3 °C respectively, may well become (9) .... hot (10) .... North African cities such as Fez are now.

2 **Decide which word or phrase (A, B, C or D) best fits each gap.**

1 Everyone in this city is in .... reducing air pollution.
A hope of B favour of C view of D case of

2 Scientists say the greatest threat to life on our planet is .... warming.
A carbon B renewable C global D fossil

3 Creating a new lake here sounds a good idea but in .... I don't think it'll work.
A progress B all C particular D practice

4 The forest fires are still burning, ... the rain that has recently fallen.
A although B whereas C despite D while

5 The results of the town council elections will be announced in ....
A short B due course C these days D future

6 We'll greatly reduce air and water pollution if we introduce .... farming methods.
A sustainable B processed C intensive
D refined

7 Plastic packaging is still used, ... the environmental harm it causes is well known.
A nevertheless B in spite of C in contrast
D even though

8 Unless the sea level stops rising, the future of these small islands must be in ....
A doubt B short C brief D trouble

3 **Make questions with the given conditional form of the verbs. Then answer these questions.**

1 What / happen / to the oceans / if / we / not / protect / them? (first conditional)
2 If / you / not / have / a car / you / miss / it? (second conditional)
3 Do you think / you / enjoy / your last holiday / more / if / you / have / more time off? (third conditional)
4 Where / you / go / next winter / if / be / very cold? (first conditional)
5 What / you / most / like / to see / if / you / go / to Australia? (second conditional)
6 If / it / sunny / last week / you / go / to the seaside / then? (third conditional)
7 What / life / be / like / today / if / we / not / invent / the internet? (mixed conditional)

4 **Complete the second sentence so that it has a similar meaning to the first sentence, using the word given. Do not change the word given. You must use between two and five words, including the word given.**

1 This city is rather less polluted than it used to be.
SO
This city isn't .... it used to be.

2 It's a good thing we remembered to bring an umbrella or we'd be very wet now.
FORGOTTEN
We'd be very wet now if .... to bring an umbrella.

3 Many scientists predict that rising sea levels will eventually cause a lot of damage.
TERM
Many scientists predict that rising sea levels will cause a lot of damage ....

4 I was very cold because I forgot to take my coat with me.
REMEMBERED
If .... my coat with me, I wouldn't have been so cold.

5 In your situation, Ben, I'd relocate to somewhere warmer.
YOU
I'd relocate to somewhere warmer ...., Ben.

6 I couldn't have finished the project without their help.
THEY
I couldn't have finished the project .... me.

Now go to Practice Extra Unit 7

UNIT 8

1 **Complete the crossword with words from Unit 8.**

Across

1 the symbol # on a keyboard
4 stop working suddenly (computer)
7 look at information on the internet
8 problem in a computer program
9 smallest living part of an animal or plant
11 change back (something on a computer)
14 use a computer program
15 put electricity into something
16 post information on Twitter

Down

2 see information using a computer
3 an online record of your thoughts
5 smallest possible unit of an element
6 spend the winter sleeping
7 extra copy of computer information
10 new information
12 information stored in a computer
13 at a greater distance from the centre

2 **Complete the sentences with these words to form collocations.**

access	charge	exploration	outer	times	video

1 Spacecraft can fly over 20 .... faster than aeroplanes.
2 If I don't .... my mobile phone, the battery will be completely flat soon.
3 Scientists have discovered a planet in .... space that in some ways is like Earth.
4 It's usually impossible for aeroplane passengers to .... the internet.
5 I'm abroad, but I can see and talk to my family in an internet café by .... conferencing.
6 The first stage in space .... , over 40 years ago, was when Sputnik 1 went into space.

3 **Fill in the gaps with *a/an* or *the*, or leave the gap blank if no article can be used.**

I can't imagine **(1)** .... life without my phone. I use it all **(2)** .... day Monday to Friday and at **(3)** .... weekend, whether I'm **(4)** .... home, in **(5)** .... classroom or out somewhere with **(6)** .... friends. Apart from making **(7)** .... calls, texting and keeping **(8)** .... eye on my social media pages, I like to keep up with **(9)** .... latest news from around **(10)** .... world, check out some of **(11)** .... most interesting videos on **(12)** .... YouTube and maybe play some computer games. Of course, **(13)** .... internet is incredibly useful when I have **(14)** .... homework to do. I'm currently doing a lot of **(15)** .... research into my favourite subject, **(16)** .... chemistry, and one day I hope to work as **(17)** .... scientist. Without doubt, **(18)** .... mobile phone is one of **(19)** .... greatest inventions ever – especially for **(20)** .... young.

4 **Complete the second sentence so that it has a similar meaning to the first sentence, using the word given. Do not change the word given. You must use between two and five words, including the word given.**

1 It's possible that they weren't informed of the problem.
MIGHT
They .... informed of the problem.

2 The company expects an increase in sales next year.
EXPECTED
An increase in sales .... next year.

3 Now scientists suggest that humans will land on Mars within our lifetime.
IT
Now .... humans will land on Mars within our lifetime.

4 Researchers believe that learning a second language can be good for your brain.
BELIEVED
It .... learning a second language can be good for your brain.

5 Many people say that the first video game was invented in the 1960s.
BEEN
The first video game .... invented in the 1960s.

6 They are making changes to the network so that it is faster.
CHANGED
The network .... so that it is faster.

Now go to Practice Extra Unit 8

UNIT 9

1 **Match the words in box A with the words in box B. Complete the sentences with six of the compound nouns.**

A

camera current drama fake gossip investigative remote set soap talent

B

affairs column control designer journalist news opera operator series show

1 Liam deserved to win the .... because he was the best performer.
2 That story about finding life on the moon sounds like .... to me.
3 I don't read serious news stories; I just like the ....
4 A good .... can uncover the truth.
5 Have you seen the new .... on TV? It will have you on the edge of your seat.
6 The .... was very skilled; she took brilliant close-up shots of the runners crossing the finish line.

2 **Read the dialogue. Then complete the reported speech version.**

Orla: You look sleepy, Rory.
Rory: Yes, I am.
Orla: Why's that?
Rory: I didn't get to sleep until very late last night.
Orla: Did you stay up watching a TV series again?
Rory: Yes, I did.
Orla: Why don't you switch off earlier?
Rory: I can't. I'm really enjoying the historical one I told you about last week.
Orla: Perhaps you can watch just a couple of episodes each evening?
Rory: OK, I'll try that.

Orla told Rory that **(1)** .... sleepy, and he said **(2)** .... When she asked him why that **(3)** .... he explained that **(4)** .... to sleep until very late the **(5)** .... night. Orla then asked him **(6)** .... up watching a TV series again and he said **(7)** .... She asked him why **(8)** .... off earlier, but he replied that **(9)** .... He said **(10)** .... the historical one **(11)** .... about the week **(12)** .... She then suggested **(13)** .... just a couple of episodes each evening. He said **(14)** .... that.

3 **Complete the second sentence so that it has a similar meaning to the first sentence, using the word given. Do not change the word given. You must use between two and five words, including the word given.**

1 'I'll pass on your CV to my producer,' said Ella.
PROMISED
Ella .... my CV to her producer.

2 'Keep it clean or it will get infected,' the doctor told him.
WARNED
The doctor .... keep it clean to prevent infection.

3 'What's the height of the mountain?' the reporter asked.
HIGH
The reporter wanted to know ....

4 'I'm sorry I turned off the news,' my brother said.
APOLOGISED
My brother .... the news.

5 'Have any good shows been added to the streaming service?' said Amber.
ASKED
Amber .... any good shows had been added to the streaming service.

6 'I never wanted to be famous,' Taylor told the interviewer.
HE
Taylor told the interviewer .... famous.

4 **Read the text below. Use the word given in capitals at the end of some of the lines to form a word that fits in the gap in the same line.**

THE ROLE OF NEWSPAPERS

The most obvious role of newspapers is to inform, by providing **(1)** .... with a wide range of facts and figures supported by photos, charts and **(2)** .... They also aim to educate, by going into news stories in far greater **(3)** .... than is possible on television or social media. A good newspaper also provides **(4)** .... with its political cartoons, crossword puzzles and humorous columns, as well as making **(5)** .... on its review pages for what to read, watch and listen to. Some say the rise of online reporting has made the press less **(6)** .... in present-day society, but newspaper **(7)** .... reply that the same was said many years ago when TV news first became popular, yet printed **(8)** .... have remained a vital source of news.

(1)	**READ**
(2)	**ILLUSTRATE**
(3)	**DEEP**
(4)	**ENTERTAIN**
(5)	**RECOMMEND**
(6)	**POWER**
(7)	**EDIT**
(8)	**PUBLISH**

Now go to Practice Extra Unit 9

UNIT 10

1 Choose the correct option.

1 They've sold out of the top I liked. I wish I *bought* / *'d bought* it last week.
2 I wish I *am* / *were* better at sport.
3 If only I *waited* / *'d waited* for the sale. I could have got that jacket for half the price.
4 I wish I *didn't* / *don't* have to go to the supermarket, but they don't deliver to my area.
5 It's quite busy where we live in the city centre. I wish we *would live* / *lived* somewhere quieter.
6 You've lost my favourite hat! I wish I *didn't* / *hadn't* lent it to you.
7 If only someone *will* / *would* come to the shop with me. I hate shopping alone.
8 I wish my parents *didn't* / *wouldn't* buy me clothes for my birthday. They don't have very good taste.

2 Complete the second sentence so that it has a similar meaning to the first sentence, using the word given. Do not change the word given. You must use between two and five words, including the word given.

1 Let's order a pizza and ask them to deliver it here.
GET
Let's order a pizza and .... here.
2 I should have walked around in those trainers before buying them.
OUT
I wish .... those trainers before buying them.
3 That horrible music they play here is really annoying.
WISH
I .... play that horrible music here.
4 The hairdresser at the shopping centre did my hair.
HAD
I .... the shopping centre.
5 I really should have listened to your advice.
ONLY
If .... to your advice.
6 The store doesn't have any of those T-shirts left, which is a shame.
OUT
I wish the store .... those T-shirts.

3 Write replies to the comments. Use *should*, *how about* or *why don't you* + causative *have* or *get* to give advice.

1 'My printer's not working.'
You should have it mended. / Why don't you have it mended? / How about having it mended?
2 'This is a lovely painting.'
3 'I can't find a suit I like for the wedding.'
4 'I dropped sauce on my coat.'
5 'My hair is getting too long.'
6 'My eyes feel sore after reading.'

4 Complete the crossword with words from Unit 10.

Across
1 one sock is an … of clothing
4 50% … means it's half the usual price
8 person who trades in something such as art
9 the opposite of tight
10 a designer … is a make of expensive clothes
13 something that is in … is available in a shop
16 clothes that are … are not for formal wear
17 be exactly the same colour or type as something else
18 you can use a … card to buy things

Down
2 large, covered shopping area for pedestrians
3 something on sale for less than its real value
5 not real
6 trendy
7 you push this round a supermarket
8 money that you owe somebody
11 strong in colour
12 make a product available for the first time
13 number of things sold
14 type of product made by a particular company
15 simple, opposite of patterned

Now go to Practice Extra Unit 10

UNIT 2

Exam task

3

4

UNIT 7

Exam task 1

1

2

UNIT 7

Exam task 2

3

4

UNIT 1

Present tenses

Present simple

The present simple is used

1 for describing routine actions or habits:
*Before breakfast, I **go** online to check my emails.* (It's my daily routine.)
*In this business, we **don't take** holidays in summer.* (Refers to every summer, not just this one.)

2 to show that a situation is permanent:
*His girlfriend **teaches** at a local primary school.* (It's a permanent job.)
*My grandparents **live** just around the corner from here.* (It's their permanent home.)

3 when something is always true, or a definite fact:
*In autumn, the trees in my garden **lose** their leaves.* (This always happens.)
*Water **freezes** at zero degrees Celsius.* (It's a scientific fact.)

Present continuous

The present continuous is used

1 to describe an action which is happening right at this moment:
*The children **are sleeping**, so we can't talk too loudly.* (They are sleeping right now.)
*Where **are** you **calling** from?* (We are on the phone right now.)

2 for a situation which is temporary, and will not last permanently:
*I**'m doing** a training course at work at the moment.* (For a fixed period, not forever.)
*We**'re staying** with Jo while we look for a flat to rent.* (We'll leave Jo's home when we find a flat.)

3 when talking about changes or developing situations:
*The number of road accidents **is increasing** year by year.* (The situation is getting worse.)
*Shopping online **is becoming** the most popular way to buy books.* (It's developing.)

4 with *always*, when we want to show that we are annoyed or surprised by an action:
*My brother **is always borrowing** my laptop without asking me.* (This irritates me!)
*That new student **is always asking** the strangest questions in class!* (It's surprising.)

5 for **future arrangements** (see Grammar reference Unit 5):
*I**'m having** dinner with Amy tomorrow night.*

The present continuous cannot normally be used with **stative verbs**, which describe a state (such as existing or feeling), as opposed to an action (such as walking or eating).

Some common stative verbs are: *agree, believe, belong, consider, consist, cost, disagree, exist, hate, have, know, like, love, matter, mean, need, own, prefer, realise, remain, remember, seem, suppose, think, understand, want.* For example:

*This car **belongs** to my uncle.* ✓ (state of possession)
~~*This car **is belonging** to my uncle.*~~
*That sound **doesn't exist** in my language.* ✓ (state of existence)
~~*That sound **isn't existing** in my language.*~~

However, some stative verbs can be used in the present continuous when they describe actions:

*John can't answer the phone because he**'s having** a shower.* ✓ (action, not state)
~~*John can't answer the phone because he **has** a shower.*~~
***Does** Claire's new apartment **have** a shower?* ✓ (state, not action)
~~***Is** Claire's new apartment **having** a shower?*~~

Present simple in time clauses

When we are talking about the future, the present simple must be used after time expressions like *when:*

*I'll send her an email when I **get** home.* ✓ (time clause after *when*)
~~*I'll send her an email when I **will** get home.*~~

Other expressions which are followed by the present simple are: *after, as soon as, before, by the time, next time, once, until.*

1 Choose the correct options to complete the text. Sometimes there may be more than one possible answer.

Many people **1** *take up / are taking up* running these days. Running is great because it **2** *helps / is helping* our general fitness. When we run, we **3** *use up / are using up* more energy than when we **4** *walk / are walking*. I **5** *go / am going* running regularly, and I like to run after work to help me relax. At the moment, I **6** *train / 'm training* for a race, so I **7** *spend / 'm spending* a lot of time out running.

2 **Complete the sentences with either the present simple or the present continuous form of the verbs in brackets.**

1 I .... for a long walk three times a week after work. (go)
2 I .... my friend Max at the cinema tonight. (meet)
3 It really annoys me when people .... to my texts. (not reply)
4 Cycling .... a more popular way to travel around cities. (become)
5 Can you call back later? Fred .... his dad in the garden at the moment. (help)
6 I'll order a takeaway for dinner. .... you .... Indian food or Chinese food? (prefer)

UNIT 2

Past tenses

Past simple

The past simple is used for past events or actions:

*He **closed** the front door, **locked** it, and **set** off to work.*
*In the end, we **decided** not to move house.*

The past simple is often used with a specific time:

*The previous director **retired** in November.*
*She **wrote** her first novel in 2001.*

Past continuous

The past continuous is used for a continued action which was happening when another action took place:

*We arrived at the theatre just as the show **was starting**.*

In many cases, the continued action is interrupted:

*When he **called**, **I was watching** my favourite soap opera.* (His call interrupted me.)

The past continuous is also often used to set the scene at the beginning of a story:

*It **was raining** hard and an icy wind **was blowing**. Alex knew the journey would be impossible.*

The past continuous cannot normally be used with stative verbs:

*My grandparents rarely **disagreed** with each other.* ✓
~~*My grandparents **were** rarely **disagreeing** with each other.*~~

For a list of common stative verbs, see Grammar reference Unit 1: present tenses.

1 **Choose the correct options to complete the sentences.**

1 While I *listened / was listening* to music, my brother was playing in the garden.
2 My friends *often phoned / were often phoning* me in the evenings.
3 While I was baking a cake, I *realised / was realising* that the recipe was wrong.
4 It was a beautiful day. The sun *shone / was shining* and the birds *sang / were singing*.
5 Simone Biles *won / was winning* four gold medals for the USA at the Rio Olympics.

2 **Complete the sentences with the past simple or past continuous form of the verbs in brackets.**

1 While I .... (pack) for my holiday, I .... (find) some old sunglasses.
2 As I .... (leave) the restaurant, I .... (realise) that I'd left my scarf behind.
3 While Mark .... (practise) the piano, his sister .... (watch) TV.
4 When we .... (hear) the protests, we all .... (stop) what we .... (do) and .... (look) out of the window.
5 My computer .... (crash) while I .... (write) my essay.

Past perfect

The past perfect is used to show that an action happened earlier than another past action:

*The police were unaware that the attacker **had** already **escaped**.* (The attacker escaped before the police realised.)

Sometimes it is not necessary to use the past perfect if it is very clear which action happened first:

*After we **finished** eating, we played cards.*

Past perfect continuous

The past perfect continuous is used for a continued action which happened before another past action:

***We'd been working** so hard that we decided to take a break.* (We took a break after a continued period of work.)

The past perfect continuous can be used to show how long an action continued up to a certain point in the past:

*When the search began, the girl **had** already **been missing** for two days.* (She was missing for two days before the search began.)

3 **Complete the sentences with the past perfect simple or continuous form of the verbs in brackets.**

1 We were furious, because we .... (wait) for over two hours before the train arrived at the station.
2 She .... (write) poetry for over three years before she finally decided to try to get some of her poems published.

3 Martha's children devoured the cake that she .... (bake) only an hour ago.
4 I must have dropped the letter that she .... (hand) to me.
5 When they got home, they discovered that their babysitter .... (already read) their toddler a bedtime story.
6 When I finally reached the front of the queue, I found out that my sister .... (pick up) the tickets an hour earlier.

4 Complete the sentences with the past perfect simple or continuous form of the verbs in brackets.

1 The waiter, who was under a lot of pressure, brought a starter that I .... (not order).
2 I had great difficulty recalling the poem I .... (try) to memorise the previous night.
3 The children excitedly collected the fruit that .... (fall) from the trees.
4 She .... (play) tennis all afternoon when we glimpsed her briefly as we walked past the park.
5 I .... (read) a chapter of my book every evening for over two weeks, so I was upset when I forgot to take my book with me on holiday.
6 He .... (live) in Paris all his life and was reluctant to move, even when he got married.

used to / didn't use to

The structure *used to* + infinitive is used for repeated actions, habits or states in the past:

*Before the internet, people **used to write** letters a lot more.*

The negative form of this structure is *didn't use to*:

*We **didn't use to have** a dishwasher in our old house.*

Used to is not normally used with time expressions which specify the duration of the action:

*I **smoked** for ten years, but then I gave up.* ✓
~~*I **used to smoke** for ten years, but then I gave up.*~~

Would + infinitive can also be used for actions and habits in the past:

*When I was a child, my dad **would** always **tell** me a story at bedtime.*

However, *would* cannot be used to talk about past states:

*This collection of paintings **used to belong** to a rich family.* ✓
~~*This collection of paintings **would belong** to a rich family.*~~
(*Belong* is a stative verb.)

5 Complete the sentences with the correct form of *used to* and the verbs in brackets.

1 I .... eating spinach when I was a child, but now I love it! (– / enjoy)
2 Her friend .... judo, but now she trains twice a week. (– / do)
3 They .... hours playing football in the park. (+ / spend)
4 My mother .... a beautiful grand piano. (+ / own)
5 .... she .... in touch with her relatives before they emigrated to New Zealand? (? / keep)
6 I .... the sound of fireworks when I was young. (– / like)

6 Tick the correct sentences. Correct the sentences with mistakes.

1 My dad would play in a band before he got married.
2 I would work in a hotel for many years in my youth.
3 When she was younger, she would enjoy playing the flute and would practise every day.
4 I would live in London near Hyde Park until I left to go to university in Nottingham.
5 When I was a kid I would play in the park with my friends until it was quite dark and my mother called me to go in.
6 I didn't use to enjoy the taste of seafood, until I had the chance to eat some fresh mussels in Scotland last year.

UNIT 3

Modal verbs

ability

To express ability in the present, we use *can* or *be able to*:

*On a clear day, you **can see** the mountains from my balcony.*
*I**'m not able to read** without my glasses.*

For general ability in the past, we use *could* or *be able to*:

*The sea was warm, so we **were able to swim** all year round.*
*In the old days you **could buy** everything at the local market.*

However, when we are talking about ability on one specific occasion in the past, we only use *be able to*, not *could*:

*Luckily we didn't get lost because Alice **was able to get** directions from someone.* ✓ (specific occasion)
~~*Luckily we didn't get lost because Alice **could get** directions from someone.*~~

1 **Complete the sentences with a modal verb from the box. One of the modal verbs is used twice.**

can	can't	could	couldn't	was able to

1 .... you ride a bike when you were five?
2 He .... get to the party on time yesterday, because his car broke down.
3 He's absolutely amazing – he's only seven and he .... speak five languages, including Greek.
4 She was relieved, because she .... find a taxi and get to the airport on time.
5 I've searched everywhere for my glasses, but I .... find them anywhere.
6 I .... lift this box – it's so heavy! Could you help me, please?

2 **Tick the correct sentences. Correct the sentences with mistakes.**

1 I wasn't able translate the text into German, because it contained too many unfamiliar expressions.
2 When the plumber showed me the bill for the repair, I didn't have enough money on me to pay for it, but fortunately I could use my credit card this time.
3 Thank you for your offer to lend me some money, but I am afraid I couldn't accept it.
4 When you finally move into your new house, you'll be able to decorate it as you wish.
5 I could taste and smell the onions for hours after the meal.
6 She could run the marathon in less than three hours, although she had not been training regularly for ten days.

possibility

To say that something is possible, we use *could*, *may* or *might*:

Without treatment, your health ***could be*** *at risk.*
Let's have dinner indoors because it ***might rain*** *later.*
I ***may be able*** *to join you later, but I can't say for sure.*

We use *could have*, *may have* or *might have* to talk about possibility in the past:

She ***could have let*** *us know about the change, but she forgot.*
They ***may have missed*** *the ferry because the traffic was bad.*
This place ***might have been*** *important in ancient times, but experts are not sure.*

impossibility

To say that something is impossible in the present, we use *can't*:

You ***can't cross*** *the river here because the bridge is closed.*

We use *can't have* or *couldn't have* to talk about impossibility in the past:

You ***can't have seen*** *James in town today because he was at home all day.*
She ***couldn't have won*** *the competition without her family's support.*

certainty

When we are certain about something, we use *must*:

You ***must be*** *exhausted after walking such a long way.*

To talk about certainty in the past, we use *must have*:

They ***must have been*** *terribly worried when their children didn't come home.*

obligation

To say that something is obligatory in the present, we often use *must* when the obligation is by the speaker:

Everyone ***must report*** *to me before they go home.*

When the obligation comes from outside, we often use *have to*:

The new law means that we ***have to pay*** *more for public transport.*

For both kinds of obligation in the past, we use *had to*:

We ***had to come*** *home by train because the airport was closed.*

no obligation / unnecessary

When there is no obligation to do something, or when something is unnecessary, we use *don't have to*, *don't need to* or *needn't*:

You ***don't have to bring*** *your own towel because everything is provided.*
You ***don't need to tell*** *me what happened. I saw it all for myself.*
We're going to eat out tonight, so you ***needn't cook*** *for us.*

We use *didn't need to* when something was unnecessary in the past, and did not happen:

We ***didn't need to pay*** *because the concert was free.* (We didn't pay because this was unnecessary.)

However, when we want to say that something unnecessary has happened, we use *needn't have*:

We ***needn't have hurried*** *because the train left late anyway.* (We hurried, but this was unnecessary.)

permission

To say that something is allowed, we use *can*:

You ***can park*** *outside the shop on weekdays.*

May is also used, but it is more formal:

***May** I **ask** where you bought that beautiful dress?*

To talk about something that was allowed in the past, we use *could*:

*When I was a child, we **could play** outside as much as we wanted.*

When something is not allowed, we use *can't* or *mustn't*:

*I'm sorry, but you **can't sit** at this table because it's reserved.*
*You **mustn't start** writing until the teacher says so.*

For things that were not allowed in the past, we use *couldn't*:

*In the old days, people **couldn't travel** abroad without a visa.*

3 Choose the correct options to complete the sentences.

1 If you don't pay attention to your skiing instructor, you *could / can* have an accident.
2 You *can't have / might have* passed the maths test, because you didn't do any revision!
3 Do we *have to / must* get up now?
4 I *must / have* try to argue less often with my younger brother.
5 The police warned me that I *can / must* never drive without insurance again.
6 When I was a child, people *couldn't / mustn't* access the internet with their mobile phones.
7 We didn't *need to / must* queue to get into the concert because we got to the venue really early.
8 You *can / must* buy lunch in the canteen or bring a sandwich if you prefer.

the right thing to do

When we want to say that something is the right or the wrong thing to do, we use *should/shouldn't* or *ought/ought not to*:

*You **shouldn't eat** too many sweets when you are on a diet.*
*People **ought to be** more careful about saving energy in the home.*

The past forms are *should have* and *ought to have*:

*You **should have asked** me before borrowing my bike.*

4 Find and correct the mistake in each sentence below.

1 She shouldn't have ate all those crisps.
2 They should arrived by now.
3 I should have listen to my friend's advice.
4 People ought waste less food.
5 You should to ask your teacher for help if you don't understand the question.

Adverbs of degree

These adverbs can be used with verbs, adjectives and other adverbs.

When we want to say 'a little', we can use *slightly* or *a bit* (less formal):

*I'm feeling **a bit** tired, so I'm going to bed now.*

When we want to say 'a lot' or 'very', we can use *absolutely, completely, extremely, really* or *totally*:

*He drove **extremely** fast all the way home.*

When we mean 'more than a little, but less than a lot', we can use *fairly, pretty, rather* or *quite*:

*We were **quite** surprised when she told us the news, even though we knew something was wrong.*

However, we normally only use *rather* with negative or surprising ideas:

*I must say I was **rather** disappointed with your exam results.*

With adjectives such as *right, sure* and *different*, ***quite*** means 'completely':

*Are you **quite** sure that you want me to tell Alex about this?*

With gradable adjectives and adverbs such as *good, happy* or *hard*, we use *extremely, fairly, quite, rather, really, slightly* or *very*:

*She was **very** angry when she heard what he had done.* ✓

(*Angry* is a gradable adjective, which means that it can be used to describe different levels of anger.)

~~*She was **absolutely** angry when she heard what he had done.*~~

With stronger (ungradable) adjectives and adverbs such as *wonderful, impossible* or *delighted*, we use *absolutely, completely, really* or *totally*:

*She was **absolutely** furious when she heard what he had done.* ✓

~~*She was **very** furious when she heard what she had done.*~~

(*Furious* is an ungradable adjective, which means that it describes an extreme state of anger which cannot have different levels.)

5 Put the words in order to make sentences.

1 a snack / I'm / going to have / before dinner. / quite hungry, / I'm / so
2 extremely nervous / the job. / I was offered / I was / but / about / in the end / my interview,
3 was / but / computer game / I bought it / rather expensive, / for my niece / The / nonetheless.
4 was / when I realised / he had lied / absolutely furious / I / that / to me.
5 behaviour / the party / very / Her / angry. / at / made me

UNIT 4

Verbs followed by *to* + infinitive or *-ing*

The following verbs are followed by *to* + infinitive: *agree, appear, choose, decide, expect, hope, learn, manage, offer, promise, refuse, seem, tend, threaten, want*:

*We **managed to finish** the report by the end of the day.*

The following verbs are followed by the *-ing* form: *admit, avoid, bother, deny, dislike, enjoy, finish, get round to, imagine, insist on, keep (on), mind, miss, suggest*:

*I don't know anyone who **enjoys doing** housework.*

Some verbs can be followed by either *to* + infinitive or the *-ing* form, with no change in meaning. These verbs include *begin, continue* and *start*:

*You may **begin writing** as soon as I say so.*

*You may **begin to write** as soon as I say so.* (The meaning is the same in both examples.)

Other verbs can be followed by either *to* + infinitive or the *-ing* form, but with a change in meaning. These verbs include *forget, go on, regret, remember, stop* and *try*:

*I **forgot to talk** to her about it.* (I didn't talk to her because I forgot.)

*I'll never **forget talking** to her about it.* (I talked to her and now I won't forget.)

*He **went on to read** a book.* (He was doing something else and then started reading a book.)

*He **went on reading** a book.* (He continued to read the same book as before.)

I ***regret to tell*** you that nobody survived the fire. (I am sorry that I am giving you this bad news.)

*I **regret telling** you that nobody survived the fire.* (I told you, and now I wish I had not told you.)

*Please **remember to switch** the lights off.* (You shouldn't forget to do this.)

*I **remember switching** the lights off.* (I switched the lights off and I remember this fact.)

*I **stopped asking** him about his son.* (I didn't ask any more questions about his son.)

*I **stopped to ask** him about his son.* (I stopped what I was doing because I wanted to ask him about his son.)

*Have you **tried changing** your diet?* (Have you experimented with eating different foods?)

*Have you **tried to change** your diet?* (Have you made an effort to change what you eat?)

1 Tick the correct sentences. Correct the sentences with mistakes.

1. He decided buy the house even though it needed to be renovated.
2. I hope to continue to improve my level of spoken English.
3. They promised visiting me in Spain after I moved there.
4. She refused to help him with his homework.
5. She expected not getting the job because the interview hadn't gone well, but the next day she received an offer.
6. The lawyers spent all night working on the case and luckily managed finish just in time.

2 Choose the correct options to complete the sentences.

1. I can't stop *to chat / chatting*. I'm in a hurry.
2. I didn't get round to *do / doing* the housework yesterday, so I'll have to do it today instead.
3. The teacher insisted on the students *being / be* on time for the school trip.
4. I admit to *lie / lying* to my parents about the time the party finished last night.
5. I regret not *accepting / accept* the offer of a job in Berlin.
6. Now that I work from home, I miss *talking / talk* to my colleagues in the office.
7. If you forget *to go / going* to the supermarket, we won't have anything for dinner.

Too and *enough*

When *too* is used before an adjective or adverb, it means 'more than we want or need':

I could tell by her smile that she was very happy. ✓

~~*I could tell by her smile that she was **too** happy.*~~ (This would mean 'happier than she wanted to be'.)

*I can't walk in these shoes because they're **too** small.* ✓

The structure *too* + adjective or adverb is often followed by *to* + infinitive:

*When we got home, we were **too tired to cook** dinner.*

Enough usually goes before a noun, but after an adjective. It usually means 'as much/many as we need':

*That plant isn't getting **enough sunlight**.*

*You will succeed if you work **hard enough**.*

Both structures are often followed by *to* + infinitive:

*We don't have **enough money to buy** a bigger house.*

3 Underline and correct the mistakes in these sentences.

1 Is the food enough hot?
2 I arrived too late catch my flight.
3 We have medicine enough for all the patients.
4 They aren't enough fit to play for the rugby team.
5 The room was enough dark to see anything.

Present perfect forms (with *for, since, already, yet* and *just*)

The present perfect can be used for an action or event that started in the past and is permanent:

***I've known** Stephen since our university days.*

It is also used for a past action or event which has a result now:

***We've** finally **finished** redecorating our house.*

However, it is not used when a past event is finished and has no connection with the present:

*When I was at school, my favourite subject **was** geography.* ✓

~~*When I was at school, my favourite subject **has been** geography.*~~ (My school days are finished and no connection is made with the present.)

For actions and events which began in the past and are still happening now, the present perfect continuous can be used:

*How long **have** you **been working** on this project?*

The present perfect continuous can be used to emphasise an action, while using the present perfect simple puts the emphasis on the result of the action:

***I've been sending** emails all morning.* (emphasis on the action)

***I've sent** 12 emails this morning.* (emphasis on the result)

We do not normally use the present perfect continuous with stative verbs:

*Animals **have existed** here for thousands of years.* ✓

~~*Animals **have been existing** here for thousands of years.*~~ (*Exist* is a stative verb.)

For a list of common stative verbs, see Grammar reference, Unit 1: present tenses.

We often use *for* and *since* with the present perfect simple and present perfect continuous. *For* is used to show the period of time during which an action or event took place, while *since* is used to show when an action or event started. They cannot be interchanged:

*We've been sitting here **for** over two hours.* ✓ (period of the action)

~~*We've been sitting here **since** over two hours.*~~

*We've been sitting here **since** lunchtime.* ✓ (time when the action started)

~~*We've been sitting here **for** lunchtime.*~~

Already is used when an event or action occurs sooner than expected:

*I can't believe we've **already** come to the end of our holiday.*

Yet is normally used with question forms and negatives. It shows that an action or event is expected, and often occurs at the end of a clause or sentence:

*I know you need the report now, but I'm afraid I haven't finished it **yet**.*

We use *just* to show that an action or event has occurred very recently:

*Tania has **just** called to say she won't be joining us tonight.*

4 Complete the sentences with either the present perfect simple or continuous form of the verbs in brackets.

1 I .... (work) on my essay all week, but I .... (not finish) it yet.
2 What .... (you do)? Your clothes are covered in mud.
3 You .... (look) exhausted recently. Have you .... (work) too much?
4 I .... (not cook) dinner yet, because I .... (read) in the garden for over an hour.
5 Have you got a plaster? I .... (play) football in the garden and I .... (cut) my knee on some stones.
6 I .... (be) to France several times this year. Every visit was really outstanding.
7 Recently the government .... (become) more aware of the need to promote language education in schools.
8 I .... (stand) on my feet all day, so I'm not really in the mood to go out.

5 **Make sentences with either the present perfect simple or continuous.**

1 Engineers / develop / technology / to carry out / many important processes.
2 He / not look at / his exam results / yet.
3 I'm exhausted! We / walk for / over four hours.
4 We all feel tired / because / not / get enough sleep / this week.
5 He / know her / since / she was three years old.
6 It rain / heavily / all day / and as a result / some roads / are flooded now.

UNIT 5

Future forms

will

Will (the future simple) is used

1 for predictions about the future:
*You'**ll feel** a lot better when you finish your exams.*
*Letters sent today **will not arrive** until next week.*
2 for predictions which are uncertain:
*I imagine they'**ll phone** you fairly soon.*
***Will** he **help** us find somewhere to stay?*
3 for sudden or spontaneous decisions:
*Is that the doorbell? I'**ll answer** it.*
*Who could help with this? I know! I'**ll give** Pete a call.*

going to

The *going to* future is used

1 for decisions or intentions about the future:
*We'**re going to take** a longer holiday next year.*
*I'**m** definitely **not going to call** him again.*
2 for predictions about the future based on evidence:
*She looks awful. I think she'**s going to be** sick.*
*You drive far too fast. You'**re going to have** an accident one of these days.*

1 **Complete the sentences with the correct form of *will* or *be going to* and a verb from the box.**

apply	ask	be	order	see	visit	watch	write

1 They .... a curry for dinner tonight.
2 .... you .... the new superhero film at the weekend?
3 **A:** Our washing machine has broken. Do you know anyone who could fix it?
B: Hmm, I .... Mark.
4 I .... for a job at the local library during the semester break.
5 We .... him in concert any more as they've cancelled the show.
6 Mark and Fiona .... their brother in Brazil next month.
7 I .... an email of complaint about the service at the hotel.
8 Your suit .... ready for collection on Thursday morning.

Present continuous

The present continuous can be used for future arrangements:
*I'**m playing golf** with my brother later.*
*They'**re leaving** the country next week.*

Present simple

The present simple can be used for future events which are fixed by a timetable or schedule:
*The last bus **leaves** at midnight.*
*The show **begins** at eight o'clock this evening.*

(For other uses of the present simple and continuous, see Grammar reference Unit 1.)

Future perfect

The future perfect is used for actions which will be completed before a particular point in the future:
*Elena **will have finished** her course by the end of July.*
***Will** you **have decided** what to do by next week's meeting?*

2 **Choose the correct options to complete the sentences.**

1 We *see / 're going to see* the new action film tomorrow. I bought the tickets online.
2 I don't think I *'ll be / am* late home. The concert finishes at eight o'clock.
3 I've got an important meeting tomorrow, so I *go / 'm going to go* to bed early this evening.
4 Our flight *departs / is departing* at 9.15 tomorrow morning.
5 **A:** We've run out of milk.
B: OK, I *'ll go / 'm going to go* and get some more.

Future continuous

The future continuous is used

1 for actions in progress in the future:
*This time next week we'**ll be sunbathing** by the pool.*
In many cases, the continued action may be interrupted:
*Don't make too much noise when you come home tonight because I'**ll be sleeping**.*
2 for expected future events:
*I'**ll be seeing** John at work tomorrow so I'll ask him then.*
3 for polite questions:
***Will you be using** the car tomorrow?*

3 **Complete the sentences with the correct form of the future perfect or the future continuous and a verb from the box.**

finish finish have join pass watch

1 This time tomorrow, I .... dinner with my friends.
2 James .... his internship by the end of August.
3 Can I call you at 1.30 pm? .... you .... lunch by then?
4 There's a film on that I want to watch tonight, so I .... TV from 8 pm to 10 pm.
5 I hope that I .... my driving test by the end of the year.
6 .... you .... the online meeting later today?

Countable and uncountable nouns

The indefinite article (*a/an*) can be used with singular countable nouns:

*There seems to be **a problem** with my laptop.*

With plural countable nouns, *(a) few, many* or *a lot / lots of* can be used:

*She doesn't have **many friends** apart from me.*

The indefinite article cannot be used with uncountable nouns:

*Let me give you **some advice**.* ✓

*Let me give you **a piece of advice**.* ✓

~~*Let me give you **an advice***~~. (*Advice* is an uncountable noun.)

Uncountable nouns do not have a plural form:

*You can find more **information** on our website.* ✓

~~*You can find more **informations** on our website.*~~

With uncountable nouns, *(a) little, much* or *a lot / lots of* can be used:

*Anything is possible if you have **a little patience**.*

4 **Tick the correct sentences. Correct the sentences with mistakes.**

1 My friends and I finally found some suitable accommodations at a reasonable rent.
2 My brother was astonished to discover that the airline charged us extra for our luggages.
3 A pollution from traffic fumes can cause some people to get ill.
4 I usually reject an advice from my aunt.
5 The company's website had little information about prices and delivery dates.
6 All of the sculptures in the exhibition are extremely valuable work of art.

5 **Choose the correct options to complete the sentences.**

1 Many experts argue that it is not wise to drink *coffee / coffees* late in the evening.
2 He considered calling the helpdesk, but finally decided he didn't need to ask for *some / any* help.
3 There's a container for recycling *cardboards / cardboard* and waste *papers / paper* behind our house.
4 Some of the news about the damage done by the floods *were / was* very upsetting.
5 The cost of the *equipment / equipments* needed to play ice hockey *is / are* beyond the reach of many people.
6 The engineers were desperately struggling to repair the *damages / damage* caused to the railway line by the storm.

UNIT 6

Relative clauses

Defining relative clauses

Defining relative clauses are used to give essential information about a noun:

*I've lost the book **which you lent me**.* (Gives essential information, defining which book we mean.)

*How can I contact those men **who helped you to move house**?* (Gives essential information, defining which men we are talking about.)

The following relative pronouns can be used in defining relative clauses: *which* or *that* (for things); *who* or *that* (for people); *where* (for places); *when* (for times); *whose* (to indicate possession):

*There are times **when I feel like quitting my job**.*

*I've always admired people **that know how to cook**.*

Sometimes, *which* can refer to the whole clause or sentence which comes before it:

*They've decided to move house, **which I think is a good idea**.*

(Refers to their decision to move, not to the noun *house*.)

If the relative pronoun in a defining relative clause is the object, it can be omitted:

*That isn't the woman **I was talking about**.* (The pronoun *who/that* is omitted.)

*What's the most beautiful place **you've ever been**?* (The pronoun *where* is omitted.)

Non-defining relative clauses

Non-defining relative clauses are used to give extra information. They are usually separated from the main clause with commas:

*The Prime Minister, **who has visited the city on three previous occasions**, will arrive here tomorrow.* (The meaning of the main part of the sentence does not change if the extra information is removed.)

*The documents are kept in the Director's office, **where they should remain at all times**.*

That cannot be used as a relative pronoun in non-defining relative clauses. However, all the other relative pronouns mentioned above can be used:

*The boy's parents, **who were very concerned**, contacted the police.* ✓

~~*The boy's parents, **that were very concerned**, contacted the police.*~~

The relative pronoun cannot be omitted from non-defining relative clauses:

*The city library, **which many residents use on a regular basis**, is expected to close next month.* ✓

~~*The city library, **many residents use on a regular basis**, is expected to close next month.*~~

1 **Choose the correct relative pronoun.**

1 Ljubljana, *which / where / whose* is the capital of Slovenia, is a city famous for its history and culture.
2 Owen, *who / whose / which* father is from Rio de Janeiro, speaks English and Portuguese fluently.
3 This camera, *who / which / where* I bought on holiday, takes absolutely superb photos.
4 Cambridge University, *which / where / whose* Stephen Hawking studied, is famous for its beautiful old buildings.
5 Mr Barrett, *who / which / where* is my biology teacher, is going to retire in the near future.
6 The film star Ryan Gosling, *which / who / whose* has starred in numerous successful films, was born in Canada.

2 **Complete the sentences with a relative pronoun.**

1 The furniture .... was damaged by yesterday's fire is being repaired.
2 The place .... the car had been abandoned was a pedestrian precinct.
3 The reason .... I was late for the training session is not of any significance.
4 The nurse .... I was hoping to see wasn't on duty when I arrived at the medical centre.
5 The man .... spoke at the meeting was very knowledgeable.
6 That's the woman .... cat likes to sleep in my garden.

3 **Rewrite each pair of sentences as one sentence using relative clauses.**

1 The music was by Beethoven. Sandra was playing the music last night.
The music which ....
2 The flute was not hers. Sandra was playing the flute in the concert.
The flute that ....
3 Luke is Sandra's music teacher. Sandra borrowed Luke's flute.
Luke, ...
4 We've just listened to Sandra's latest recording. Sandra's recording is in the top ten in the classical charts.
We've just listened ....
5 Sandra's mother is very proud of her. Sandra's mother was in the audience tonight.
Sandra's mother, ...
6 Tomorrow, Sandra is going back to London. Sandra goes to music school in London.
Tomorrow, Sandra is ....

Purpose links

To express purpose, we use the structures *so that* and *in order that*, followed by a subject and a verb, either positive or negative:

I lent him some money ***so that he could*** *get a taxi home.*

Put your jacket on ***so that you don't get*** *cold.*

After *so*, it is possible to omit *that*:

I lent him some money ***so he*** *could get a taxi home.*

Put your jacket on ***so you*** *don't get cold.*

In order that is more formal:

The trial will be postponed until next month ***in order that*** *all the evidence can be collected.*

We can also use the structures *so as to* and *in order to*, followed by a verb in the infinitive:

They moved to Wales ***in order to*** *be closer to their family.*

The negative forms are *so as not to* and *in order not to*:

I walked upstairs very quietly, ***so as not to*** *wake the children.*

4 Put the words in order to make sentences.

1 she could / spent / in Toulouse / She / improve / her French. / a semester / so that
2 is taking part in / he can improve / skills. / in order that / his / a training course / He / project management
3 early / rush-hour traffic. / I / the office / the / in order to / left / avoid
4 washed / so as not to / her housemates. / dirty dishes / Martha / all of / annoy / her
5 warm clothes / in order not to / should / in the winter / catch a cold. / You / wear

UNIT 7

Conditional forms

Conditional sentences usually consist of a main clause and a conditional clause which begins with *if* or *unless*:

If I don't hear from her by tomorrow, *I'll call the police.*

It is possible to reverse the order of the clauses:

I'll call the police ***if I don't hear from her by tomorrow.***

The **first conditional** is used when we are talking about a possible future event. The present simple appears in the conditional clause. In the other clause, we use *will, may, might* or *could*:

If you ***call*** *me tomorrow,* ***I'll give*** *you all the information.*

The situation ***could*** *become dangerous unless immediate action* ***is taken.***

The **second conditional** is used when we are talking about a present or future event which is unlikely, imaginary or impossible. The past simple appears in the conditional clause. In the other clause, *would, might* or *could* is used:

If she ***found*** *out where he was, she* ***might try*** *to find him.*

They ***wouldn't behave*** *like that unless something* ***was*** *wrong.*

If I ***were*** *you, I* ***would wait*** *for a while before contacting them.*

We use the **third conditional** when we are talking about the imaginary result of a situation in the past. The past perfect is used in the conditional clause. In the other clause, we use *would, might* or *could* with *have* and the past participle:

I ***wouldn't have come*** *if I* ***had known*** *that you were ill.* (I didn't know you were ill, so I came.)

If Mike ***hadn't spent*** *so much time playing computer games, he* ***could have passed*** *his exams.* (He didn't pass his exams because he spent so much time playing computer games.)

Sometimes we use **mixed conditionals**, which include parts of both second and third conditional sentences. For example, when we imagine the present result of a situation in the past, we use the past perfect in the conditional clause, but complete the sentence with a second conditional form:

If Jim ***hadn't been*** *such a careless driver, he* ***would*** *still* ***be*** *with us today.* (Jim was a careless driver and as a result, he is not with us today.)

When we are talking about the imaginary result of a present or permanent situation, we use the past simple in the conditional clause, but complete the sentence with a third conditional form:

He ***wouldn't have been able*** *to help you if he* ***wasn't*** *a doctor.* (He was able to help you because he's a doctor.)

1 Complete the sentences with the first or second conditional form of the verbs in brackets.

1 If she .... (be) late, we .... (have to) leave without her.
2 If I .... (be) you, I .... (buy) that smartphone.
3 If you .... (come) this way, the manager .... (see) you now.
4 If I .... (have) more time, I .... (not be) late for my meeting.
5 Unless the weather .... (improve) significantly, we .... (have to) cancel the barbecue.
6 I .... (go) on a round-the-world cruise if I .... (win) the lottery.

2 **Choose the correct verb tense.**

1 If my sister .... to lend me some money, I wouldn't have bought that expensive car.
   A didn't agree
   B doesn't agree
   C hadn't agreed

2 I wouldn't have gone on that guided tour if you .... it to me.
   A didn't recommend
   B don't recommend
   C hadn't recommended

3 He would have bought a new suit for his friend's wedding if he .... his credit card at home.
   A wouldn't leave
   B didn't leave
   C hadn't left

4 If you .... for your teacher's support, she would have willingly helped you in any way she could.
   A had asked
   B asked
   C ask

5 I would have been extremely disappointed if you .... to the party.
   A don't come
   B hadn't come
   C wouldn't have come

6 If he .... rushing to get to his job interview, he wouldn't have put on the wrong shoes.
   A wasn't
   B hadn't been
   C wouldn't be

3 **Complete the third conditional sentences with the verbs in brackets.**

1 If you .... (not / arrive) late at the train station, we .... (not / miss) our train to Newcastle.

2 If they .... (come) home from the party at a reasonable time, they .... (not / get up) so late.

3 If he .... (work) harder during his internship, he .... (might get) that amazing job as a journalist.

4 If you .... (be) born in Montreal, you probably .... (learn) to speak two languages.

5 If she .... (not board) that flight to Brazil, she .... (never meet) her future husband.

6 He .... (catch) a taxi from the airport if he .... (have) enough money.

Comparison of adjectives and adverbs; superlative forms

We use the suffix *-er* to form the comparative of most one-syllable adjectives:

*They felt a lot **calmer** once they knew their children were safe.*

*The weather is **hotter** in the south of the country.*

The superlative form of these adjectives ends in *-est*:

*That's the **kindest** thing she's ever said to me.*

Some short adjectives and adverbs have irregular comparative and superlative forms. *Better* and *best* are the comparative and superlative forms of *good* and *well*; *worse* and *worst* are the comparative and superlative forms of *bad* and *badly*; *further* and *furthest* are the usual comparative and superlative forms of *far*.

One- and two-syllable adjectives which end in *-y* have comparative forms ending in *-ier*:

*She looks much **prettier** now that she's had her hair cut.*

The superlative form of these adjectives ends in *-iest*:

*July tends to be the **driest** month of the year in my country.*

More is normally used to form the comparative of adjectives and adverbs with two or more syllables:

*There's nothing **more irritating** than losing your keys.*

The superlative of these adjectives and adverbs is formed with *most*:

*Of all the presentations we heard today, yours was the **most carefully** prepared.*

When we want to say that two things are the same, we often use the structure *as … as* with either an adjective or an adverb:

*The new traffic system is just **as slow as** the old one.*

The structure *not as / not so … as* can be used with either an adjective or an adverb to compare two things which are not the same:

*Her new novel is **not as complicated as** the previous one.*

Less can also be used, with the same meaning:

*Her new novel is **less complicated** than the previous one.*

The superlative form of *less* is *least*:

*Henry is the **least successful** of the three brothers.*

4 **Complete the sentences with the correct comparative or superlative form of the words in brackets.**

1 Today is the .... (good) day we've had this month.
2 She goes on holiday .... (often) than anyone else I know.
3 This maths puzzle is the .... (complicated) I've ever completed.
4 That musical was the .... (memorable) theatre performance I've ever attended.
5 This is the .... (hot) summer on record. It's really sweltering!

5 **Put the words in order to make sentences with the comparative or superlative.**

1 Her musical talent / than / has always / her sister's. / greater / been /
2 were as impressive / the scores / His results / the competition / as / of his nearest rival. / throughout /
3 The lecturer is / since he started / less / attending conferences / available to his students / every month.
4 The plants / are not / as fast / as my friends predicted. / growing /
5 Her interest in / considerably / than / history is / greater now / it was / at the beginning of her degree.
6 ideally want. / close to them / Their daughter doesn't live / as / quite / as they would /
7 than / There are slightly / living in / more people / five years ago. / the village /
8 more / than by plane. / It's / to travel by train / considerably / environmentally friendly /

Contrast links

However, nevertheless and *on the other hand* can be used to express contrast. They often come at the beginning of the sentence and are usually separated from the rest of the sentence with a comma:

This problem is clearly getting worse. ***However****, nobody seems to want to do anything about it.*

When *on the other hand* is used, the first sentence or paragraph often begins with *on the one hand*:

On the one hand*, the problem is clearly getting worse.* ***On the other hand****, nobody seems to be doing anything about it.*

In contrast and *by contrast* indicate contrast between two things. They are also usually separated from the rest of the sentence with a comma:

Traditional fuels can harm the environment. ***In contrast****, solar power is far less damaging.*

Although and *even though* also express contrast, but they introduce a clause which contains a subject and a verb. They cannot be followed by a comma and they cannot be used when the sentence only has one clause:

Some governments are refusing to take action ***although*** *the situation is urgent.* ✓

~~*Some governments are refusing to take action.* ***Although****, the situation is urgent.*~~

While and *whereas* are followed by a subject and verb, and can be used to express a contrast between two things:

A letter can take days to arrive, ***whereas*** *an email can be sent in a few seconds.*

Despite and *in spite of* have a similar meaning to *although*, but they must be followed by an *-ing* form or a noun / noun phrase:

Despite having some advantages*, solar power is not widely used in my country.* ✓

Despite its advantages*, solar power is not widely used in my country.* ✓

~~***Despite it has advantages****, solar power is not widely used in my country.*~~

If we add *the fact (that)* after *despite* or *in spite of*, we can finish the clause in the same way as with *although*:

Recycling is essential, ***although it takes time****.*

Recycling is essential, ***in spite of the fact that it takes time****.*

6 **Tick the correct sentences. Correct the sentences with mistakes.**

1 Michael didn't get a sports scholarship. Even though, he's really good at basketball.
2 Despite he had an injury last year, Scott was able to compete in the world championships.
3 In spite we left the house really early, we still missed our flight.
4 Fran really enjoyed the summer camp although it rained most days.
5 In spite of the fact that she practised every day, she didn't pass her driving test.

UNIT 8

Passive forms

The passive is formed using the correct form of the auxiliary verb *be* and a past participle:

Several parts of the city ***were damaged*** *in the storm.*

The auxiliary and the past participle may be separated, for example by an adverb:

Several parts of the city ***were badly damaged*** *in the storm.*

The passive is often used in formal written English, for example, in news reports, academic texts, or scientific or technical writing:

Water ***is pumped*** *through the system by a high-performance electric motor.*

The passive is sometimes formed using the auxiliary *get*, but this is informal and is most common in spoken English:

There wasn't enough room in the car, so Janet ***got left*** *behind.*

If we want to say who or what did the action, we use the preposition *by*:

A new medical treatment is being developed ***by scientists.*** (Scientists are developing a new medical treatment.)

The passive is often used when we don't know who did something:

The woman ***was attacked*** *on her way home from work.* (Her attacker is unknown.)

It can also be used to show that an event itself is more important than the person or thing which caused it:

He will not be playing because he ***was injured*** *during last week's match.* (The injury and its consequences are more important than the cause.)

We also use the passive when we don't need or don't want to say who did something:

A 20-year-old man ***was arrested*** *yesterday.* (It is obvious that the police arrested him.)

In more formal English, an impersonal passive can be formed using *it* and a verb such as *believe, consider, expect, know, report, say* or *think*:

It is thought *that the President will arrive tomorrow.* (People think the President will arrive tomorrow.)

An impersonal passive can also be formed with verbs such as *believe, consider, feel, know* or *think*. However, in this type of passive structure, the passive verb is followed by *to* + infinitive, not *that* + clause:

People ***believe that he is*** *guilty.* ✓ (active)

He ***is believed to be*** *guilty.* ✓ (impersonal passive)

~~*He* ***is believed that*** *he is guilty.*~~

When we use this structure to report something which happened in the past, the passive verb is followed by *to* + perfect infinitive (*have* + past participle):

People ***think that he took part*** *in the robbery.* ✓ (active verb reporting a past event)

He ***is thought to have taken part*** *in the robbery.* ✓ (impersonal passive with perfect infinitive)

~~*He* ***is thought that he took part*** *in the robbery.*~~

1 Make the sentences passive.

1. A member of the hotel staff brought my breakfast to my room.
2. You can find lots of bargains in the second-hand shop.
3. You can buy bus tickets from the driver.
4. People thought that protesters were to blame for the graffiti.
5. Someone took my wallet out of my coat pocket.
6. They've changed the lock on my front door.

2 Choose the correct option.

1. The old paintings .... by expert art historians.
   A were restored
   B was restored
   C been restored
2. My handbag with my money and phone .... at the railway station.
   A been stolen
   B were stolen
   C was stolen
3. The woman in the photograph .... for questioning by the police.
   A had wanted
   B gets wanted
   C is wanted

4 Your theatre tickets .... and you can collect them from the box office on the day of the show.
A had been reserved
B have been reserved
C have reserved

5 The roof of their house .... badly damaged in the storm.
A been
B had
C got

6 They .... for fraud.
A were arrested
B been arrested
C arrested

Articles

We use the **indefinite article** (*a/an*) when we mention a singular countable noun for the first time:

Just as I turned the corner, I saw ***a car*** *coming towards me.*

We also use *a/an* when talking about people's jobs:

She has been working as ***a doctor*** *for more than 20 years.*

The indefinite article also appears in some expressions with numbers:

We have seen ***a 20 per cent*** *drop in sales this year.*

We use the **definite article** (*the*) when we have already mentioned something, or when it is common knowledge:

At the zoo, we saw lions, tigers and elephants. ***The tigers*** *were my favourite.* (They have been mentioned previously.)

Do you mind if I open ***the window****?* (We both know which window.)

We also use *the* when there is only one of something:

I think you should tell ***the manager*** *about this.*

The definite article is used with superlatives:

That's ***the most ridiculous*** *thing I've ever heard.*

The is also used with inventions, types of animal, and musical instruments:

The computer *was an important invention of the 20th century.*

The wild goat *can be found in mountain areas.*

My mother forced me to learn ***the violin.***

When used with an adjective, *the* can indicate a certain group of people:

This problem does not affect ***the rich.*** (rich people)

No article is used when we are talking in general and in the plural, or with abstract nouns:

My city has never been popular with ***tourists.***

To be a good parent, you need to have ***patience.***

When we talk about sports or certain illnesses, no article is used:

She's absolutely brilliant at ***tennis.***

Scientists have not yet found a cure for ***cancer.***

However, some common illnesses are exceptions to this rule:

If you go out without a jacket you might catch ***a cold.***

No article is needed before certain nouns in expressions with *to*, including *to bed*, *to work*, *to prison* and *to school*.

3 **Complete the sentences with definite or indefinite articles.**

1 I heard .... loud noise in .... attic.
2 I think that .... man driving .... car is .... member of .... British royal family.
3 They are looking for .... apartment on .... outskirts of town.
4 What's .... tallest building in the world?
5 The government is building more affordable housing for .... poor.
6 She's .... tour guide in one of .... most beautiful towns in Austria.

4 **Choose the correct options to complete the sentences.**

1 Could you go to *the / a* library and collect *the / a* book I ordered?
2 The company has bought two new computers for its employees. *The / A* laptop is for *the / a* new intern and *the / a* desktop is for *the / a* CEO's personal assistant.
3 My sister is much better at *the / –* volleyball than me, but she can't play *the / –* guitar as well as I can.
4 *The / A* mirror in *the / a* hallway is *the / a* largest in *the / a* whole house.
5 He's just been awarded *a / an* university degree in History.
6 *The / A / –* housing can be quite cheap in some parts of *the / a / –* France.

UNIT 9

Reported speech and reporting verbs

Tenses in reported speech

When direct speech is reported in the past, verb tenses often change. Verbs in the present simple often change to the past simple:

*'The boss **is** really disappointed with your work.'*

*She explained that the boss **was** really disappointed with my work.*

Verbs in the present continuous change to the past continuous:

*'We**'re watching** TV at Dave's house.'*

*They said they **were watching** TV at Dave's house.*

Verbs in the present perfect change to the past perfect:

*'I**'ve finished my** essay.'*

*She said she **had finished** her essay.*

Verbs in the past simple often change to the past perfect:

*'I **tried** to call you three times.'*

*He said he **had tried** to call me three times.*

Many modal verbs do not change when they are reported, but *can* changes to *could*, and *may* changes to *might*. When we are talking about obligation, *must* often changes to *had to*:

*'You **must tidy** your room before going out.'*

*She said I **had to tidy** my room before going out.*

In the future simple, *will* changes to *would*:

*'I**'ll let** you know as soon as possible.'*

*He said he **would let** us know as soon as possible.*

However, a change in verb tense does not always occur, especially when the situation is still the same when the verb is reported:

*'I **don't eat** meat.'*

*He told us that he **doesn't eat** meat.* (This is still true now.)

It isn't always necessary to change verbs from the past simple to the past perfect:

*'As a boy, I **played** tennis every day.'*

*He told me he **played** tennis every day as a boy.* ✓

*He told me he **had played** tennis every day as a boy.* ✓

Other changes

Some other words may change when direct speech is reported. For example, pronouns and expressions of time and place may be different:

*'I'll meet **you here tomorrow**.'*

*He promised to meet **me there the following day**.*

Reported questions

In reported questions, the subject comes before the main verb (not after the main verb, as in direct questions). This means that reported questions have the same order as statements:

*'**I'm** from Brazil.'* (statement)

*'Where **are you** from?'* (direct question)

*I asked her where **she was** from.* ✓ (reported question)

~~*I asked her where **was she** from.*~~

The auxiliary verbs *do, does* and *did* are not used in reported questions:

*'What time **did** you get up?'*

*They asked me what time **I had got up**.* ✓

~~*They asked me what time **did I get up**.*~~

When 'yes/no' questions are reported, we add either *if* or *whether*:

'Did you enjoy your meal?'

*He asked us **if** we had enjoyed our meal.* ✓

*He asked us **whether** we had enjoyed our meal.* ✓

~~*He asked us **had we** enjoyed our meal.*~~

Reporting verbs

Reporting verbs can be divided into categories according to the grammatical patterns which come after them.

Some verbs, including *agree, claim, decide, offer, promise, refuse* and *threaten*, are followed by *to* + infinitive:

'I do not wish to comment on what happened.'

*He **refused to comment** on what happened.*

Other verbs, including *advise, ask, beg, forbid, invite, order, persuade, remind, tell* and *warn*, are followed by an object + *to* + infinitive:

'Don't forget to bring an umbrella.'

*She **reminded me to bring** an umbrella.*

Some verbs, including *admit, deny, recall, recommend* and *suggest*, are followed by the *-ing* form:

'It wasn't me who stole the money.'

*He **denied stealing** the money.*

Verbs such as *claim, complain, confess, decide, deny, explain, insist, mention, promise, recommend, reply, suggest* and *threaten* can be followed by (*that* +) a clause:

'I'll call you back by the end of the day.'

*She **promised that she would call** me back by the end of the day.*

Some other verbs are followed by a verb + preposition + *-ing*. These include *apologise for, insist on* and *advise against*:

'I'm really sorry I was so horrible to you.'

She ***apologised for being*** *so horrible to me.*

Accuse is slightly different, because it is followed by an object + preposition + *-ing*:

'We think you lied about your experience.'

They ***accused me of lying*** *about my experience.*

1 Complete the reported speech with the verbs in the correct tense and any other words necessary.

1 'I work in the marketing department.' → He said he .... in the marketing department.
2 'I'm having a late lunch.' → She phoned to say that she .... a late lunch.
3 'I've never ridden a motorbike.' → He told me that he .... a motorbike.
4 'I got food poisoning from the meat I ate.' → She suggested that she .... food poisoning from the meat that she ....
5 'I'll ring as soon as I get home.' → He promised that he .... as soon as he ....
6 'I can play the guitar, but I can't play the piano.' → She told me that she .... play the guitar but that she .... play the piano.

2 Choose the correct option, A or B.

1 He explained that he .... higher than anyone else in his class.
A could jump B can jump
2 My sister said that she .... some candles for the cake, if we wanted some.
A might buy B may buy
3 He whispered that he .... swim.
A can't B couldn't
4 She told them that they .... better in their exams this year.
A must do B had to do
5 He stated that he .... to go to the cinema than the theatre.
A would prefer B will prefer
6 The teacher told the pupils they .... their calculators in the exam.
A mustn't use B had not to use

UNIT 10

Adverbs of manner and opinion

When adverbs are used to describe how something happens, they are called **adverbs of manner**:

They didn't like each other at first but after a while they got on ***brilliantly****.*

He spoke ***calmly****, without showing how nervous he was.*

Adverbs such as *obviously* or *sadly* can be used to show our opinion of what is being said:

Obviously*, parents are responsible for looking after their* children.

Sadly*, they had to come home early because Martin got ill.*

Other adverbs which can be used in this way are: *actually, clearly, hopefully, interestingly, personally, strangely, surprisingly* and *unfortunately.*

As shown in the examples above, adverbs of manner and opinion may occur at the beginning, middle or end of a sentence or clause. However, they almost never appear between a verb and its object:

He ***slowly*** *took his phone out of his pocket.* ✓

Slowly*, he took his phone out of his pocket.* ✓

He took his phone out of his pocket ***slowly****.* ✓

~~*He took* ***slowly*** *his phone out of his pocket*~~. (*His phone* is the object of *took*.)

Adverbs of opinion are sometimes used between commas to show that the speaker is commenting on the whole clause or sentence:

We have found that a number of drivers, ***unfortunately****, fail to respect the speed limit.*

1 Tick the correct sentences. Correct the sentences with mistakes.

1 Hopefully, we will all pass our exams and be able to celebrate at the end of the year.
2 The teacher explained quickly the task to the students.
3 The little girl signed her name beautifully on the picture she had drawn.
4 Unfortunately, many people don't understand the importance of eating a healthy diet.
5 Susan sang happily her favourite song as she got ready to go out.
6 The children devoured the meal hungrily.

Wish and if only

To express regret about a past situation, we can use *wish* or *if only* + past perfect:

***He** now **wishes he hadn't bought** a second car.* (He bought a second car, but now he regrets it.)

To talk about a present situation which we would like to change, we use *wish* or *if only* + past simple. *If only* is used when we feel very strongly:

***If only I lived** closer to my office.* (I don't live close to my office, but I would like to.)

To talk about something which we would like to happen in the future, we use *wish* or *if only* + subject + *could* + infinitive:

***I wish I could see** her again.* (I would like to see her again in the future.)

***If only I could see** her again.* (I feel very strongly that I would like to see her again in the future.)

When we use *wish* or *if only* + *would* instead of *could*, there is a sense that we are annoyed or frustrated:

***If only they would stop** making so much noise when I'm trying to sleep.* (It is annoying that I can't sleep because of the noise they are making.)

We cannot use *wish* + *would* + infinitive if the subject of *wish* is the same as the subject of *would*:

***She wishes she could get** better marks at school.* ✓

~~***She wishes she would get** better marks at school.*~~ (*She* is the subject of both *wish* and *would*.)

2 Complete the sentences with verbs in the past simple, with *could* + infinitive or with *would* + infinitive.

1 I wish I .... (had) a really well-paid job in the media industry.
2 If only I .... (meet) some people who are adventurous like me.
3 I wish that dog outside .... (stop) barking. I'm getting a headache!
4 If only he .... (start) studying harder for his exams.
5 I wish I .... (have) more time to meet up with my friends.
6 If only my mother .... (not keep) asking me if I've tidied my room.

3 Choose the correct options to complete the sentences.

1 I wish I *would be / was* better at maths.
2 If only he *could stop / would stop* playing his drums so loudly when I'm trying to work.
3 If only I *knew / would know* how to drive a car.
4 I wish I *could play / would play* the piano better.
5 He wishes he *knew / could know* how to cook Indian food.
6 If only the dog *wouldn't roll / didn't roll* in the mud every time we went out.

Causative *have* and *get*

We can use causative *have* when we ask or pay someone to do something for us:

*My parents **had their living room redecorated** last year.* (They paid someone to redecorate their living room.)

Causative *have* is formed with:

subject + *have* + object + past participle

***My parents are going to have their living room redecorated**.*

In informal or spoken English, we sometimes use *get* instead of *have*:

*I can't meet you this afternoon because **I'm getting my hair cut**.* (I'm paying someone to cut my hair.)

We can also use this structure when we want to say that something unpleasant has been done to us:

*Our neighbours **had their car stolen** when they were on holiday.*

4 Complete the sentences with the correct form of *have* or *get*.

1 I've just .... my boots mended at the shoe shop in the centre of town.
2 We have just .... the groceries delivered that we ordered online.
3 I'm going to .... my dress dry cleaned for the party.
4 She .... her daughter to tidy her room by giving her pocket money.
5 He .... his smartphone stolen while he was on the train.
6 She .... her nails done tomorrow.
7 We have just .... a new kitchen put in to our house.
8 She .... her tablet repaired by the IT specialist.

Infinitive	Past simple	Past participle
break	broke	broken
bring	brought	brought
broadcast	broadcast	broadcast
build	built	built
choose	chose	chosen
cost	cost	cost
cut	cut	cut
deal	dealt	dealt
draw	drew	drawn
fly	flew	flown
forget	forgot	forgotten
grow	grew	grown
hear	heard	heard
hit	hit	hit
hold	held	held
mean	meant	meant
pay	paid	paid
rise	rose	risen
shake	shook	shook
sing	sang	sung
sink	sank	sunk
sleep	slept	slept
spend	spent	spent
spill	spilt	spilt
steal	stole	stolen
swear	swore	sworn
teach	taught	taught
wear	wore	worn
win	won	won

WRITING PART 1: ESSAY

1 **Read the exam task. What question should you answer? What ideas should you include?**

In your English class you have been talking about the environment. Now, your English teacher has asked you to write an essay.

Write your essay using **all** the notes and giving reasons for your point of view.

Will environmental problems be worse in 20 years?

Notes

Write about:

1 pollution

2 climate change

3 your own idea

2 **Study the model answer. What extra idea does it include?**

3 **Read the essay question. Then decide which ideas would be relevant to include in the essay.**

We shouldn't spend so much money on exploring space. Do you agree?

1 It costs a huge amount of money to send rockets into space.
2 Rockets have extremely powerful engines.
3 There are more important problems in the world that we should spend money on.
4 We can learn a lot about our own planet and solar system.
5 People first landed on the moon in 1969.
6 A lot of people in the world don't have food or shelter.
7 I would love to go into space one day.
8 Some important scientific experiments can be carried out in space.

4 **Look at the plan for a student's essay on the question in Exercise 3. Decide which paragraph the correct sentences from Exercise 3 could go in.**

Introduction
[1]......... Is it worth the money?

Arguments against exploring space
[2]........., ...

Arguments for exploring space
[3]........., ...

Conclusion
We can learn things from exploring space, but it's probably a luxury the world can't afford.

MODEL ANSWER

[1]In my opinion, [2]it is possible that environmental problems will be worse in 20 years. We already face a large number of serious environmental problems and, if steps are not taken to tackle them, they will become even more serious.

[3]Firstly, there is already a huge amount of pollution in the world, for example from cars, lorries and planes. There is also a big problem with the amount of rubbish that we produce, which often ends up in the sea.

Secondly, [4]our modern way of life produces harmful gases which are causing the planet to become warmer. This is a very serious problem for animals such as polar bears, [5]which may die out if the ice that they live on melts.

Finally, the world's population is growing rapidly and this will put even more pressure on the Earth's resources. More people means more food production, more pollution and more waste.

[6]In conclusion, the world faces some very serious environmental problems which will definitely be worse in 20 years if nothing is done to solve them. [7]However, I am optimistic that scientists and politicians will find ways to improve the situation.

[1]Use phrases to express your own opinion.

[2]Start with a general introduction to the topic.

[3]Use words and phrases to organise your essay and make it clear when you are introducing a new topic.

[4]Give information which is relevant to the topic.

[5]Give reasons to support your arguments and opinions.

[6]End with a clear conclusion.

[7]Use linking words to add similar or contrasting ideas.

5 **Read the essay question. Then choose the best introduction and conclusion. Why is it the best one?**

Do you think it is better to watch films in the cinema or at home?

1 Introductions

A There are loads of amazing films nowadays. Personally, I love science-fiction films and I often watch them with my friends.

B Watching a film on the big screen at the cinema is certainly very impressive. But in my opinion, there are also advantages to watching films at home with friends.

C Going to the cinema is quite expensive, and some people can't afford it. Also, some small towns don't have a cinema.

2 Conclusions

A To sum up, I hardly ever go to the cinema because there isn't one very close to where I live. But I often watch movies with my friends at the weekend.

B On balance, some people prefer going to the cinema to watch films, and some people prefer to watch films at home. There are lots of different reasons for this, for example, some people can't afford to go to the cinema.

C In conclusion, I would say that for most films, it is more enjoyable to watch at home with a few friends. However, for films with a lot of special effects, it is worth the trip to a cinema to see these on the big screen.

6 **Study the words and expressions in the *Key language* box.**

KEY LANGUAGE FOR ESSAYS

Ordering your ideas:

firstly, secondly, finally

Expressing your opinion:

in my opinion, in my view, I would say that, personally, I think

Giving reasons:

because, as, since

Giving results or consequences:

consequently, as a result, therefore, for this reason

Giving examples:

for example, for instance, such as, one example of this is

Linking similar ideas:

in addition to this, furthermore, moreover

Linking contrasting ideas:

however, on the one hand / on the other hand, in contrast, although, whereas

Giving a conclusion:

in conclusion, to sum up, on balance

7 **Choose the correct options to complete the sentences.**

1 In my opinion, computers are essential in schools *as / for this reason* students need them to find information.

2 It is clearly necessary to test new medicines, but *in my opinion / therefore* this doesn't justify using animals.

3 Cars create a lot of pollution in city centres. *In addition to this / Consequently,* they can cause accidents.

4 There are several reasons why I am against exams. *Finally / Firstly,* they only test what someone can remember on one particular day.

5 Sports *such as / furthermore* tennis and football are more sociable than running.

8 **Read the exam task and use the table to plan your essay.**

In your English class you have been talking about city life. Now, your English teacher has asked you to write an essay.

Write an essay using **all** the notes and giving reasons for your point of view.

Some people believe that cycling is the best way to travel around cities. Do you agree?

Notes

Write about:

1 health

2 safety

3 your own idea

	Ideas	Useful phrases
Introduction		
Paragraph 1		
Paragraph 2		
Paragraph 3		
Conclusion		

9 **Write your essay. Remember to write between 140 and 190 words.**

10 **Check your essay and make changes if necessary.**

- Have you answered the question in the task?
- Have you included the two ideas in the task and added your own idea?
- Have you included only relevant information?
- Have you started with an introduction and ended with a conclusion?
- Have you ordered your ideas into paragraphs?
- Have you given reasons for your ideas and opinions?
- Have you used words and phrases to link ideas?
- Have you used between 140 and 190 words?

WRITING PART 2: EMAIL / LETTER

1 **Read the exam task. Who should you write an email to? What should you write about in your email? What questions should you answer?**

You have received this email from your English-speaking friend, Jo.

> I guess you've been in your new home for about a month now. All your old friends are really keen to know how you're getting on. What's your new home like? And are there lots of exciting things to do in the city? Also, have you made plenty of new friends?
>
> Write and tell me all about it!
>
> Jo

Write your **email** in **140–190** words.

2 **Study the model answer. Does it answer all the questions in Jo's email? Is the tone formal or informal?**

3 **Read this task. Then decide if the sentences below are true or false.**

You see this notice in your college.

> Our college wants to organise an event this summer to raise money for schools in developing countries. Below are some of our ideas. Please email me to let me know which you think is the best idea and why. Please also tell us how we should organise the event, to make sure it is a success.
>
> 1 a fun sports day 2 a quiz evening 3 a concert
>
> Thank you for your help.
>
> Anna Bradley, Principal

Write your **email**.

1 You need to write a notice about the event.
2 You have to choose one idea.
3 You should explain your reasons for choosing this.
4 You should suggest a date for the event.
5 Your email is to the college principal.
6 You should use an informal tone.

4 **Choose the four sentences that are suitable to include in your email to the principal in Exercise 3. Why are they suitable?**

1 I think it's a great idea to raise money for schools in developing countries.
2 I would suggest that a fun sports day would be the best option.
3 I think a quiz evening would be amazing!
4 Loads of people enjoy listening to live music.
5 Concerts are extremely popular with lots of people of different ages.
6 I think it would be a good idea to keep the ticket price fairly low.
7 Why don't you serve food during the event, too?
8 I'm sure that the event will be a huge success and hopefully it will raise a large amount of money.

MODEL ANSWER

[1]Hi Jo,

[2]It was great to hear from you! I miss all my old friends, but I'm getting used to living here in Manchester now.

[3]My new flat is amazing! It's modern and quite big, and it's got a lovely balcony which looks out over a park. There's also a large living room with comfortable sofas and our new huge TV! My room's quite small, but I don't mind that because I'm out during the day, so I only use it for sleeping.

[4]Manchester's a really lively city. Did you know it's the biggest university city in Britain, so there are loads of young people here. There's always something new and exciting to do. I've discovered some amazing music venues where there are live bands.

[5]I've been lucky with friends and I've met some really nice people here. I'm seeing some of them this evening, to go to the cinema, and I know [6]you'll get on with them when you meet them. When are you going to come and visit me? Let me know when you're free and we can fix a date.

[7]See you soon,

Ali

[1]*Use a suitable greeting.*

[2]*Give a reason for writing.*

[3]*Answer the first question.*

[4]*Answer the second question.*

[5]*Answer the third question.*

[6]*In an informal email/letter, use informal words and phrases.*

[7]*Use a suitable ending phrase.*

5 Choose the correct options in this formal email.

(1) *Dear Ms Copeland, / Hi Anne,*

I am writing **(2)** *because of / in response to* your advertisement for staff to work in your hotel this summer. I am **(3)** *currently / at the moment* studying hotel management at college and **(4)** *would love to work / would be interested in working* in your hotel.

I have **(5)** *learnt all about / studied different aspects of* hotel work as part of my course, and I also have some experience of hotel work as I **(6)** *was employed / had a job* in a large international hotel in Spain for six weeks last summer. I worked mainly as a waiter, but also **(7)** *gained some experience as / had a go as* a receptionist when the regular receptionist was ill.

I am friendly and hardworking, and work well as part of a team. I also understand that in a hotel, **(8)** *keeping the customer happy / customer satisfaction* is the most important thing.

(9) *I would be grateful if you would / Please will you* consider me for a position in your hotel.

(10) *I look forward to hearing from you. / Write soon!*

Joseph Brown

6 Study the words and expressions in the *Key language* box.

KEY LANGUAGE FOR FORMAL EMAILS AND LETTERS

Opening a formal email/letter:

Dear (Mr/Mrs/Ms Edwards), Dear Sir/Madam,

Giving reasons for writing:

I am writing in response to … I saw your notice/advert in …

Referring to something mentioned in the letter/notice/advert:

Your letter/notice/advert mentioned that … Your letter/notice/advert asked for …

Making suggestions / giving advice:

It would be a good idea to … It might be sensible to … You might like to consider …

Offering to do something:

I would be able/willing to … if necessary.

Making requests:

Would it be possible for you to … ?

Asking for information:

Could you give me some information on … ? Could you let me have more details about … ?

Apologising:

I would like to apologise for …

Closing a formal email:

Yours sincerely (after *Dear Mr Edwards*), *Yours faithfully* (after *Dear Sir/Madam*), *I look forward to hearing from you, Kind regards*

Tip: Only use *Mrs* if you are sure that the woman you are writing to is married. Otherwise, use *Ms*.

7 Correct the mistakes in the sentences from formal and informal letters/emails.

1. It was great hear from you.
2. Why you don't come and visit me in July?
3. I would able to help with the arrangements.
4. I look forward hearing from you.

8 Read the exam task and use the table to plan your letter.

You see this advertisement in your local English-language newspaper.

Staff wanted for summer work

We require staff to work with our English-speaking guests in our busy hotel this summer.

We are looking for people for the following roles:

- Waiter
- Coffee-bar assistant
- Receptionist

Write to Maria Simpson at Top Beach Hotel saying which job interests you and why, and explain why you would be suitable for the job.

Write your **letter** in **140–190** words.

	Ideas	Useful phrases
Writing to?		
Formal or informal?		
Opening phrase		
Point 1		
Point 2		
Point 3		
Ending		

9 Write your letter. Remember to write between 140 and 190 words.

10 Check your letter and make changes if necessary.

- Have you covered all the points in the task?
- Have you used an appropriate formal or informal tone?
- Have you used a range of phrases for giving advice, making suggestions, etc.?
- Have you used a suitable opening and ending?
- Have you used a wide range of language?
- Have you used between 140 and 190 words?

WRITING PART 2: REVIEW

1 **Read the exam task. What should you write a review of? What points should you include? Where will people read your review?**

You see this notice in an English-language magazine.

> **Film reviews wanted**
>
> What films have you seen recently? Write a review of a film you have seen, explaining what it was about and whether you enjoyed it or not. Tell us whether or not you think other people would enjoy it.
>
> The best reviews will be published in next month's magazine.

Write your **review**.

2 **Study the model answer and answer the questions.**

1 Does the review cover all the points in the task?
2 Did the writer enjoy the film?
3 Who does the writer think will enjoy the film?
4 Is the language in the review formal and neutral, or informal and friendly?

MODEL ANSWER

[1]*Black Panther*

I watched the film *Black Panther* for the first time last week. [2]It's a superhero film, in the same genre as *Superman* and *Spiderman*, and has been extremely popular around the world.

[3]Although I am not usually a big fan of superhero films, [4]I was really impressed with this one. The story is fairly traditional, with the hero T'Challa (*Black Panther*) defeating the evil Killmonger, who is trying to gain power over the whole world. [5]But the action is gripping and the special effects are spectacular. Chadwick Boseman, who plays T'Challa, acts superbly, and really brings the comic-book character to life. The brilliant costumes and music also really help make the film a great spectacle.

[3]On the negative side, [6]I felt that there was sometimes a bit too much violence, which makes it unsuitable for young children, and of course you have to accept that the plot is slightly predictable because the good guy will always win.

In spite of this, [7]I loved the film and [8]anyone who enjoys fantasy movies will definitely like it.

[1]includes the name of the film as the title
[2]briefly describes the film in the introduction
[3]is organised into clear paragraphs, which focus on positive and negative aspects
[4]uses a range of phrases to express a personal opinion
[5]praises positive features and says why the film is good
[6]includes some negative features, to give a balanced view
[7]clearly states the writer's opinion in the conclusion
[8]includes a recommendation, saying who would enjoy the film

3 **Read the review task. Then look at the two student plans. Which plan is better? Why?**

> **Reviews wanted!**
>
> What shopping websites have you used recently? Write a review of a shopping website that you have used. Say what you bought, how pleased you were with the product, and talk about any problems you experienced. Say whether you would recommend the site to others.

A

Introduction
name of website TechWorld, and basic information (what they sell)
What I bought (a new tablet)

My experience
The website – why I like it (easy to use, good prices)
The product – why I was pleased with it (good quality)

A few problems
slow delivery, missing case, but they dealt with this quickly

Recommendation
great website for anyone who is looking for a low-priced tablet or other device

B

Introduction
Why I chose to use this website (looking for a cheap tablet, easier to buy online than go into town)

The website
How I found out about it, how I chose my tablet, problem of slow delivery

Games
Why I like it (I needed a new tablet for playing games)

Conclusion
I'm very pleased with my new tablet and it was very cheap

4 **We often use adjectives or phrases to give our opinion about something in an indirect way. Match the beginnings and endings of the sentences.**

1 I was disappointed to
2 We were delighted that
3 I'm absolutely thrilled with
4 The tent isn't as big
5 The food was even better
6 There weren't enough

a my new camera.
b seats around the pool for all the guests.
c find that the screen was cracked.
d than I expected.
e as it looked on the website.
f we had a room with a view of the sea.

5 **In a review we often use words to express contrast. Complete the sentences with words from the box.**

although despite however spite though

1 The weather was terrible, but in .... of this, we thoroughly enjoyed our stay at the resort.
2 Even .... it was rather expensive, we really enjoyed our time at the museum.
3 I would advise anyone to check out this website, ... the problems that I experienced.
4 .... the service was quick and friendly, the food was a little disappointing.
5 The website stated that the bag was black. ...., when it arrived it was grey.

6 **Study the words and expressions in the *Key language* box.**

KEY LANGUAGE FOR REVIEWS

Praising something:

It is one of the best … I have ever … , The … was absolutely perfect, The … was even better than I expected, I was pleased/delighted to find that … , It was a nice surprise to find that … ,

Criticising:

The … was rather disappointing, The advertisement said … , but in fact … , I was a little disappointed to find … , There weren't enough …

Recommending:

Anyone who likes … will really enjoy … , Don't miss the chance/opportunity to … , I'm sure everyone will really enjoy … , If you get the chance to see/buy/try … , you should definitely do it, I would advise anyone to …

Advising someone against something:

I would suggest finding a better … than this, I would strongly advise against eating/reading/watching/buying this … , My advice is to avoid this …

7 **Choose the correct options to complete the sentences.**

1 This show was even better *than* / *as* I expected.
2 The dessert was rather *disappointed* / *disappointing*.
3 Anyone who enjoys crime novels *will* / *can* love this book.
4 Don't *lose* / *miss* the opportunity to visit this theme park.
5 I would suggest *using* / *to use* a different website.
6 I would strongly *advise* / *suggest* against staying at this campsite.

8 **Read the exam task and use the table to plan your review.**

You see this advertisement on a travel website.

Reviews wanted!

What holiday resorts have you been to recently?

Write a review describing the resort, explaining why you did or didn't enjoy your stay there and saying whether it is good value for money.

The best reviews will be published on our website.

Write your **review**.

Paragraphs	Ideas	Useful phrases
Description of the resort		
Why I enjoyed / didn't enjoy it		
Good value for money?		
Recommendation		

9 **Write your review. Remember to write between 140 and 190 words.**

10 **Check your review and make changes if necessary.**

- Have you covered all the points in the task?
- Have you organised your ideas clearly into paragraphs?
- Have you given your own opinion clearly?
- Have you ended with a recommendation?
- Have you used descriptive adjectives and adverbs to make your writing interesting?
- Have you used a friendly tone?
- Have you used between 140 and 190 words?

WRITING PART 2: ARTICLE

1 Read the exam task. What should you write an article about? What points should you include? Where will people read your article?

> You see this notice in an English-language magazine.
>
> **Articles wanted**
>
> My hobby
>
> Write an article about your hobby. Say what it is, how you started doing it, and why you enjoy it.
>
> The best articles will appear in our magazine next week.
>
> Write your **article**.

2 Study the model answer and answer the questions.

1 Does the article cover all the points in the task?
2 How many paragraphs does it have?
3 How many direct questions does it ask the reader?
4 Is it written in a formal or an informal style?

MODEL ANSWER

[1]The thrill of the stage

[2]I'll never forget the first day I stepped onto a real theatre stage. I knew immediately that this was my hobby for life! I'm now a member of my local drama club. We put on two shows every year and have a lot of fun while doing so!

[3]I first started acting by chance. A friend of mine was interested in joining a drama club, and I agreed to go along with her, to give her a bit of support. [4]And I loved it from the first day!

First, drama is [5]incredibly challenging. [6]Not only do you have to learn what you're going to say, but also understand the character you're playing, their role in the play, and then communicate that to the audience.

[7]Another thing I love about drama is how sociable it is. I've made so many good friends at the drama club, and spending time with them working towards a shared goal is extremely rewarding. And in addition to all of this, [8]what could beat the thrill of appearing under the lights, in front of a cheering crowd?

[1]has an interesting title
[2]has a first sentence which interests the reader and encourages them to read more
[3]is organised into clear paragraphs, each with a topic sentence
[4]gives the writer's opinions
[5]uses creative language with strong meanings
[6]gives examples to support the ideas
[7]uses structures to add emphasis
[8]ends with a question or a lively final sentence

3 It is important to choose a title and first sentence which will engage your reader and encourage them to read more. Choose the best title and first sentence for an article about Nelson Mandela. Why is it the best?

A Nelson Mandela
I really admire Nelson Mandela because of everything he achieved in South Africa.

B A peaceful transformation
Can you imagine one person bringing peaceful change to a whole country?

C An important figure in South Africa
Nelson Mandela is a very important figure in the history of South Africa.

4 The first sentence in each paragraph (the topic sentence) gives the topic of the paragraph. Match the topic sentences (a–e) with the paragraphs from an article about a favourite place to visit. There are two topic sentences you don't need.

a The people here are incredibly warm and welcoming.
b This is a lovely, relaxing place.
c I first discovered this place about five years ago.
d One thing I really love is the stunning scenery.
e If you love good food, this is a great place to visit.

1 .... When you look in one direction, you can see the beautiful beach and the clear blue sea. In the opposite direction, there are lovely views of the mountains, which have snow on their peaks all year round.

2 .... You can find delicious local cheeses, and plenty of fresh fruit and vegetables. And of course there's fresh fish which the fishing boats bring in each day, and which is perfectly cooked in the restaurants by the beach.

3 .... They always have time to stop and chat and they seem genuinely keen for you to enjoy your stay. You can always find someone to help if you have any problems, too.

5 **In an article, it is important to use creative words with strong meanings, to make your writing more interesting. Replace the bold words and expressions in the sentences with the creative words with similar meanings from the box.**

absolutely essential   fascinated by
freezing   huge   packed   terrifying

1 Like a lot of people, I was **interested in** the castle's history.
2 The city centre is always **crowded** with tourists.
3 His first film was a **big** success.
4 I always enjoy watching my local football team play, even when the weather's **cold**.
5 The drive up the narrow mountain road was quite **scary** at times.
6 A good fitness programme is **really necessary** if you're serious about losing weight.

6 **You can use structures to emphasise your ideas and opinions in an article. Complete each second sentence so it has a similar meaning but has more emphasis.**

1 I admire his determination.
What ..*I admire is*.. his determination.
2 I like the freedom you get when you go hiking.
The thing .... the freedom you get when you go hiking.
3 Her honesty really surprised me.
One thing .... her honesty.
4 I will never forget our evening barbecues on the beach.
What .... our evening barbecues on the beach.
5 I noticed how happy everyone looked.
The thing .... how happy everyone looked.

7 **Study the words and expressions in the *Key language* box.**

KEY LANGUAGE FOR ARTICLES

Catching the reader's attention:
Have you ever … ? I want to tell you about … It's the best …
Ordering ideas:
first(ly), second(ly), finally
Linking similar ideas:
moreover, in addition to this
Linking contrasting ideas:
while, whereas
Linking results:
therefore, which means
Emphasising ideas:
What I love/admire the most is … , The thing I like best is …
Giving your opinion:
In my opinion, For me, As far as I'm concerned

8 **Complete the sentences with one word in each space.**

1 .... me, sailing is the best sport in the world!
2 Painting is relaxing, creative and fun, and .... addition to this, you can earn a bit of money by selling your paintings.
3 As far .... I'm concerned, cooking is the best hobby.
4 Hiking isn't expensive, ... means that anyone can do it.
5 I want to .... you about something amazing that happened to me last year.
6 .... I love most is watching live shows in a theatre.

9 **Read the exam task and use the table to plan your article.**

You see this notice on an English-language fitness website.

Articles wanted
Staying healthy
How important is your health to you? What do you think are some of the best ways to stay fit and healthy?
The best articles will appear on our website next month.

Write your **article**.

	Ideas	Useful phrases
How important is health to me?		
Good diet		
Exercise		

10 **Write your article. Remember to write between 140 and 190 words.**

11 **Check your article and make changes if necessary.**

- Have you covered all the points in the task?
- Have you organised your ideas clearly into paragraphs?
- Have you got an interesting title and first sentence?
- Have you given your own opinions clearly?
- Have you used creative vocabulary with strong meanings?
- Have you used structures to add emphasis?
- Have you used between 140 and 190 words?

WRITING PART 2: REPORT

1 **Read the exam task. Who is the report for? What points should you include?**

> A group of English-speaking students wants to visit your city. The group leader has asked you to write a report that includes the following information:
> - the best time of year to visit
> - some interesting places to visit in your city
> - the best way to get around the city
>
> Write your **report**.

2 **Study the model answer. Does it cover all the points in the exam task?**

MODEL ANSWER

Introduction

[1]The aim of this report is to make recommendations for a group of students who are interested in visiting York.

[2]The best time of year to visit

York can be cold during the winter, and extremely busy with tourists during the summer. However, the spring is often warm and the city is quiet, so this is a good time to visit. [3]For this reason, I usually encourage my friends to visit in April or May.

[4]Places of interest

The city has numerous attractions which reflect its long and fascinating history. [5]The must-see places are the city walls, the tiny streets in the Shambles area of the old city and the Castle Museum.

Transport

York is a small city, and easy to get around on foot. However, [6]I would strongly recommend buying a York Pass, which not only includes entry to the top attractions, but also allows travel on the Hop-on, Hop-off tourist bus. It therefore offers [7]a practical and good value transport option.

[7]Conclusion

To sum up, I am sure the students will enjoy seeing the sights in York, and I look forward to welcoming them when they come.

[1]Start with a general introduction which gives the aim of the report.

[2]Use clear headings for the different points.

[3]Include a small amount of personal information to make the report interesting to read.

[4]Avoid repeating the exact words in the input.

[5]Use a neutral tone for most of the report, and avoid expressing your feelings.

[6]Make recommendations.

[7]End with a conclusion.

3 **Read the exam task. Then match the headings with three paragraphs from the report.**

> Your English teacher wants to take your class for a meal to celebrate the end of the year and has asked you to suggest a restaurant in your area. Describe a restaurant that you know and say why it would be popular with your classmates.
>
> 1 The restaurant 2 Advantages of this restaurant 3 Why it would be popular

a
The food is all freshly cooked and the dishes are reasonably priced. There are often daily specials, which are especially good value. In addition to this, there is a separate room at the back of the restaurant which is excellent for large groups.

b
Students will like it because the staff are always welcoming and there is an informal, friendly atmosphere. People in the class have different likes and needs, and there is a good choice of dishes for everyone, including some excellent vegetarian options. Most people will also be unable to resist the delicious desserts.

c
The restaurant is called Dario's and is located on North Street, quite close to the college. It serves a range of Italian food, including pizzas and pasta.

4 **Which personal information would it be useful to include in the report in Exercise 3? Why?**

A My cousin doesn't usually like Italian food, but he enjoyed his meal there.
B I eat there quite frequently and am always surprised at how low the final bill is.
C I can get there quite easily from my flat because the bus service is excellent.
D I know one of the waiters who works there, and he has confirmed that the food is excellent.

5 **Choose the best introduction and conclusion for the report in Exercise 3. Why is it the best one?**

Introductions

A In this report I'm going to recommend the best Italian restaurant for our class meal.

B This report describes the advantages and disadvantages of a particular restaurant and discusses whether it would be suitable for a class meal.

C This report aims to give information about a restaurant that I know and explain why it would be a good choice for a class meal.

Conclusions

A In conclusion, I strongly recommend Dario's because it offers a range of tasty food at good prices and has adequate space to cope with a large group.

B To sum up, Dario's is my favourite restaurant and I'd love to go there with the class.

C On balance, Dario's offers several advantages, especially the desserts, but it also has a few disadvantages.

6 **We often use passive forms in reports to make the tone neutral. Complete the passive sentences with the correct words.**

1 People often recommend this restaurant for large groups.
This restaurant .... for large groups.

2 People consider this hotel to be one of the best in the area.
This hotel .... one of the best in the area.

3 We expect that around 30 students will attend this event.
It .... that around 30 students will attend this event.

4 People have suggested that a new sports centre should be built.
It .... that a new sports centre should be built.

5 We recommend waterproof clothes for the hiking trip.
Waterproof clothes .... for the hiking trip.

7 **Study the words and expressions in the *Key language* box.**

KEY LANGUAGE FOR REPORTS

Introductions:

The aim/purpose of this report is to … , This report aims to … , This report looks at …

Giving advantages and disadvantages:

One advantage is … , One disadvantage is … , One problem with this is …

Linking similar ideas:

in addition to this, furthermore, moreover

Linking contrasting ideas:

however, on the one hand / on the other hand, in contrast, although, whereas

Making recommendations:

I would recommend … , I strongly recommend … , I have no hesitation in recommending …

Giving a conclusion:

in conclusion, to sum up, on balance, all things considered

8 **Correct the mistakes in the sentences. Look at punctuation and spelling as well as language mistakes.**

1 The aim for this report is to discuss the problems with public transport in Leeds.

2 There are some excellent shops in the shopping centre. In adition to this, there are a number of very good cafés and restaurants.

3 There are very few buses that come to the college moreover the ones that do come are expensive.

4 I have no hesitation in recomending the New Forest for a walking trip.

5 All things consider, the Old Duck would be an excellent choice of hotel.

6 In conclusion I would strongly recommend a new car park in the city centre.

9 **Read the exam task and use the table to plan your report.**

The local council wants to improve the shopping centre in your town. Your English teacher has asked students to write a report about the shopping centre, explaining which shops are popular and why, and recommending ways to improve it.

Heading	Ideas	Useful phrases
Introduction		
Conclusion		

10 **Write your report. Remember to write between 140 and 190 words.**

11 **Check your report and make changes if necessary.**

- Have you covered all the points in the task?
- Have you organised your ideas under clear headings?
- Have you included only relevant information?
- Have you started with an introduction and ended with a conclusion?
- Have you used words and phrases to link ideas?
- Have you used a formal, neutral tone?
- Have you used between 140 and 190 words?

Speaking bank

SPEAKING PART 1

1 Read about Part 1 of the Speaking paper.

In Part 1 of the Speaking paper, an examiner asks you personal questions about familiar topics. In Part 1:

- you are with another candidate, but you only speak to the examiner, not the other candidate
- an examiner asks you questions about yourself, and you answer
- the questions are about everyday topics such as your family, your hometown, likes and dislikes, your work or studies, free time, travel, celebrations and your future plans

2 Read the tips.

To get a good mark in Part 1 of the Speaking paper:

- you should listen to the questions carefully and make sure you answer the exact questions the examiner asks you
- you should use full sentences to answer the questions
- you should add reasons, examples or extra information to support your answers
- you should express your own opinions
- if you don't understand a question, you can ask the examiner to repeat it
- you should try to relax and answer the questions in a natural way

3 Read some typical Part 1 questions. Match each question with a topic (a–e).

1 What do you like about your hometown?
2 What kind of job would you like to do in the future?
3 How do people usually celebrate New Year in your country?
4 When do you usually spend time with your family?
5 What do you normally do at the weekend?
6 Tell us about an enjoyable trip that you went on.
7 Which country would you most like to visit?
8 Which subject did you most enjoy when you were at school?
9 What's the most important festival in your country?
10 What do you enjoy doing in your free time?

a Personal and family life
b Hobbies and free time
c Work and studies
d Travel
e Celebrations

4 28 Read and listen to Sofia's answers to four of the questions in Exercise 3. Does she add more information to every answer?

MODEL ANSWER

Examiner: What do you like about your hometown?
Sofia: [1]Well, I'm from Milan, in the north of Italy. It's a big city, and I enjoy living there because there's always lots to do, like going to the cinema or music concerts. There are also a lot of young people there, [2]so I like that as well.
Examiner: What do you enjoy doing in your free time?
Sofia: Well, I'm quite a sporty person, so I do a lot of exercise. [3]For example, I go to the gym two or three times a week, and I play tennis. I also enjoy spending time with my friends.
Examiner: Which country would you most like to visit?
Sofia: I would love to go to Australia. [4]The reason for this is that I like hot weather and I love going to the beach. The beaches in Australia look amazing. I also think the way of life in Australia is quite relaxed, having barbecues and things like that, so I think I'd enjoy that.
Examiner: Which subject did you most enjoy when you were at school?
Sofia: [5]Could you repeat that, please?
Examiner: Yes. Which subject did you most enjoy when you were at school?
Sofia: That was definitely geography, because I'm really interested in different countries, and I love learning about how people live in other parts of the world. [6]I had a very good geography teacher at school too, and I think he made the subject very interesting.

[1]Use full sentences in your answer.
[2]Give your own opinions.
[3]Add examples to support your answers.
[4]Add reasons to support your opinions.
[5]Ask the examiner to repeat a question if necessary.
[6]Add extra information to make your answer longer.

5 **The questions the examiner asks may be about the past, present and future, and it is important to listen carefully and answer correctly. Read six more questions. What do they ask about? Write *past*, *present* or *future*.**

1 Tell us about your last holiday or trip. ....
2 How often do you watch TV? ....
3 Which sport would you like to try? ....
4 What things do you usually buy online? ....
5 Which famous person would you most like to meet? ....
6 What kinds of food did you dislike when you were younger? ....

6 **Choose the most suitable verb form to complete the answers to the questions in Exercise 5.**

1 I.......... to Spain last month with some friends.
A 've been **B** would love to go **C** went
2 I.......... TV very often.
A don't watch **B** didn't watch **C** 'm not going to watch
3 I.......... skiing because I think it's really good fun.
A once tried **B** 'd like to try **C** love
4 I usually.......... clothes online.
A bought some **B** buy my **C** didn't buy many
5 I.......... Ariana Grande because I think she's an amazing singer.
A 've never met **B** meet **C** 'd love to meet
6 I.......... ice cream!
A hated **B** hate **C** 'd hate

7 **Write the words and expressions from the box next to the correct function.**

also	as well	because	for example	for instance
like	plus	such as	the reason for this is that	too

1 adding extra information ....
2 giving a reason ....
3 giving an example ....

8 29 **Choose the correct options to complete Dan's answers to three more questions. Listen and check.**

Examiner: In what ways do you think you will use English in the future?
Dan: I think I'll use English for my job in the future. **(1)** *The reason for this is that / Such as* I want to work for an international company, so probably everyone will speak English to each other. I'll probably use it for travelling **(2)** *too / also*, because I'd like to travel and visit lots of different countries.
Examiner: What do you usually do on your birthday?
Dan: I usually see my family on my birthday **(3)** *also / because* they like to wish me a happy birthday and they might have presents for me. Then in the evening I usually get together with some friends and do something, **(4)** *as well / like* go for a meal together.
Examiner: What kind of music do you enjoy listening to?
Dan: I really enjoy R&B music. **(5)** *For instance, / Too* I like American singers like Rihanna. I'm **(6)** *as well / also* keen on classical music because I find it very relaxing.

9 **Practise answering some of the Part 1 questions in this section. Try to relax and talk about yourself in a natural way.**

SPEAKING PART 2

1 Read about Part 2 of the Speaking paper.

In Part 2 of the Speaking paper, you are given a one-minute 'long turn'. In Part 2:

- the examiner will give you two photos on a similar topic and ask you to compare them and answer a question
- the question you have to answer is written above the photos
- you speak on your own for around one minute, and no one will interrupt you
- your partner will talk about a different set of photos
- when your partner has finished speaking, the examiner will ask you a question about your partner's photos. You will have around 30 seconds to answer this question.

2 Read the tips.

To get a good mark in Part 2 of the Speaking paper:

- you should compare the two photos and say what is similar and different about them, rather than just describing them
- you should always make it clear which photo you are talking about
- you should focus equally on both photos, rather than just talking about one of them
- you should speculate about what is happening in the photos and how the people are feeling
- you should make sure you allow enough time to answer the question after you have finished comparing the photos
- you should listen carefully while your partner is answering, so you can answer the question the examiner will ask you

3 Read the exam task and look at the photos. What topic connects the two photos? What question do you have to answer?

Examiner: In this part of the test I'm going to give each of you two photographs. I'd like you to talk about your photographs on your own for about a minute, and also to answer a question about your partner's photographs. Ana, it's your turn first. Here are your photographs. They show people on holiday. I'd like you to compare the photographs and say why you think the people chose these holidays.

4 30 **Read and listen to the model answer. Does the student say why the people have chosen the holidays?**

MODEL ANSWER

[1]Both pictures show people on holiday, but they're different kinds of holidays. [2]The people in the first photo are in the countryside, [3]whereas the second photo shows a big city. [4]It looks as if the people in the first photo are on a walking holiday, because they've got backpacks and a map. [3]On the other hand, the other people are probably doing some sightseeing. They seem to be up in a tower, and they're taking a selfie. Another difference is that the people in the city [5]look happy and relaxed, whereas the people in the countryside look worried. I think they might be lost. They don't look as happy as the people on the city break. I think the people in the first photo must enjoy walking. [6]Maybe they chose this holiday because they enjoy being in the countryside. I think the people in the second photo enjoy city life, so [6]I guess they probably chose to visit this city because there are lots of interesting things to see.

[1]Say what is similar about the two photos.

[2]Make it clear which photo you are talking about.

[3]Use linking words to compare the photos and say what is different about them.

[4]Speculate about what the people are doing.

[5]Say how you think the people are feeling.

[6]Answer the question when you have finished comparing the photos.

5 31 **Complete the sentences for comparing and contrasting photos with the words from the box. Listen and check.**

as	both	difference	different	other	whereas

1 .... pictures show people on holiday.
2 They're .... kinds of holidays.
3 The people in the first photo are in the countryside, ... the second photo shows a big city.
4 On the .... hand, the other people are probably doing some sightseeing.
5 Another .... is that the people in the city look happy and relaxed.
6 They don't look .... happy as the people on the city break.

6 32 **Match the beginnings and endings of sentences for speculating about photos. Listen and check.**

1 It looks as
2 They're probably doing
3 They seem to
4 They look
5 I
6 They must enjoy
7 Maybe they
8 I guess

a be up in a tower.
b think they might be lost.
c if they're on a walking holiday.
d walking.
e some sightseeing.
f happy and relaxed.
g they probably chose to visit this city because there are lots of interesting things to see.
h chose this holiday because they enjoy being in the countryside.

7 33 **Look at the exam task question and the two photos on page 132. Then listen to three students making mistakes when they complete the task. Match each speaker (1–3) with the mistake that they make (A–D). There is one answer you don't need.**

A describes what they can see in both photos, but doesn't compare and contrast them
B focuses too much on one photo
C doesn't give any personal opinions about the photos
D compares and contrasts the photos, but doesn't answer the question

Here are your photographs. They show people preparing food. I'd like you to compare the photographs and say how the people might be feeling about the food they are preparing.

How might the people be feeling about the food they are preparing?

8 34 **Read the task and look at the photos. Complete the task, then listen to the model answer and compare your answers.**

Here are your photographs. They show people working. I'd like you to compare the photographs and say what you think might be difficult about the people's jobs.

What might be difficult about the people's jobs?

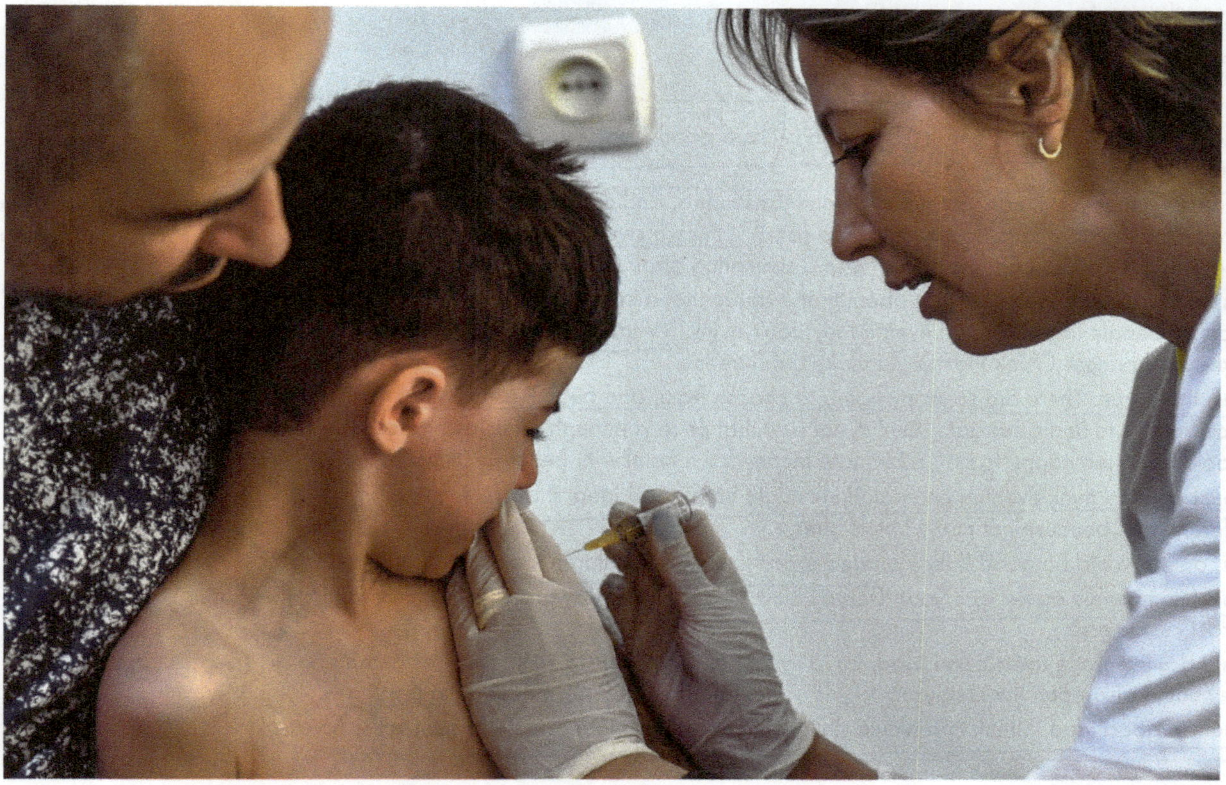

SPEAKING PART 3

1 Read about Part 3 of the Speaking paper.

Part 3 of the Speaking paper lasts for about three minutes, and you work with a partner. In Part 3:

- the examiner will explain an imaginary situation to you, then give you a piece of paper with written prompts that show different ideas or possibilities
- you must talk with your partner and discuss the prompts, giving your opinions about the different prompts
- you do not have to discuss all the prompts, but you should discuss most of them
- there is no right or wrong answer to the task
- the examiner will then ask you to try to reach agreement about something, and you do this with your partner
- you do not *have* to reach agreement with your partner, but you should try

2 Read the tips.

To get a good mark in Part 3 of the Speaking paper:

- you should talk to your partner and listen to your partner – it is important to have a conversation with your partner, rather than just expressing your own ideas
- you should make suggestions and respond to suggestions that your partner makes
- you should express your own opinions on the different prompts and respond to your partner's opinions
- you should give reasons for your opinions
- you should try to reach agreement with your partner when the examiner asks you to

3 Read the exam task and read how the examiner will introduce it. What question do you have to discuss? How many prompts are there for you to discuss?

I'd like you to imagine that a hotel wants to attract more guests. Here are some ideas they're thinking about. Talk to each other about why these ideas would attract more guests to the hotel.

a swimming pool

evening entertainment

reduced prices

How might these things attract more guests to a hotel?

tennis courts

an award-winning chef in the restaurant

4 35 Read and listen to Paul and Eva completing the task. How many of the prompts do they discuss? Do they both express their opinions?

MODEL ANSWER

Paul: [1]Shall we start with tennis courts? This sounds like a good idea. A lot of people like playing tennis.

Eva: [2]I can see what you mean, but not everyone likes tennis, and a lot of people go on holiday to relax, so they perhaps don't want to do sport. [3]I think a swimming pool might be a better idea, because people of all ages can use a swimming pool. Do you agree?

Paul: Yes, you're right. I hadn't thought about that. I agree that a swimming pool's a good idea because people like to sit by it even if they don't swim. [1]What do you think about the idea of reduced prices? I think that would make a difference.

Eva: [5]Yes, that's true. There are so many hotels to choose from, and people usually look at the price and try to find a bargain. But I'm not sure that price is enough on its own because people are often happy to pay a bit more money for a hotel with better facilities.

Paul: [5]Yes, I agree. I think evening entertainment might be a good idea, though. That's a bit different, too, because not many hotels offer it.

Eva: Yes, and it would be good if they offered entertainment for children too, not just adults.

Paul: [5]Yes, I completely agree with you. [4]Do you think that having an award-winning chef would attract customers?

Eva: Yes, I do. Everyone loves good food, but a lot of hotels don't have very good restaurants. They could also open the restaurant to everyone, but offer cheaper prices for guests.

Paul: [5]That's a good idea. I think that would definitely encourage more people to stay at the hotel.

[1]Make suggestions to move the discussion to the different prompts.

[2]Use polite expressions if you disagree with your partner.

[3]Give your own opinion, and give reasons to support it.

[4]Ask for your partner's opinion.

[5]Use a range of different expressions to agree with your partner.

5 36 **Read the second task that the examiner gives the students, then read and listen to the students completing the task. Do they reach agreement?**

Examiner: Now you have about a minute to decide which idea would be best for the hotel.

Eva: So, what do you think would be best for the hotel?

Paul: I'd suggest either the swimming pool or the evening entertainment. Both those things are easy for people to see when they look on the website, and I think they would both be popular with guests.

Eva: Well, I think everyone enjoys a swimming pool, especially children and young people. But on the other hand, most people only use a swimming pool in the summer, whereas evening entertainment can continue all year, and, like we said, they could offer different entertainment for different ages.

Paul: That's true, so shall we choose the evening entertainment?

Eva: Yes, let's go for that.

6 37 **Listen to extracts from three more pairs of students completing the task in Exercise 3. What mistakes do the students make? Match each pair (1–3) with a common mistake (A–D). There is one mistake you don't need.**

A The students talk about one prompt for too long, so don't have enough time to talk about the other prompts.

B The students talk for too long individually, don't listen to each other, and don't ask for each other's opinions.

C The students interrupt each other.

D The students talk about things that are not relevant to the task.

7 38 **Match the beginnings and endings of the sentences to make suggestions. Listen and check.**

1 It might be a good
2 Perhaps they
3 Tennis courts sound
4 They could
5 I would say that

a like a good idea.
b idea to offer reduced prices.
c offer entertainment for children, too.
d an award-winning chef would be a good idea.
e should have a swimming pool.

8 39 **Choose the correct options to complete the questions you can use to ask your partner's opinion. Listen and check.**

1 *Do / Are* you agree?
2 What *are / do* you think about the idea of a swimming pool?
3 *Will / Would* you agree with that?
4 *Do / May* you think that's true?

9 40 **Complete the expressions for agreeing and disagreeing with words from the box. Listen and check.**

agree	better	but	mean	right	sure	that's	think

1 I .... so, too.
2 Yes, ... true.
3 Yes, you're ....
4 I .... with you.
5 I can see what you ...., but I think a swimming pool might be a .... idea.
6 I'm not .... about that.
7 Yes, that's true, ... on the other hand, entertainment would also be popular.

10 41 **Read and listen to the expressions for reaching agreement. (a) Which two expressions can you use to encourage your partner to reach agreement with you? (b) Which expression shows that you have reached an agreement?**

1 I'd suggest either the swimming pool or the evening entertainment.
2 Are you OK with that?
3 My choice would be the reduced prices.
4 So, shall we choose the evening entertainment?
5 Yes, let's go for that.

11 42 **Read an exam task and practise answering it with a partner. Listen and compare your ideas.**

I'd like you to imagine that some people are discussing modern technology. Here are things that some people say it would be difficult to live without. Talk to each other about why it would be difficult to live without these things.

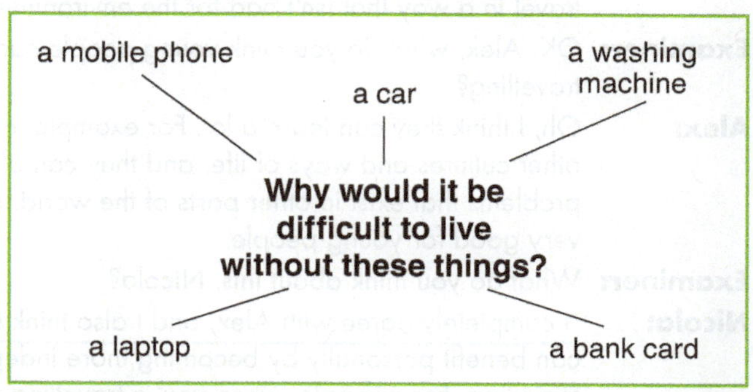

12 43 **Read the second part of the exam task and practise answering it with a partner. Listen and compare your ideas.**

Now you have about a minute to decide which thing people would find it the most difficult to live without.

SPEAKING PART 4

1 Read about Part 4 of the Speaking paper.

Part 4 of the Speaking paper lasts for about four minutes, and you work with a partner. In Part 4:

- the examiner will ask you questions on the general topic that you have talked about in Part 3
- the questions ask you to express your opinion rather than give information
- the examiner will ask you questions individually, but they may also bring your partner into the discussion after you have answered a question
- the examiner may also ask you to reply to your partner's opinions

2 Read the tips.

To get a good mark in Part 4 of the Speaking paper:

- you should express your opinions and give reasons and examples to support your opinions
- you should avoid giving short answers and should always give more information to expand your answers
- you should listen carefully when your partner is speaking, so that you can give your opinion on what they have said if you are asked

MODEL ANSWER

Examiner: Alex, some people say that travel is bad for the environment. Do you agree?

Alex: Yes, I do because [1]I think that when people travel they use fuel, for example in a plane or a car, and that's very bad for the environment. [2]They also create a lot of rubbish, for example if they have a picnic on the beach, and that's bad for the environment too.

Examiner: What do you think, Nicola?

Nicola: Well, I agree with Alex that travel can be bad for the environment, but on the other hand, I'd say that you *can* be a responsible tourist. [3]For example, I prefer to travel by train because it's better for the environment, and I never leave rubbish. So I think it's possible to travel in a way that isn't bad for the environment.

Examiner: OK. Alex, what do you think young people can learn by going travelling?

Alex: Oh, I think they can learn a lot. For example, they can learn about other cultures and ways of life, and they can also see some of the problems that exist in other parts of the world. I think that travelling is very good for young people.

Examiner: What do you think about this, Nicola?

Nicola: [4]I completely agree with Alex, and I also think that young people can benefit personally by becoming more independent when they go travelling. For example, when you're travelling you might have to deal with some difficult situations, and if you do this successfully, it can give you a lot of confidence.

[1]Make suggestions to move the discussion to the different prompts.

[2]Give reasons and examples to support your opinions.

[3]Talk about your own likes, dislikes and preferences.

[4]Agree and disagree with your partner, and respond to what they say.

3 Read some typical Part 4 questions on the topic of travel and holidays. Do all the questions ask about opinions?

What is the advantage of going on holiday with friends, rather than with family?
Some people say that tourism is bad for an area. What do you think?
What places are popular for holidays in your country?
Some people say travel is bad for the environment. Do you agree?
What do you think young people can learn by going travelling?

4 🔊 44 Read and listen to Alex and Nicola discussing two of the questions in Exercise 3. Choose the sentence which describes how they answer.

A They each give their own opinions, but don't listen to each other.

B They listen to each other and respond to what the other says.

5 Listen to three more pairs of students answering Part 4 questions. What mistakes do the students make? Match each pair (1–3) with a common mistake (A–D). There is one mistake you don't need.

A The students' answers are too short, and they don't add more information.
B The students don't listen to each other, so they can't respond to what the other says.
C The students talk about things that are not relevant to the task.
D The students interrupt each other.

6 Read the tip. Then listen to three students answering Part 4 questions on the topic of food. What extra question does each student have in their mind?

- Sometimes it can be difficult to think of things to say in answer to a Part 4 question. To help, it can be useful to keep question words in your mind: *Why? How? When? Where?* Asking yourself these questions can help you think of extra things to say.

7 Sometimes the examiner might ask you a question that you haven't thought about before. Look at the model answers and notice the strategies that the students use.

MODEL ANSWERS

1
Examiner: Do you think online shopping will ever replace going to shops?
Student: [1]Hmm, let me think. That's an interesting question. I'm not sure that online shopping will ever replace going to the shops because there are some things that people like to see or try before they buy them.

2
Examiner: Do you think that some people spend too much time shopping?
Student: [2]Well, it's true that some people spend quite a lot of time shopping. I guess for some people shopping is almost like a hobby. But I think that if they've got plenty of money to spend, then it isn't a problem for them to spend a lot of time in the shops. But I think it's a problem for people who don't have much money, because they might spend too much if they spend a lot of time shopping.

3
Examiner: Is it better to go shopping alone or with friends?
Student: [3]I think that there are some advantages to shopping alone, for example, you can find things more quickly and you probably don't spend as much money. On the other hand, shopping with friends is more fun because you can chat about things and go for a coffee together. So I think I would probably say that shopping with friends is better for this reason.

[1]Use expressions to give yourself time to think about your ideas, then give your opinion.

[2]Start with a general statement about the topic of the question, then develop the idea and give your opinion.

[3]Give one point of view and then the opposite point of view, then give your own opinion.

8 Listen to three students answering Part 4 questions about health and fitness. Match each student with the strategy (1–3) from Exercise 7 that they use.

9 Practise answering these Part 4 questions. Listen and compare your answers.

1 Some people say that there will be no shops in 20 years because people will buy everything online. Do you agree?
2 Are there advantages to living in the countryside rather than a big city?
3 Why do you think that so many people dream of becoming a celebrity?
4 How do you think people benefit from going on holiday?

Speaking bank – functional language

USEFUL LANGUAGE FOR PART 1

Asking for repetition

Could you say that again, please?

I'm sorry, could you repeat that?

I'm afraid I didn't catch that.

Sorry, what did you say after … ?

Pardon?

Sorry?

Giving reasons and explanations

the reason is …

(that's) because …

… so …

what I mean is …

that's to say …

in other words …

the point I'm making is …

Giving examples

for example …

for instance …

such as …

like …

… say …

a case in point is …

a good example of this is …

USEFUL LANGUAGE FOR PART 2

Saying which photo you're talking about

The top picture shows …

In the other photo there are …

In the one below, it looks as if …

Both pictures show …

In both photos there are …

Describing similarities and differences

This picture shows … , but that one …

In both pictures there's … , though in this one …

One difference between the pictures is that …

In one respect the pictures are quite similar because …

The two situations are completely different because …

They are similar in that they both show …

The biggest difference between them is that this one shows … , but the other one …

Comparing

This looks far more … than that.

The … in this photo look much more … than those.

What's happening in this photo is just as … as what's going on there.

Doing … like that isn't so … as …

These people are … a lot more … than those are.

Giving your opinion

In my opinion, …

I'd say that …

Well I think …

It seems to me …

Well, my own feeling is that …

I'm convinced that …

My own view is that …

Adding points of similarity and difference

Another similarity/difference is …

And something else that's different is …

Another thing that's not quite the same is …

They also differ in that …

They're alike in another way in that …

USEFUL LANGUAGE FOR PART 3

Agreeing

Right. Yes, I agree with that.
I think so, too.
That's a great idea.
Yes, you're absolutely right.
That's just what I was thinking.

Politely disagreeing

Perhaps, but what about … ?
I'm not so sure. Don't you think … ?
I think I'd rather …
It might be better to …
I'm not really that keen on …
I don't really agree …
I don't think we agree, so let's leave it at that.
Let's just agree to disagree.

Giving reasons for disagreeing

That's because …
Well, the thing is …
The problem with that one is …
The main reason is that …
For one thing, … And for another, …

Keeping going

Shall we move on to the next one?
What about this one?
Let's go on to the next one.
What do you think of this idea?
How do you feel about that one?

Reaching a decision

Which do you think would be best?
So which shall we choose?
Are we both in favour of that one?
Shall we have these two, then?
OK, we're agreed.
Right, those are the ones we'll choose.
I don't think we agree, so let's leave it at that.
Let's just agree to disagree.

USEFUL LANGUAGE FOR PART 4

Asking for opinions

What do you think?
Do you agree with that?
What's your opinion?
What are your feelings about this?
How do you feel about … ?
What do you reckon?

Asking for reasons

Any particular reason?
Could you tell me why?
Is that because … ?
Why do you think so?

Trying to change someone's opinion

But don't you think that … ?
Yes, but isn't it true that … ?
Though wouldn't you agree that … ?
Yes, but on the other hand …
But isn't it possible that … ?
Perhaps another way of looking at it would be …

Interrupting politely

Could I say something here?
Do you mind if I add to that?
If I could just make a point here.
I'd just like to say something about that.
Yes, I'd like to comment on that.

Adding points

And another thing is …
Apart from that, …
As well as that, …
Even better, …
Just as importantly, …
Not only that, …
Then there's …
Worse still, …
There's also the fact that …

Phrasal verb builder

Phrasal verbs consist of a verb with a preposition or adverb or both. The meaning of the phrasal verb is different from the meaning of its separate parts. The following are all phrasal verbs:

Phrasal verb	Definition
to be into sth	to be interested in something
to book sb into	to reserve a place for somebody at a hotel/event
to break up	to finish school/college at the end of the term/year
to bring up	to introduce (a topic in a discussion)
to burst out	to suddenly start doing something (laughing/crying)
to calm sb down	to stop somebody feeling angry, upset or excited
to check in	to arrive and register at a hotel or airport
to check out	to leave a hotel after paying and returning your room key
to cheer up	to become happy
to copy out	to write a written text again on a piece of paper
to devote sth to sb	to use time, energy, etc. for a particular purpose
to drop out	to fail to complete something (a university course / a race)
to fall behind	to not make progress
to get away	to leave or escape from a person or place
to get back	to return
to get on	to board a plane/train/ferry/bus
to get through	to complete successfully
to go away	to go on holiday
to go over	to examine or look at something in a careful or detailed way
to hand in	to give something (homework) to a teacher
to hand out	to give something (worksheet) to each of a number of people
to keep up with	to progress or travel at the same rate/speed as others
to listen up	to pay attention
to look through	to quickly read
to make up	to invent

Phrasal verb	Definition
to pick out	to identify (details)
to point out	to direct someone's attention to someone or something
to pull out	to drive from the side of the road onto a different part of the road
to pull over	to drive to the side of the road and stop
to pull up	to stop in a vehicle
to read out	to read words aloud so that other people can hear
to read up	to spend time reading in order to find out information about something
to refer to	to talk or write about somebody or something, especially briefly
to rub out	to erase
to run into sb	to meet someone you know when you are not expecting to
to run into sth	to crash into something (in a vehicle or on a bike)
to set out	to start a journey
to shut up	to stop talking or making a noise, or to make somebody stop doing this
to speak up	to speak loudly and distinctly or to express an opinion freely
to stand for	to mean
to stand up for	to defend
to stay over	to sleep overnight (often at someone's house)
to stop over	to stay somewhere for one night or more when you are travelling to somewhere else
to take off	to leave the ground and fly (of an aircraft)
to take up	to become interested or engaged in a pursuit
to talk sb into sth	to persuade someone to do something
to talk sth over	to discuss a problem or situation with someone, often to find out their opinion or to get advice before making a decision about it
to tell sb off	to express disapproval to someone for doing something bad
to turn up	to arrive or appear somewhere, usually unexpectedly

Wordlist

adj = adjective, *adv* = adverb, *n* = noun, *v* = verb,
pv = phrasal verb, *prep* = preposition, *exp* = expression
Note: the numbers show which page the word or phrase first appears on in the unit.

UNIT 1

adventurous *adj* (12) willing to try new or difficult things, or exciting and often dangerous things
aggressive *adj* (12) behaving in an angry and violent way towards another person
ambitious *adj* (11) having a strong wish to be successful, powerful or rich
amused *adj* (9) showing that you think something is funny
artistic *adj* (12) able to create or enjoy art
bossy *adj* (11) describes someone who is always telling people what to do
cautious *adj* (12) describes someone who avoids risks
cheeky *adj* (12) slightly rude or showing no respect, but often in a funny way
childish *adj* (11) (disapproving) If an adult is childish, they behave in a way that would be expected of a child.
competitive *adj* (12) wanting very much to win or be more successful than other people
confidence *n* (12) when you are certain of your ability to do things well
decisive *adj* (11) describes someone who is able to make decisions quickly and confidently
demanding *adj* (7) needing a lot of time, attention or energy
depressing *adj* (7) making you feel unhappy and without hope for the future
disorganised *adj* (11) describes someone who is not good at planning or organising things
emotional *adj* (12) having and expressing strong feelings
energetic *adj* (12) having or involving a lot of energy
enthusiastic *adj* (12) showing enthusiasm, a feeling of energetic interest in a subject or activity
foolish *adj* (12) unwise, stupid or not showing good judgement
grab *v* (7) to take the opportunity to get, use or enjoy something quickly
greedy *adj* (12) wanting a lot more food, money, etc. than you need
head to *pv* (7) to go in a particular direction
impatient *adj* (11) describes someone who is easily annoyed by someone else's mistakes or because they have to wait for someone else
irritating *adj* (10) making you feel annoyed
motivated *adj* (7) very enthusiastic or determined because you really want to do something
optimistic *adj* (11) hopeful; believing that good things will happen in the future
pessimistic *adj* (12) thinking that bad things are more likely to happen
practical *adj* (11) describes someone who is able to provide effective solutions to problems
puzzling *adj* (7) difficult to explain or understand
reasonable *adj* (11) using good judgement and therefore fair and practical
relieved *adj* (9) happy that something unpleasant has not happened or has ended
respectful *adj* (12) showing respect for someone or something
schedule *n* (7) a list of planned activities or things to be done, showing the times or dates when they are intended to happen or be done
sensitive *adj* (11) easily upset by the things people say or do; understanding what other people need, and being helpful and kind to them
stunning *adj* (7) extremely beautiful or attractive
sympathetic *adj* (13) describes someone who shows, especially by what they say, that they understand and care about someone's suffering
task *n* (7) a piece of work to be done
thoughtful *adj* (11) kind and always thinking about how you can help other people
unpredictable *adj* (11) likely to change suddenly and without reason

UNIT 2

at ease *exp* (20) relaxed
at first sight *exp* (20) when you first see someone or something
authentic *adj* (15) If something is authentic, it is real, true or what people say it is.
be attracted to *exp* (20) If you are attracted by or to someone, you like them.
break somebody's heart *exp* (20) to make someone who loves you very sad, usually by telling them you have stopped loving them
convenience food *n* (16) food that is almost ready to eat when it is bought and can be prepared quickly and easily
counter *n* (15) a long, flat, narrow surface in a shop, bank, restaurant, etc. at which people are served
critic *n* (15) someone whose job is to give their opinion about something, especially films, books, music, etc.

cuisine *n* (15) a style of cooking
get on somebody's nerves *exp* (20) to annoy someone a lot
go off *pv* (21) If a warning device goes off, it starts to ring loudly or make a loud noise.
heat up *pv* (16) to make something hot or warm, or to become hot or warm
hygienic *adj* (16) clean, especially in order to prevent disease
junk food *n* (16) food that is unhealthy but is quick and easy to eat
keep somebody company *exp* (20) to stay with someone so that they are not alone
leave somebody alone *exp* (20) to stop speaking to or annoying someone
lose touch *pv* (20) to stop communicating with someone, usually because they do not live near you now
packaging *n* (16) the materials in which objects are wrapped before being sold
portion *n* (16) the amount of a particular food that is served to one person, especially in a restaurant or a shop which sells food ready to be eaten
premises *n* (15) the land and buildings owned by someone, especially by a company or organisation
propose to *pv* (20) to ask someone to marry you
ready meal *n* (15) a meal cooked and bought at a shop but taken somewhere else, often home, to be heated and eaten
reviewer *n* (15) someone who writes articles expressing their opinion of a book, play, film, etc.
sit-down meal *n* (16) A sit-down meal is served to people who are sitting at a table.
struggle *v* (15) to be in danger of failing or being defeated
take somebody/something for granted *exp* (20) If you take situations or people for granted, you do not realise or show that you are grateful for how much you get from them.
vegan *adj* and *n* (16) not eating, using or including any animal products; a person who does not eat or use any animal products

UNIT 3

adamant *adj* (23) impossible to persuade, or unwilling to change an opinion or decision
ashamed of *exp* (28) feeling guilty or embarrassed about something you have done
asset *n* (23) a useful or valuable quality, skill or person
capable of *exp* (28) having the ability, power or qualities to be able to do something
collaboration *n* (23) the situation of two or more people working together to create or achieve the same thing
conscious of *exp* (28) aware that a particular thing or person exists or is present
familiar with *exp* (28) knowing something or someone well
fed up with *exp* (28) bored, annoyed or disappointed, especially by something that you have experienced for too long
be flattered *v* (23) to feel very pleased and proud because someone has said good things about you or has made you feel important
have nothing to do with *exp* (28) to have no connection or influence with someone or something
in connection with *exp* (28) on the subject of something
in need of *exp* (28) having to have something that you do not have
in place of *exp* (28) instead of someone or something
in relation to *exp* (28) in connection with something
in response to *exp* (28) as an answer or reaction to something
in terms of *exp* (28) used to describe which particular area of a subject you are discussing
in view of *exp* (28) because of a particular thing, or considering a particular fact
initiative *n* (23) a new plan or process to achieve something or solve a problem
involved in *exp* (28) included in something
lose sight of *exp* (23) to not consider something, especially because you have forgotten about it
obliged to *exp* (28) forced to do something or feeling that you must do something
obsessed with *exp* (28) unable to stop thinking about something; too interested in or worried about something
prepared to *exp* (28) willing, or happy to agree to do something
renovate *v* (23) to repair and improve something, especially a building
required to *exp* (28) when it is necessary for you to do something
sensitive to *exp* (28) easily upset by the things people say or do
sort of *exp* (28) one of a group of things which are of the same type or which share similar qualities
be supposed to *v* (28) to be expected to be something; to be considered by many people to be something; intended or expected to
sustainable *adj* (23) causing little or no damage to the environment and therefore able to continue over a period of time
tangible *adj* (23) real and not imaginary; able to be shown, touched or experienced
the trouble with *exp* (28) used to say what is wrong with someone or something
with regard to *exp* (28) in connection with

UNIT 4

abstract *adj* (30) used to refer to a type of painting, drawing or sculpture that uses shapes, lines and colour in a way that does not try to represent the appearance of people or things
absurd *adj* (37) stupid or unreasonable; silly in a humorous way
bizarre *adj* (38) very strange and unusual
bother *v* (33) to make the effort to do something
breathtaking *adj* (37) extremely exciting, beautiful or surprising
camera operator *n* (30) someone whose job it is to control a camera
cast *n* (30) the actors in a film, play or show
costume *n* (30) a set of clothes worn in order to look like someone or something else, especially for a party, film or play
count on *pv* (31) to be confident that you can depend on someone
delightful *adj* (37) very pleasant, attractive or enjoyable
depend on *pv* (31) to trust someone or something and know that they will help you or do what you want or expect them to do
dreadful *adj* (37) very bad, of very low quality, or shocking and very sad
exceptional *adj* (37) much greater than usual, especially in skill, intelligence, quality, etc.
fine *adj* (37) excellent or much better than average
focus on *pv* (31) to give a lot of attention to one particular person, subject or thing
get round to *pv* (33) to find time to do something that you have intended or would like to do
go on *pv* (35) to continue
impressive *adj* (36) If an object or achievement is impressive, you admire or respect it, usually because it is special, important or very large.
log on *pv* (31) to connect a computer to a computer system by typing your name, so that you can start working
lyrics *n* (30) the words of a song, especially a pop song
moving *adj* (37) causing strong feelings of sadness or sympathy
mysterious *adj* (37) strange, not known or not understood
outstanding *adj* (37) excellent; clearly very much better than what is usual
plot *n* (36) the story of a book, film, play, etc.
poor *adj* (37) not good, being of a very low quality, quantity or standard
portrait *n* (30) a painting, photo, drawing, etc. of a person or, less commonly, of a group of people
predictable *adj* (37) happening or behaving in a way that you expect and not unusual or interesting
producer *n* (30) a person who makes the practical and financial arrangements needed to make a film, play, or television or radio programme
regret *v* (33) to feel sorry about a situation, especially something sad or wrong, or a mistake that you have made
rehearse *v* (30) to practise a play, a piece of music, etc. in order to prepare it for public performance
rely on *pv* (31) to need a particular thing or the help and support of someone or something in order to continue, to work correctly, or to succeed
remarkable *adj* (37) unusual or special and therefore surprising and worth mentioning
scene *n* (30) a part of a play or film in which events happen in one place
script *n* (30) the words of a film, play, broadcast or speech
set *n* (30) a place where a film or play is performed or recorded, and the pictures, furniture, etc. that are used
shoot *v* (30) to use a camera to record a video or take a photo
slow-moving *adj* (37) developing or changing very slowly
solo *n* (30) a musical performance done by one person alone, or a musical performance in which one person is given special attention
soundtrack *n* (30) the sounds, especially the music, of a film, or a separate recording of this
studio *n* (30) a room where an artist paints or a musician practises
superb *adj* (37) of excellent quality; very great
take on *pv* (31) to accept a particular job or responsibility
tend *v* (33) to be likely to behave in a particular way or have a particular characteristic

UNIT 5

academic *adj* (40) relating to schools, colleges and universities, or connected with studying and thinking, not with practical skills
apprenticeship *n* (40) a period of time working for a skilled person, often for low payment, in order to learn that person's skills
Bachelor's degree *n* (40) a first degree at college or university
charm *n* (43) a quality that makes you like or feel attracted to someone or something
commerce *n* (43) the activities involved in buying and selling things
consultant *n* (42) someone who advises people on a particular subject
current *adj* (39) of the present time

duty *n* (45) something that you have to do because it is part of your job, or something that you feel is the right thing to do
earnings *plural n* (43) the amount of money that someone is paid for the work they do
graduate *v* (40) to complete a first university degree successfully
highly *adv* (39) very, to a large degree, or at a high level
institution *n* (45) a large and important organisation, such as a university or bank
intuition *n* (43) an ability to understand or know something immediately based on your feelings rather than facts
inventor *n* (42) someone who has invented something or whose job is to invent things
lecturer *n* (42) someone who teaches at a college or university
line manager *n* (42) the person who is directly responsible for managing the work of someone else in a company or business
management *n* (44) the group of people responsible for controlling and organising a company; the control and organisation of something
Master's degree *n* (40) an advanced college or university degree
novelist *n* (42) a person who writes novels
overtime *adv* (43) (time spent working) after the usual time needed or expected in a job
postgraduate *adj* (40) used to refer to university studies or students at a more advanced level than a first degree
production *n* (43) the process of making or growing goods to be sold
promotion *n* (43) the act of raising someone to a higher or more important position or rank
self-employed *adj* (40) not working for an employer but finding work for yourself or having your own business
supplier *n* (42) a company, person, etc. that provides things that people want or need, especially over a long period of time
take off *pv* (39) to suddenly start to be successful or popular
take on *pv* (39) to employ
take out a loan *exp* (39) to borrow a sum of money, often from a bank, which has to be paid back, usually together with an extra amount of money that you have to pay as a charge for borrowing
take to *pv* (39) to start to like someone or something
take up *pv* (43) to start doing a particular job or activity
thesis *n* (40) a long piece of writing on a particular subject, especially one that is done for a higher college or university degree
trade *n* (40) a job, especially one that needs special skill, that involves working with your hands
traineeship *n* (40) a period when someone is trained in the skills needed for a particular job
undergraduate *n* (40) a student who is studying for their first degree at a university or college
unlike *prep* (39) different from someone or something

UNIT 6

bruise *n* (46) a dark area on your skin where you have been hurt
be coming up *pv* (49) to be happening soon
cure *v* (46) to make someone with an illness healthy again
diving *n* (50) the sport of jumping into water or swimming under water
eat up *pv* (49) to eat all the food that you have been given
facility *n* (53) a place, especially including buildings, where a particular activity happens
fracture *n* (46) a break or crack in something hard, especially a bone
graze *n* (46) an injury on the surface of your skin caused by rubbing it against something rough
heal (up) *v* (46) to make or become well again, especially after a cut or other injury
health care *n* (46) the providing of medical services
helmet *n* (50) a strong hard hat that covers and protects the head
illness *n* (46) a disease of the body or mind
infection *n* (46) a disease in a part of your body that is caused by bacteria or a virus
injection *n* (46) the act of putting a liquid, especially a drug, into a person's body using a needle and a syringe (= small tube)
injury *n* (46) physical harm or damage to someone's body caused by an accident or an attack
mental health *n* (46) the condition of someone's mind, and whether or not they are suffering from any mental illness
pitch *n* (50) an area painted with lines for playing particular sports, especially football
plaster *n* (46) a small piece of sticky cloth or plastic that you use to cover and protect a cut in the skin
psychological *adj* (46) relating to the human mind and feelings
recovery *n* (46) the process of becoming well again after an illness or injury
slope *n* (50) a surface or piece of land that is high at one end and low at the other
speak up *pv* (49) to speak in a louder voice so that people can hear you
specialist *n* (46) someone who has a lot of experience, knowledge, or skill in a particular subject

sprain *n* (46) an injury to a joint (= a place where two bones are connected) caused by a sudden movement

stitch *n* (46) a length of special thread used to join the edges of a deep cut in the flesh

sum up *pv* (49) to describe or express the important facts or characteristics about something or someone

surgeon *n* (46) a doctor who is specially trained to perform medical operations

therapeutic *adj* (46) causing someone to feel happier and more relaxed or to be more healthy

thermometer *n* (46) a device used for measuring temperature, especially of the air or in a person's body

treat *v* (46) to give medical care to someone for an illness or injury

treatment *n* (46) the use of drugs, exercises, etc. to cure a person of an illness or injury

use up *pv* (49) to finish a supply of something

well-being *n* (46) the state of feeling healthy and happy

wound *n* (46) a damaged area of the body, such as a cut or hole in the skin or flesh made by a weapon

UNIT 7

the Arctic *n* (56) the very cold area around the North Pole

bear in mind *exp* (60) to remember a piece of information when you are making a decision or thinking about a matter

carbon footprint *n* (56) Someone's carbon footprint is a measurement of the amount of carbon dioxide that their activities produce.

climate change *n* (55) the way the world's weather is changing

coastal *adj* (56) positioned on or relating to the coast

conservation *n* (56) the protection of plants and animals, natural areas, and interesting and important structures and buildings, especially from the damaging effects of human activity

consumption *n* (54) the amount used or eaten

dam *n* (59) a wall built across a river that stops the river's flow and collects the water, especially to make a reservoir (= an artificial lake) that provides water for an area

degradation *n* (54) the process in which the beauty or quality of something is destroyed or spoiled

fossil fuel *n* (56) fuels, such as gas, coal and oil, that were formed underground from plant and animal remains millions of years ago

global warming *n* (56) a gradual increase in world temperatures caused by polluting gases such as carbon dioxide which are collecting in the air around the Earth and preventing heat escaping into space

greenhouse gas *n* (55) one of several gases, especially carbon dioxide, that prevent heat from the Earth escaping into space, causing the greenhouse effect

guideline *n* (55) information intended to advise people on how something should be done or what something should be

high-visibility/high-vis *adj* (59) easy to see in all conditions because of being a very bright colour

ice cap *n* (56) a thick layer of ice that permanently covers an area of land

impact *n* (54) a powerful effect that something, especially something new, has on a situation or person

in all *exp* (60) with everything added together to make a total

in doubt *exp* (60) If the future or success of someone or something is in doubt, it is unlikely to continue or to be successful.

in due course *exp* (60) at a suitable time in the future

be in favour *exp* (60) to support or approve

in practice *exp* (60) in reality rather than what is meant to happen

in progress *exp* (60) happening or being done now

in the long term *exp* (60) for a long period of time in the future

in the meantime *exp* (60) until something expected happens, or while something else is happening

mild *adj* (61) describes weather that is not very cold or not as cold as usual

mountainous *adj* (56) having a lot of mountains

play a part in *exp* (60) to help to achieve something

processed *adj* (55) Processed food has had some sort of chemical or industrial treatment in order to cook it, preserve it, or improve its taste or appearance.

refined *adj* (55) A refined substance has been made pure by removing other substances from it.

regulation *n* (60) an official rule that controls how something is done

renewable *adj* (56) Renewable forms of energy can be produced as quickly as they are used.

solar panel *n* (59) a device that changes energy from the sun into electricity

solar power *n* (56) electricity produced by using the energy from the sun

sophisticated *adj* (54) A sophisticated machine or system is very advanced and works in a clever way.

spill *n* (56) an amount of something that has come out of a container

think tank *n* (55) a group of experts brought together, usually by a government, to develop ideas on a particular subject and to make suggestions for action

tropical *adj* (56) from or relating to the area between the two tropics

waste *n* (56) unwanted matter or material of any type, especially what is left after useful substances or parts have been removed

UNIT 8

absorb *v* (65) to take something in, especially gradually

air conditioning *n* (65) the system used for keeping the air in a building or vehicle cool

antiquarian *adj* (63) connected with the trade, collection or study of old and valuable or rare objects

application *n* (67) a computer program that is designed for a particular purpose

atom *n* (64) The smallest unit of any chemical element, consisting of a positive nucleus surrounded by negative electrons. Atoms can combine to form a molecule.

bookmark *n* (67) a record of the address of an internet document on your computer so that you can find it again easily

breakthrough *n* (64) an important discovery or event that helps to improve a situation or provide an answer to a problem

broadband *n* (62) a system that makes it possible for many messages or large amounts of information to be sent at the same time and very quickly between computers or other electronic devices

browse *v* (63) to walk around a shop looking at several things without intending to buy any of them; to look at information on the internet

bug *n* (67) a mistake or problem in a computer program

cell *n* (64) the smallest basic unit of a plant or animal

charge *v* (67) to put electricity into an electrical device such as a battery

crash *v* (67) If a computer or system crashes, it suddenly stops operating.

data *n* (67) information, especially facts or numbers, collected to be examined and considered and used to help decision-making, or information in an electronic form that can be stored and processed by a computer

database *n* (62) a large amount of information stored in a computer system in such a way that it can be easily looked at or changed

desktop *n* (62) a type of computer that is small enough to fit on the top of a desk

discovery *n* (64) the process of finding information, a place or an object, especially for the first time, or the thing that is found

electronics *n* (64) the scientific study of electric current and the technology that uses it

element *n* (64) a simple substance which cannot be reduced to smaller chemical parts, e.g. hydrogen

faint *adj* (67) not strong or clear; slight

file sharing *n* (62) the activity of putting a file from your computer onto a special place on your computer so that other people can copy it, or look at it using the internet

gas *n* (64) a substance in a form like air that is neither solid nor liquid

handset *n* (62) the outer part of a mobile phone that does not include the battery or the sim card

hard disk *n* (67) a device that is fixed inside a computer and is used to store programs and information

hashtag *n* (62) used on social media for describing the general subject of a Tweet or other post

image *n* (64) a picture or photograph, especially one shown on a computer or television screen

innovation *n* (64) (the use of) a new idea or method

instant messaging *n* (62) a type of service available on the internet that allows you to exchange written messages with someone else who is using the service at the same time

interact *v* (69) to communicate with or react to

living *adj* (64) alive now

prove *v* (67) to show that something is true

ringtone *n* (62) the sound that a phone makes, especially a mobile phone when someone calls it

run *v* (67) If you run a computer program, you use it on your computer.

store *v* (67) to keep information on a computer

substance *n* (64) material with particular physical characteristics

theory *n* (67) a formal statement of the rules on which a subject of study is based or of ideas which are suggested to explain a fact or event or, more generally, an opinion or explanation

times *adv* (67) multiplied by

touchscreen *n* (62) a computer screen that you touch to get information, buy something, etc.

undo *v* (67) to remove the good or bad effects of an action or several actions

update *n* (65) new information

wave *n* (65) the pattern in which some types of energy, such as sound, light and heat, are spread or carried

UNIT 9

biased *adj* (72) showing an unreasonable like or dislike for a person based on personal opinions

boom *v* (71) to increase or become successful and produce a lot of money very quickly

broadcasting *n* (72) when programmes are sent out on television or radio

commercial *n* (72) an advertisement which is broadcast on television or radio

constructive *adj* (71) If advice, criticism or actions are constructive, they are useful and intended to help or improve something.

convincing *adj* (71) able to make you believe something that is true or right

editor *n* (72) a person who corrects or changes pieces of text or films before they are printed or shown, or a person who is in charge of a newspaper or magazine

episode *n* (72) one of the single parts into which a story is divided, especially when it is broadcast on the television or radio

faith *n* (71) great trust or confidence in something or someone

fake news *n* (72) false stories that appear to be news, spread on the internet or using other media, usually created to influence political views or as a joke

foresee *v* (71) to know about something before it happens

get somebody down *pv* (71) If something gets you down, it makes you feel unhappy or depressed.

go viral *v* (72) to become very popular very quickly

headlines *plural n* (72) the lines of words printed in large letters as the title of a story in a newspaper, or the main points of the news that are broadcast on television or radio

investigative journalist *n* (72) a type of journalist who tries to discover information of public interest that someone is trying to hide

myth *n* (71) a commonly believed but false idea

network *n* (72) a large system consisting of many similar parts that are connected together to allow movement or communication between or along the parts or between the parts and a control centre

newsreader *n* (72) someone who reads out the reports on a television or radio news programme

objective *adj* (72) based on real facts and not influenced by personal beliefs or feelings

over the moon *exp* (71) to be very pleased

podcast *n* (72) a radio programme that is stored in a digital form that you can download from the internet and play on a computer or smartphone

pop up *v* (72) to appear or happen, especially suddenly or unexpectedly

presenter *n* (72) someone who introduces a television or radio show

press *n* (72) newspapers and magazines, and those parts of television and radio which broadcast news, or reporters and photographers who work for them

propaganda *n* (72) information, ideas, opinions or images, often only giving one part of an argument, that are broadcast, published or in some other way spread with the intention of influencing people's opinions

publication *n* (72) the act of making information or stories available to people in a printed form

quiz show *n* (77) a TV or radio programme based on a game or competition in which you answer questions

reality TV show *n* (72) a television programme about ordinary people who are filmed in real situations, rather than actors

scriptwriter *n* (72) a person who writes the words for films or radio or television broadcasts

set designer *n* (72) a person who decides which pictures, furniture, etc. will be used when a film or play is performed or recorded

spot *v* (71) to see or notice someone or something, usually because you are looking hard

streaming *n* (72) the activity of listening to or watching sound or video directly from the internet

tabloid *n* (72) a type of popular newspaper with small pages which has many pictures and short simple reports

well meaning *adj* (71) wanting to have a good effect, but not always achieving one

UNIT 10

absurd *adj* (84) stupid and unreasonable, or silly in a humorous way

bargain *n* (78) something on sale at a lower price than its true value

be out of *v* (78) to have no more of something

bizarre *adj* (84) very strange and unusual

brand *n* (78) a type of product made by a particular company

breathtaking *adj* (84) extremely exciting, beautiful or surprising

budget *adj* (78) very cheap

casual *adj* (78) describes clothes that are not formal or not suitable for special occasions

catalogue *n* (80) a book with a list of all the goods that you can buy from a shop

clash *v* (78) If colours or styles clash, they look ugly or wrong together.

consumer *n* (78) a person who buys goods or services for their own use

dealer *n* (78) a person who trades in something

debit card *n* (80) a small plastic card which can be used as a method of payment, the money being taken from your bank account automatically

debt *n* (80) something, especially money, that is owed to someone else, or the state of owing something

delightful *adj* (84) very pleasant, attractive or enjoyable

designer label *n* (78) something made by a famous company that makes expensive clothes, bags, etc.

disgraceful *adj* (84) very bad

dreadful *adj* (84) causing fear, shock or suffering

exceptional *adj* (84) much greater than usual, especially in skill, intelligence, quality, etc.

exchange *v* (78) to take something back to the shop where you bought it, and change it for something else

fake *adj* (78) not real, but made to look or seem real

fine *adj* (84) excellent or much better than average

formal *adj* (78) Formal language, clothes and behaviour are suitable for serious or official occasions.

furious *adj* (84) extremely angry

genuine *adj* (78) If something is genuine, it is real and exactly what it appears to be.

guarantee *n* (80) a promise that something will be done or will happen, especially a written promise by a company to repair or change a product that develops a fault within a particular period of time

ideal *adj* (84) without fault; perfect, or the best possible

in stock *exp* (78) available to buy

launch *v* (78) to begin, or to introduce a new plan or product

loose *adj* (78) (of clothes) not fitting closely to the body

massive *adj* (79) very large in size, amount or number

matching *adj* (78) having the same colour or pattern as something else

on offer *exp* (80) If goods in a shop are on (special) offer, they are being sold at a lower price than usual.

out of stock *exp* (78) not available to buy

outstanding *adj* (84) clearly very much better than what is usual

patterned *adj* (78) with a design made from repeated lines, shapes or colours on the surface

pre-owned *adj* (78) not new; having been owned in the past by someone else

purchase *n* (78) something that you buy

reflect *v* (78) to show, express or be a sign of something

run out *pv* (83) to finish, use or sell all of something so that there is none left

sale *n* (78) an occasion when goods are sold at a lower price than usual

sales *n* (78) the number of products sold

sell out *pv* (83) If a supply of something sells out, there is no more of that thing to buy.

severe *adj* (84) causing very great pain, difficulty, worry, damage, etc.; very serious

shopkeeper *n* (78) a person who owns and manages a small shop

sophisticated *adj* (78) having a good knowledge of culture and fashion

stay out *pv* (83) to not come home at night, or to go home late

stunning *adj* (84) extremely beautiful or attractive

suit *v* (78) (usually of a colour or style of clothes) to make someone look more attractive

superb *adj* (84) of excellent quality; very great

supplier *n* (78) a company, person, etc. that provides things that people want or need, especially over a long period of time

take out *pv* (83) to get money from a bank account

throw out *pv* (83) to get rid of something that you do not want any more

tight *adj* (78) Clothes or shoes that are tight fit the body too closely and are uncomfortable.

tremendous *adj* (84) very great in amount or level, or extremely good

trolley *n* (80) a small vehicle with two or four wheels that you push or pull to transport large or heavy objects

try out *pv* (83) to use something to discover if it works or if you like it

turn out *pv* (83) to happen in a particular way or to have a particular result, especially an unexpected one

uncompetitive *adj* (78) not involving or encouraging competition

unfashionable *adj* (78) not modern or popular

vintage *adj* (78) of high quality and lasting value, or showing the best and most typical characteristics of a particular type of thing, especially from the past

vivid *adj* (84) very brightly coloured

wear somebody out *pv* (83) to make someone extremely tired

Exam information

Part/Timing	Content	Exam focus
Reading and Use of English 1 hour 15 minutes	**Part 1** A modified cloze text containing eight gaps and followed by eight multiple-choice items. **Part 2** A modified open cloze text containing eight gaps. **Part 3** A text containing eight gaps. Each gap corresponds to a word. The stems of the missing words are given beside the text and must be changed to form the missing word. **Part 4** Six separate questions, each with a lead-in sentence and a gapped second sentence to be completed in two to five words, one of which is given as a 'key word'. **Part 5** A text followed by six multiple-choice questions. **Part 6** A text from which six sentences have been removed and placed in a jumbled order after the text. A seventh sentence, which does not need to be used, is also included. **Part 7** A text, or several short texts, preceded by ten multiple-matching questions.	Candidates are expected to demonstrate the ability to apply their knowledge of the language system by completing the first four tasks; candidates are also expected to show understanding of specific information, text organisation features, tone, and text structure.
Writing 1 hour 20 minutes	**Part 1** One compulsory essay question presented through a rubric and short notes **Part 2** Candidates choose one task from a choice of three task types. The tasks are situationally based and presented through a rubric and possibly a short input text. The task types are: • an essay • an article • a letter or email • a review • a report	Candidates are expected to be able to write using different degrees of formality and different functions: advising, comparing, describing, explaining, expressing opinions, justifying, persuading, recommending and suggesting.
Listening Approximately 40 minutes	**Part 1** A series of eight short unrelated extracts from monologues or exchanges between interacting speakers. There is one three-option multiple-choice question per extract. **Part 2** A short talk or lecture on a topic, with a sentence-completion task which has ten items. **Part 3** Five short related monologues, with five multiple-matching questions. **Part 4** An interview or conversation, with seven multiple-choice questions.	Candidates are expected to be able to show understanding of attitude, detail, function, genre, gist, main idea, opinion, place, purpose, situation, specific information, relationship, topic, agreement, etc.
Speaking 14 minutes	**Part 1** A conversation between the examiner (the 'interlocutor') and each candidate (spoken questions). **Part 2** An individual 'long turn' for each candidate, with a brief response from the second candidate (visual and written stimuli, with spoken instructions). **Part 3** A discussion question with five written prompts. **Part 4** A discussion on topics related to Part 3 (spoken questions).	Candidates are expected to be able to respond to questions and to interact in conversational English.

The authors and publishers would like to thank the following contributors:
Grammar on the move: Lucy Passmore and Jishan Uddin
Grammar reference: Peter May and Bryan Goodman-Stephens
Writing and Speaking Bank: Sheila Dignen

The authors and publishers are grateful to the following for reviewing the material during the writing process: Italy: Gabriella Granata, Jane Ritter; Mexico: Montserrat Rodriguez Pastor; Spain: David Ghatei, Claire Martine Moloney

This coursebook is informed by the Cambridge English Corpus - a multi-billion word collection of examples of spoken and written English. We use our corpus to answer questions about English vocabulary, grammar and usage. Along with this, we collect and analyse learner writing. This allows us to clearly see how learners from around the world are similar and different in how they acquire and use language. These insights allow us to provide tailored and comprehensive support to learners at all stages of their learning journey.

The authors and publishers acknowledge the following sources of copyright material and are grateful for the permissions granted. While every effort has been made, it has not always been possible to identify the sources of all the material used, or to trace all copyright holders. If any omissions are brought to our notice, we will be happy to include the appropriate acknowledgements on reprinting and in the next update to the digital edition, as applicable.

Key: U = Unit, GR = Grammar Reference, R = Review, REV = Revision, SB = Speaking Bank, VM = Visual Materials.

Text

U1: Text adapted from 'A day in the life of a student in Canada' by Becky Bradley, 18.10.2018. Copyright © Becky Bradley. Reproduced with kind permission; **U2:** Text adapted from 'Star chef learnt to cook by watching YouTube', *The Times*, 15.07.2018. Copyright © 2006 The Times/ News Licensing. Reproduced with permission. **U3:** The Guardian for the adapted text from 'Sustainable tourism: why the Faroe Islands closed for maintenance' by Tim Ecott, The Guardian, 08.05.2019. Copyright © 2020 Guardian News & Media Ltd. Reproduced with permission; **U4:** The Guardian for the adapted text from 'Lights, camera … and actions to becoming a successful filmmaker' by Krysten Resnick, *The Guardian*, 06.10.2015. Copyright © 2020 Guardian News & Media Ltd. Reproduced with permission; **U6:** The Guardian for the adapted text from 'Blue spaces: why time spent near water is the secret of happiness' by Elle Hunt, The Guardian, 03.11.2019. Copyright © 2020 Guardian News & Media Ltd. Reproduced with permission; **U7:** The Guardian for the adapted text from 'Healthy diet means a healthy planet, study shows' by Damian Carrington, The Guardian, 28.10.2019. Copyright © 2020 Guardian News & Media Ltd. Reproduced with permission; **U8:** MailOnline for the adapted text from 'Local bookshop that failed to sell a single book in a day for the first time in 100 years is 'completely overwhelmed' by more than £1,000 worth of online orders after a viral Twitter post, by Harriet Johnston, *MailOnline*, 15.01.2019. Copyright © 2020 MailOnline. Reproduced with permission; **U10:** The Guardian for the adapted text from 'Is buying vintage clothing the most eco way to shop?' by Ellie Violet Bramley, The Guardian, 25.04.2019. Copyright © 2020 Guardian News & Media Ltd. Reproduced with permission.

Photography

The following images have been sourced from Getty Images..

U1: Ariel Skelley/The Image Bank; Ariel Skelley/DigitalVision; Monty Rakusen/Cultura; Colorblind Images LLC/DigitalVision; Dougal Waters/DigitalVision; pixelfit/E+; Westend61; **U2:** Buena Vista Images/Stone; Jakraphan Inchukul/Moment; Eugene Mymrin/Moment; lisegagne/E+; Maskot; PhotoAlto/Ale; Ventura/ PhotoAlto Agency RF Collections; Oscar Wong/Moment; imran kadir photography/Moment Unreleased; PeopleImages/E+; **U3:** Westend61; Ian Vargas/EyeEm; Davide Seddio/Moment; Kitti Boonnitrod/Moment; Gavin Hellier; UniversalImagesGroup/Universal Images Group; Tom Merton/OJO Images; jaminwell/E+; MARCO BERTORELLO/AFP; **U4:** guruXOOX/iStock/Getty Images Plus; Taiyou Nomachi/DigitalVision; Mint Images RF; Zero Creatives/Image Source; momcilog/E+; Klaus Vedfelt/DigitalVision; Tara Moore/Stone; **U5:** poba/E+; mixetto/E+; Robert Daly/OJO Images; PeopleImages/E+; Monty Rakusen/Cultura; Kentaroo Tryman/ Maskot; sturti/E+; South_agency/ E+; gilaxia/E+; Elke Selzle/Photographer's Choice RF; **U6:** Luis Alvarez/ DigitalVision; JohnnyGreig/E+; Fuse/Corbis; pixdeluxe/E+; GlobalStock/E+; Fajrul Islam/Moment Unreleased"; Thomas Barwick/DigitalVision; Simon M Bruty/Getty Images Sport; **U7:** Erik Isakson; fcafotodigital/E+; Pgiam/ E+; andersen_oystein/E+; Feng Wei Photography/Moment; Image courtesy of Jeffrey D. Walters/Moment Open; Owen Franken/Stockbyte; Gary John Norman/The Image Bank; **U8:** Carol Yepes/Moment; Jose Luis Pelaez/Photodisc; filadendron/E+; Tetra Images; alvarez/E+; **U9:** Klaus Vedfelt/DigitalVision; swissmediavision/ E+; tomazl/E+; SOPA Images/LightRocket; Rick Kern/WireImage; Sean Drakes/Getty Images Entertainment; Roberto Ricciuti/Getty Images Entertainment; Maremagnum/Corbis Documentary; Daniel Boczarski/ WireImage; **U10:** Alistair Berg/DigitalVision; Tom Werner/DigitalVision martin-dm/E+; Nicola Katie/E+; **REV2:** Juanmonino/E+; **REV5:** Francesco Bergamaschi/Moment; **VM:** Thomas Barwick/Stone; filadendron/E+; Mischa Keijser/Cultura; Subin Pumsom/EyeEm; SolStock/E+; izusek/E+; **GR:** Alexander Spatari/Moment; holgs/iStock/ Getty Images Plus; primeimages/E+; lechatnoir/E+; kali9/E+; **SB:** Tim Graham/Getty Images News; George Rose/Getty Images News; ullstein bild; Monty Rakusen/Cultura; Monty Rakusen/Cultura; DANIEL MIHAILESCU/ AFP.

Front cover photography by Betsie Van Der Meer/Stone/Getty Images.

Animations

Grammar animation Video production by QBS Learnings. Voiceover by Dan Strauss.

Audio

Audio production by IH Sound LTD and Leon Chambers.

Typesetting

Typeset by Hyphen S.A.